Adolescent Volcanoes

by the same authors

Little Volcanoes
Helping Young Children and Their Parents to Deal with Anger
Warwick Pudney and Éliane Whitehouse
ISBN 978 1 84905 217 7
eISBN 978 0 85700 595 3

of related interest

Starving the Anger Gremlin
A Cognitive Behavioural Therapy Workbook on
Anger Management for Young People
Kate Collins-Donnelly
ISBN 978 1 84905 286 3
eISBN 978 0 85700 621 9

How to Be Angry
An Assertive Anger Expression Group Guide for Kids and Teens
Signe Whitson
Foreword by Dr Nicholas Long
ISBN 978 1 84905 867 4
eISBN 978 0 85700 457 4

Anger Management Games for Children
Deborah M. Plummer
Illustrated by Jane Serrurier
ISBN 978 1 84310 628 9
eISBN 978 1 84642 775 6

Working with Anger and Young People
Nick Luxmoore
ISBN 978 1 84310 466 7
eISBN 978 1 84642 538 7

Feeling Like Crap
Young People and the Meaning of Self-Esteem
Nick Luxmoore
ISBN 978 1 84310 682 1
eISBN 978 1 84642 819 7

Helping Adolescents and Adults to Build Self-Esteem
A Photocopiable Resource Book
Deborah M. Plummer
ISBN 978 1 84310 185 7
eISBN 978 1 84642 051 1

Art Therapy and Anger
Edited by Marian Liebmann
ISBN 978 1 84310 425 4
eISBN 978 1 84642 810 4

Adolescent Volcanoes

Helping Adolescents and their Parents to Deal with Anger

Warwick Pudney and Éliane Whitehouse

Foreword by Max Abbott

Jessica Kingsley *Publishers*
London and Philadelphia

Every effort has been made to trace copyright holders and to obtain their permission for the use of copyright material. The authors and the publisher apologise for any omissions and would be grateful if notified of any acknowledgements that should be incorporated in future reprints or editions of this book.

Originally published in New Zealand as *Adolescent Volcanoes* by The Peace Foundation, the operating name of The Foundation for Peace Studies Aotearoa/New Zealand

This edition published with revisions in 2014
by Jessica Kingsley Publishers
73 Collier Street
London N1 9BE, UK
and
400 Market Street, Suite 400
Philadelphia, PA 19106, USA

www.jkp.com

Library of Congress Cataloging in Publication Data
Pudney, Warwick.
  Adolescent volcanoes : helping adolescents and their parents to deal with anger / Warwick Pudney and
Éliane Whitehouse ; foreword by Professor Max Abbott. -- [Revised edition].
    pages cm
  "Originally published in New Zealand as Adolescent volcanoes by the Peace Foundation."
  ISBN 978-1-84905-218-4 (alk. paper)
  1. Anger in adolescence. 2. Anger--Management. I. Whitehouse, Éliane. II. Title.
  BF724.3.A55P83 2014
  155.5'1247--dc23
                        2013032115

British Library Cataloguing in Publication Data
A CIP catalogue record for this book is available from the British Library

ISBN 978 1 84905 218 4
eISBN 978 0 85700 596 0

To our own children who taught us so much about adolescence:
Jenny Pudney, Richard Pudney and Nick Pudney,
Elizabeth Whitehouse and Alan Whitehouse

Contents

Foreword by Professor Max Abbott   13

ACKNOWLEDGEMENTS   15

PREFACE   17
Notes   17

Introduction: How This Book Can Be Useful   18

PART 1 HELPING PARENTS AND CAREGIVERS   19

Chapter 1 Adolescents, Parents and Power   **20**
It's all about power and how it changes hands!   20
Parent power and adolescent power   20
Parent power   21
Adolescent power   22
Powerlessness of parents   22
Powerlessness of adolescents   24
The relationship of the four states of power and powerlessness   25
Abuse and powerlessness   29
New power and the possibility of revenge   31
Counselling and parenting in new power relationships   32
Power and hurt   32
Clearing resentment (and anger) and letting go   33
The process   33
Power equalising   34

Chapter 2 The Development of Adolescence and Anger in Society   **36**
Same needs, different worlds   36
A history of adolescence   38

Chapter 3 Anger Between Generations   **43**
Improving understanding between parents and teenagers   43

Chapter 4 Communication   **49**
Holding families and building relationships   49
Reasserting standards, rules and protocols   50
Remembering the positive   51
Listening so that kids will talk   52
The payoff   55
Relational situations   56

Chapter 5 Adolescence: The Transition Event   **59**
Introduction to adolescence   59
Powerlessness   62
Mothers and daughters   63
Mothers and sons   63
Fathers and daughters   64
Fathers and sons   65
Who am I?   66
15–17-year-olds   66
From 17 to independence   67

Growing past adoration and contempt 67
Sexuality 68
Music 69
18–20-year-olds 69
Summary 74

Chapter 6 Negotiating and Problem Solving **75**
Negotiating the way to adulthood 75
Thinking 76
Balancing memories with reality 77
Speaking for yourself 77
Avoiding judgements and parental commands 78
Trading 78
Labelling 82
Negotiating 83

Chapter 7 Anger, Shame, Blame and Games **84**
Adults coping with their own anger 84
Differences in male and female anger 86
The need for an anger vocabulary 87
What 'games' are played around anger? 88
The anger rules 90
Suggestions for the caregiver for when the teenager feels angry 91
Summary 92

Chapter 8 Helping Adolescents with their Anger **93**
Anger at mothers and fathers 93
Angry sons and daughters 98
The anger scale 99
The adolescent anger flow chart 101
Bullying: how adults can help 113
Working with a victim 115
Growing up a winner 117
Summary 120

Chapter 9 Positive Limit Setting **124**
Setting limits positively 124
Contracts vs punishments 125
Contracting 126
Positive reinforcement 128
Consistency 128
Responsibility 129

Chapter 10 When Parents Separate **133**
Good reasons for feeling angry 133
What helps to make a clean break? 134
Summary 136

Chapter 11 When Parenting an Adolescent Feels Like an Impossible Task **137**
Support available 137
Summary 139

Chapter 12 Special Circumstances **140**
Adolescent anger and special circumstances 140
Suicide and despair 140
Sexuality 142

Chapter 13 Being an Adolescent in Two Cultures or Being Different **144**
Adolescents living with two cultures 144
How parents can help themselves to understand 144
Difficulties that adolescents with two cultures can face 145

Chapter 14 Self-Care for Adults who Live and Work with Adolescents   **149**
     Tips for managing your stress as parents   149

PART 2 HELPING ADOLESCENTS   151

Chapter 15 Rights and Responsibilities   **152**
     Rights of adolescents   152

Chapter 16 Ways of Managing Anger for Adolescents   **170**

Chapter 17 Managing Triggers, Time Out and Chill Down   **188**
     Triggers   188

Chapter 18 Communicating Better   **216**

Chapter 19 Warrior Training   **222**
     Being a 'warrior'   222

Chapter 20 Self-Abuse and Other Abuse   **234**
     What is abuse? What can you do about it?   234

Chapter 21 Expressing Anger   **255**
     Transferring anger and authority   255

Chapter 22 Making Life Better   **263**

     SUMMARY OF KEY CONCEPTS   282

     ABOUT THE AUTHORS   286
     Warwick Pudney   286
     Éliane Whitehouse   286

     BIBLIOGRAPHY   287

Handouts

The roles and primary functions of parents   41

Talking so that kids will listen   54

Family meal times   58

Activity for parents   81

Some common reasons adolescents feel angry with either mother or father   94

The most common reasons given for anger at mothers and fathers   97

Anger flow chart   102

Triggers for parents   110

The healthy family checklist   122

Four levels of muscle with the mouth   130

Rights of adolescents   153

Things I will need to back up my rights   155

Responsibilities   156

Rules of my bedroom   158

Students' problems   160

'Problem' teachers   162

Genealogy   164

The importance of your family   165

Feeling 14 for boys   167

Feeling 16 for girls   168
T-shirt message: choose your slogan for a T-shirt   169
Early warning signs of feeling anger in your body   171
The anger scale   174
Anger scripts   175
Cycle of abuser and loser   177
Tracking loser and winner behaviour   179
What do I really want?   180
Transferring anger   182
Bottling anger   184
Soothing and calming anger   186
My hooks (triggers)   192
Triggers for adolescents   193
Triggers worksheet   195
Time Out: Choosing Time Out or 'Time In' control of myself   196
Time Out   198
Time Out at home: Adults and adolescents   199
Time Out for schools   201
Escalators in action: Easy steps to being a loser in relationships   202
Adolescent escalators used by parents   203
Parent escalators used by adolescents: Handling personal conflict   205
De-escalators: Handling personal conflict   207
De-escalators in action: Easy steps to dealing with a loser/aggro parent   209
De-escalating in action: Easy steps to being a winner as a parent   210
Staying cool   211
Automatic loser button   212
Big picture – little picture: Will you win a small fight or win the big picture?   213
Are you being bullied? What can you do?   214
Training your adults to communicate   217
Basic communication – the four-part phrase   219
What helps me to communicate?   220
Warriors   223
'Warrior' training lesson 1: Shields   226
My personal shield   228
'Warrior' training lesson 2: Swords   229
'Warrior' training lesson 3: Bows   230
'Warrior' training lesson 4: The korowai training   231
Design in your head or draw your korowai of protection   233
Preventing abuse of myself and others   237
The monster within   239
The internal success coach   240
Lying and stealing   241
Letting go of the guilt   242
Tagging   244
Smoke screen – smoking   245
Why children, adolescents and young adults drink alcohol   246

The effects of alcohol   248

Coping with loss and hurt   250

Change and grief   252

What you need to know about marijuana   253

Do you hold your anger in?   257

How do you express your anger outwardly?   258

Heavy metal rage   259

Express it in song   260

Movies   261

Expression of feelings: How do you feel today?   264

Dream-catcher   266

Keeping a journal   268

Positive self-talk: Saying good things to yourself in your head   273

Self-esteem: Good things about me   274

Payback: The consequences of living with revenge and resentment   275

Hot penning   277

Getting money plan   278

Vision for a world without aggro   279

What do I want for my future? Making plans for the life I deserve   280

Foreword

Anger is part of everyday life. It is a natural human response to threats, hurt or loss of various kinds. Through anger we detect important things within ourselves, relationships and the wider world that we need to understand and possibly change so that we can grow and have more satisfying lives. Anger is a healthy emotion. As the authors of this book say, it helps us 'speak out about injustice to ourselves and others, it motivates us, it energises us, it protects us'. Anger does all these things but also has the potential to trigger behaviour of abuse and violence, directed outward onto others or inward on oneself. Consequences ripple through relationships, families and communities. These consequences are usually bad, reflected at the extremes in homicide and suicide statistics. Violence begets violence. Most people who abuse were abused. Abuse today becomes abuse tomorrow, extending into future generations.

There is no simple fix to breaking generational cycles and reducing abuse and violence. Many factors contribute, including growing economic and social inequalities within and between countries. Prevention requires action at many levels. While the mass media typically focus on what is going wrong, many good things are happening. Anger is no longer such a taboo topic. Governments, NGOs, government agencies and educational organisations, communities, families and individuals are taking steps to address abuse, its causes and consequences.

There is much in the modern world for youth to be angry about. Young people often see injustice in their personal life situations and in wider society. The transition from childhood to adulthood has become even more protracted and fraught in recent decades. Anger is an inherent part of this process and learning how to channel and draw on it in positive ways is a significant challenge. It is also a challenge for parents and other people who are close to adolescents. Sitting alongside and hearing an angry youth, while difficult for many, is an act of nurture, care and investment in their mental health and future. Listening well is the most healing tool available to parents and helping professionals. It has the power to dissipate excessive emotion, generate empathy and create a beginning place for hope, security and problem solving.

Adolescent Volcanoes helps towards understanding the causes for feelings of anger and assists to build clear responsibility for what the parent or adolescent does with that anger and their subsequent behaviour. It shows how clear boundaries, for not hurting others, can be set. Through illustrations and exercises, skills are taught for emotional engagement, communication, self-affirmation, problem solving and resolving old and new issues. Parents not infrequently benefit from the same management and skills. Old issues including past abuse and repressed anger can present additional challenges including hopelessness, depression and self-abuse. Key outcomes sought include establishing an understanding relationship and building skills and awareness to change behaviour. In my past professional experience I welcomed anger when it emerged, especially in a client locked in deep depression. It took time for me to learn this and not feel threatened. Anger is energising, opening the way to access what lies beneath, to naming it and finding positive ways to move forward. Anger heard and attended to can make the rest of life much lighter, positive and caring.

Warwick Pudney and Éliane Whitehouse have a produced an excellent resource that I am confident will be of great value to people from the various professions that work with young people in health, education, criminal justice and other settings.

Professor Max Abbott
Pro Vice-Chancellor and Dean, Faculty of Health and Environmental Sciences, Co-director, National Institute for Public Health and Mental Health Research, Professor of Psychology and Public Health, Past President and Senior Consultant, World Federation for Mental Health

Acknowledgements

Thanks to:

- The adolescent clients of Man Alive who shared their anger and pain
- Our clients who retell their adolescence in later life
- The schools that trialled and contributed material
- AUT University, Auckland
- The NZ Peace Foundation for believing in the cause

A thought for parents and adolescents

You are only
grown up when you
stop blaming your parents.
You are only
a responsible parent when you
stop blaming your children.

Warwick Pudney

Preface

It is our wish that this book be used as fully and appropriately for your clients as possible. That means that the professional helper uses their own existing knowledge and skills, uses their own cultural and social context and matches what is useful from this book to the client's context.

We believe that it is rarely just the adolescent's anger that needs to be noticed, and usually it's the parent's, caregiver's, employer's, teacher's or even professional helper's anger that needs to be given attention as well. We suggest that teachers, caregivers, counsellors and helping professionals read the book right through and do some of the exercises themselves to understand the themes of the book and make sure you have a good self-awareness of anger and its expression.

The book can also be used as a 'first aid' resource when anger-related problems occur. We hope that you can use the contents to appropriate supply copied pages for clients to use independently. Pages that invite photocopying are marked with a tick.

At the bottom of relevant pages we have indicated the 'Key concepts' being addressed. These can be turned into learning objectives in a lesson or counselling plan.

This book has been written especially for assisting adolescents. Obviously it will also have relevance to adults and children. Some pages invite your interaction. They can be photocopied, talked to, or done in your mind as you read. Invite parents to use the material also.

Notes

Examples from the authors' clients are used throughout the book. All names and some contexts have been changed so identities can be protected.

Children are not always looked after by parents. This book is written for anyone who has some responsibility for adolescents; from youth group leaders, teachers, foster parents, grandparents, afterschool programmes, school leaders, to specialists such as social workers, counsellors, psychologists, therapists, nurses and police. For convenience we will use the term 'parents and caregivers' to cover those roles of care and concern.

Warwick Pudney and Éliane Whitehouse

Introduction
How This Book Can Be Useful

For the last three generations in the Western world, adolescence and anger have seemed to go together. We expect adolescents to get angry at some point and to rebel. Unfortunately we have negative associations about both. It seems to be bad to be 'adolescent' and bad to be 'angry'. We'd like to suggest neither is bad. In our modern world adolescence is a normal stage and anger a normal emotion, necessary in small amounts for successful living. Anger helps us move from childhood and to claim the power of an adult and it's necessary to motivate us to speak out about injustice to ourselves and to others. Anger motivates us, energises us and protects us. We need it in small amounts when we have been hurt, had a loss or are afraid of a potential hurt or loss. It is a normal feeling that all humans have. What's not so good is when a person lives that way most of the time or behaves abusively. The fact that this is often more of a Western phenomenon begs some questions also about what we might not be giving to our children and young people that makes this stage difficult.

Feeling angry *all the time* is not good for us. Anger is a stressful emotion and too much stress damages our bodies and is really hard to live with. Abuse often accompanies anger. Abuse is not anger, but a behaviour, and is outside of our bodies – unlike anger which is inside our bodies.

Abuse hurts other people and damages things, people and relationships. We are really clear that no parent or adolescent should have to endure abuse.

It's never OK to be abusive to others. We are also clear that if an adolescent is abusive, it's not OK to be abusive back.

This book is about building understanding, safety, security and relationship. Over the past century we have created the condition of adolescence. It will benefit us all if we do our best to help our young people through this life stage. We will have less violence and crime, less youth suicide and the next generation of children will have better parents.

PART 1

HELPING PARENTS AND CAREGIVERS

CHAPTER 1

Adolescents, Parents and Power

It's all about power and how it changes hands!

Anger is an emotion that is associated with powerlessness and power. Anger appears when we feel powerless and we can use it to regain power and establish safety and autonomy. At a time of life when the major task is becoming autonomous and finding identity (Erickson 1980) it is understandable that anger is going to be more visible and a key part of the developmental operation. Anger is an important part of being an adolescent. Feeling angry with adolescents from time to time is also a natural response.

Parents have a lot of power which has been vested in them by a society that expects them to use it wisely to bring our kids up and to train them to be people that fit into adult social life in a way that maximises who they are. Adolescence however is the period of time when that power is challenged and carefully handed over to the adolescent as they learn to handle an adult world. Successful transitions give us good citizens. Successful transitions give adolescents responsible, respectful use of power in a manner that makes them resilient, happy and independent and hopeful of their future. An analysis of the power exchange can assist in understanding the use of parental power in the past and how it can be transitioned in the horse-trading of power that leads to strong adulthood for our adolescents.

Let's look at adult power and then set it beside adolescent power.

Adolescent power	Parent power
Adolescent powerlessness	Parent powerlessness

Parent power and adolescent power

Parents and adolescents both have power, but of a different kind. Our culture is a youth culture, in which we value the power of youth, newness and fresh approaches and we devalue aging and older ways. Parents, however, have great power in knowledge, money and parental control.

The power of one is the powerlessness of the other. When parents are feeling powerless and fearful they use their power over adolescents to feel better. Adolescents use their power in the same way. Both parents and adolescents may use their power to hit back when they feel powerlessness. It's useful to talk about our powerlessness and find respectful ways of negotiating deals.

Adolescents need to earn power from parents in order to mature. Parents need to give power gradually. They also might need to deal with their jealousy of youth and fear of their aging and decreasing looks and opportunity. Both parties need to respect the other.

Parent power

Most parents have most of the following power:

- Cooking, deciding the food eaten by others

- Greater verbal skills

- Economic and financial power

- Knowledge of how to get financial power

- House ownership/occupancy

- Legal custody and care of (and possibly access to) people under 16

- Connections to the rest of society

- Emotional knowledge from experience and education

- Organisation of the family

- Setting moral standards and holding values for the family

- Givers of care have the power to withdraw love and care

- Initiators of spiritual practice

- Managing family relationships (especially mother roles)

- Organising the home

- House-buying choice

- Deciding location of where to live (country, town, street)

- Usually they have control of all rooms except the adolescent's bedroom

- Power to withdraw provision of needs

- Power to withdraw the protection they provide

- Control of ideas, values, images, attitudes

- Managing the interface with the extended family

- Managing supportive networks

- Being better informed about the world

- Control of money

- Control of sexual activity in the home

- Organising personal needs of the family

- Owning the car, boat, machinery

- Assuming authority through expectations of society

Compare parent power with adolescent power and imagine how these power bases may play against each other.

Adolescent power

- Physical fitness
- Youthful strength and agility
- Endurance
- Optimism
- Technological knowledge
- Fresh, flexible minds
- Easier learning of new concepts
- Spontaneity
- Youthful looks
- Permission to misbehave, drink, act up, take risks
- Loudness
- Hope and aspiration
- More job options
- Exciting new attitudes
- Favoured in a youth culture
- Sport opportunity and physical expression
- Sexual activity
- Mobile lifestyles
- Entitlement to anger
- Less responsibility
- Emotionally alive and expressive
- Moral idealism and hope
- Creativity
- Good health
- Excited about the world and the future
- Marketing power of youth
- Understand and accept things easily

Both adults and adolescents also lack power in other areas. It's useful to name and contrast these as there is likely to be an expression of anger associated with experiencing these states.

Powerlessness of parents

A sense of powerlessness is what many parents react from.

- Lack of respect by adolescents who may see them as outdated in a youth culture
- Family support services overloaded
- Youth culture drawing adolescents away
- Understanding of role and gender – intergenerational differences
- Values uncertainty due to change
- Own skills and knowledge is becoming outdated
- Support for adolescents needing to stay home for education
- Unsure of how to do spiritual guidance
- Trapped in urban sprawl by high mortgages
- Periods of parenting alone or from a distance
- Single incomes

- Dealing with the dependence of youth while they demand independence
- General pressure to supply adolescent consumer needs without resources to do that
- Lack of respect for age
- Lack of extended family support
- Preoccupation with money, jobs, self-realisation
- School fees
- Often uncertain on how to relate
- Fear of relating to others adolescents (false accusation, jealousy)
- Guilt at working too hard
- Unemployment
- Lack of enough money
- Relationship break-up and discord
- Lack of own parenting
- Held responsible by social services and government departments while not having control of adolescent
- Availability and lack of control of their adolescent's access to drugs
- Fear of adolescent not liking or leaving them
- Dependency on the adolescent for service, affirmation or love
- Have dependent aged parents
- Long work hours
- Roles more stereotyped and rigid

- Mid-life crisis
- Reducing job options
- Tied to kids and house
- Not so many choices for occupation
- Less status for being older
- Nurture work not valued
- Provider work not recognised and invisible
- Technical ignorance
- Stale partner relationship
- Sexual boredom
- Have to appear nice and respectable
- Less body fitness and beauty
- Fear of youth
- Fear of newness
- Fixed thinking
- Attachment to property
- Unable to be childish
- Out of touch with youth and technical reality
- Work fixated
- Lied to by youth
- Wrestling with increased change
- Childcare role finishing
- Disillusioned with the world and mid-life
- Often bored
- More fearful as one ages
- Hard to party
- Supposed to have made it

Powerlessness of adolescents

- Lack of respect from adults who may see them as competition

- Governments and councils make little provision for them

- Search for identity when there is a lack of bonded mentors and authentic models

- Role and gender uncertainty due to changes

- Values uncertainty due to change

- Change and uncertainty in skills required for living

- Large debts for tertiary study

- Little spiritual guidance

- Reduced connection to nature due to economic and urban sprawl

- One parent or no parents: reduced care, modelling and home income

- Forced dependence on parents for education

- Increased advertising targeting adolescents

- General pressure to consume without resources to do that

- Blamed for community damage

- Lack of community mentoring and initiatory experience

- Parents preoccupied with money, jobs and 'self-realisation'

- Insulting regulation by high schools

- Not taken seriously as a social voice

- Lack of positive male community

- Lack of appropriate education learning styles (e.g. kinaesthetic and experiential)

- Non-useful education (skills and subjects that will not be used when other skills are needed)

- Lack of mentoring to support young adults

- Unemployed parents

- Lack of money

- Parental break-ups, parental discord

- Fragmented homes

- Lack of fathering

- Hurting and no one to talk to easily

- Can't communicate with adults

- Low pay or small income

- Sexual risks

- Disconnected from nature

- Eating disorders

- Body image problems

- Girls: being beauty objects

- Boys: macho image, needing to appear powerful

- Reduced understanding by parents

- Alcohol available to dull pain and fear

- Unemployment, especially if no skills
- Self-abuse with alcohol and drugs is easy and modelled in the media
- Parental ignorance
- Increased dependence on adults mainly due to study
- Greater complexity of modern-day adolescence
- Crises are frequent
- Risk-taking, accidents and deaths
- Need for constant stimulation and screen engagement
- High suicide rate
- 'I'-centredness of culture is exploited
- Shaky identity

- Fragile self-esteem
- Naive, idealistic and sensitive questioning of the world
- Feeling the need to eat as directed by the media
- Feeling the need to behave as directed by the media
- Feeling the need to dress as directed by the media
- Relational ignorance and naivety
- Shamed by peers and elders
- Developing emotional skills
- Great emotional vulnerability
- Poor communication skills
- Owning little property
- Unwanted pregnancy/ fatherhood
- Wanting approval of adults

The relationship of the four states of power and powerlessness

The four states of adolescent and parental power and powerlessness may be positioned as in Figure 1.1.

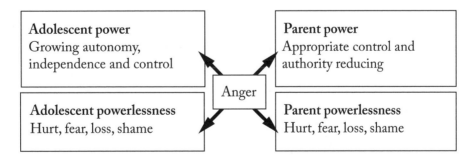

Figure 1.1 The four states of adolescent and parental power and powerlessness

Key points for the model:

The power of one is the powerlessness of the other

People often feel angry when they feel powerless

Parents decrease and adolescents increase power

Adolescence is the time of challenging power to reduce present and past powerlessness

Example: conflict over personal space

Rex (14) feels like he has no power over anything when at home. He feels angry about his parents' frequent intervention into his bedroom and their demands to keep it neat and tidy. What he wants is some control over his space and some autonomy.

Rex's mother feels hurt and distant from her son when he stops all touch, affection and hugs and when he spends even more time in his room. She increases her visits and interventions into his bedroom with complaints about its condition.

When conflict takes place there is an inclination for us to use our powerful zone in a 'power over' manner. This is a domination model that always ends up with dissatisfaction as the other is reduced to their 'powerlessness' sector and will feel angry and so seek to re-establish a better feeling by going into power competition.

A 'power with' model and a 'power assist' model are recommended throughout this book.

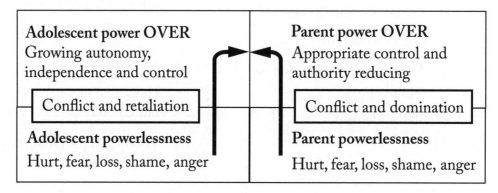

Figure 1.2 Domination or 'power over' model

Key points for the model:

We use our power zone to take power over the 'other' to reduce our powerlessness

Conflict and domination don't work as people get further apart

Conflict and competition don't leave people happy

Example: conflict over staying out late

Because he is afraid of severe limitations which he has experienced before, Simon tells (not asks) his mother (who depends emotionally on him) that he is going to a concert which finishes at midnight and that he won't be home till 1am. His mother is immediately fearful and angry at her possible loss of control and moves to take parental power to stop him going. Simon refuses to accept her dictate. He says nothing more and disappears that evening in defiance of his mother and leaves a note to say he is staying at his friend's place that night.

Having established that both adults and adolescents have power and powerlessness we can notice some patterns:

1. Both parents and adolescents have different ways of feeling powerful and may do so with or without taking power over the other. Sometimes that power is controlling and abusive.

2. It is because of our powerlessness that we feel angry and anger gives us the power and energy to seek to rectify the powerlessness.

3. Parents and adolescents will both use power (parent power or adolescent power) from their power assets in order to re-establish a sense of internal or external power and so lose the uncomfortable sense of powerlessness that is associated with hurt, loss (or sadness), fear, shame.

4. Anger becomes the conveyance vehicle to the powerful zone.

5. The easiest way of dealing with powerlessness is not a battle or asserting yourself via the power assets that you have, but sharing the vulnerability of that position and asking the other person/s for assistance.

6. This assumes a level of good will or suggests that that good will needs to be restored.

Throughout this book the 'power assist' model is what is being recommended where parents and adolescents show listening and kindness to each other when a power–powerlessness position is encountered. The attitude is one of help, co-operation and care. It requires a willingness to speak about the powerlessness being experienced.

We also recommend the 'power with' model where parents and adolescents show listening and respect to each other when in a power–power position and a sharing of the different aspects of power takes place between them. This requires trust and mutual respect.

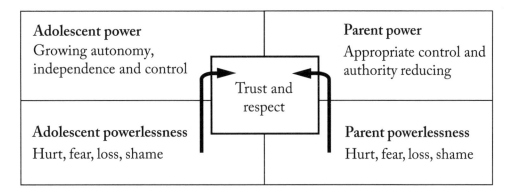

Adolescent power Growing autonomy, independence and control	Parent power Appropriate control and authority reducing
Adolescent powerlessness Hurt, fear, loss, shame	Parent powerlessness Hurt, fear, loss, shame

(Trust and respect)

Figure 1.3 The 'power with' model

Key points for the model:
Honesty about powerless feelings from both parties
Kindness and assistance with each other's powerless feelings
Growing respect and equality

Example: a 'power with' agreement

Mike goes to his father and asks for the car so that he can go on an education field trip. His father considers (his power) his previous experience of Mike, Mike's current state of mind, limitations, strengths, his own trust levels, his son's openness to him on who will be with him, and his own powerlessness (Mike's power) in knowing that his son has enough money to buy his own car. In this case Mike's father decides that he wants a trusting 'power with' agreement rather than competition.

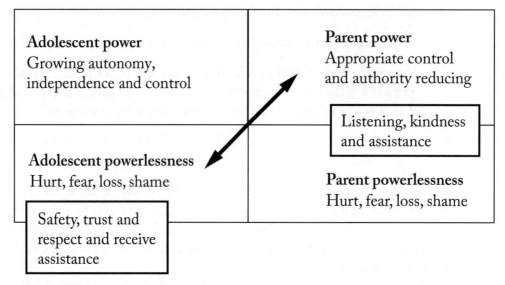

Figure 1.4 The 'power assist' model

Key points for the model:

One party can tell the other party about powerlessness and knows it won't be used against them

Powerful party helps powerless party and may even feel angry for the powerless person

Powerless party receives the assist

Example: dealing with trauma

Rachael has sufficient trust and previous experience of being respected and listened to, that she is prepared to risk telling her father about running away from an attempted rape in a car on a date. Her father listens with shock then kindness and assists her in her sobbing and trauma. He takes her to get professional counselling. He identifies with her and feels her pain and then feels angry for her. He later considers what additional action a responsible parent should take in this situation about the offender, considering also his daughter's grief and fear of public shame.

> **Key concepts**
>
> ♦ People respond to powerlessness by feeling angry.
>
> ♦ Anger is OK. People feel angry for a reason.
>
> ♦ Behind anger is hurt and powerlessness.
>
> ♦ Trust and respect are vital to power sharing or assistance.
>
> ♦ It's never OK to abuse others with 'power over' attempts and domination.
>
> ♦ We need to talk about our powerlessness, not try to 'power over' back.
>
> ♦ We need to listen to people's powerlessness.

Abuse and powerlessness

Read this real case to yourself or to an adolescent or parent. If you are a teacher, show each paragraph separately and discuss each one before progressing to another. Listen to understanding building and judgements changing.

After each paragraph, stop and check out your *judgements* and *feelings*.

1. Tim is 17. He is busted by cops for driving under the influence of alcohol. He goes to court and has his licence taken from him and he pays a fine.
    What do you think about that?

2. Tim was busted because he drove his mother's car to his girlfriend's party. He left at 12.30am and came back twice; he was wheel spinning outside and once he hit the curb taking off. He was very drunk. On the third visit at 3.30am he stopped in the middle of the cul-de-sac with the motor running and fell asleep in the driver's seat. His girlfriend's father came out and tried to wake him. He couldn't. He rang the police.
    What do you think about Tim now?

3. The cops came. They verbally abused him, calling him foul names, and pushed him around. He did not resist arrest and did not talk back. They made him sit in the road then took him off to a cell for the night. He was released on bail next morning.
    What do you think about that?

4. Tim liked to spend time with his girlfriend, Robyn. She was the only one who seemed to listen to him and understand him. He could tell her things that he couldn't tell anyone else. He couldn't speak to his mum and dad. He found it hard to talk to his male friends. He found it hard to cope without Robyn, in fact he depended on her. He found it hard to go home that night and would have really liked to have stayed.
    What do you think now?

5.   Tim's parents were angry with him. They were embarrassed, disappointed and shamed. They yelled at him. The car was forbidden. Tim's dad beat him up. He was a big man. He'd beaten him up all his life. He did it to discipline him and teach him a lesson.

        What do you think now?

6.   Tim hated being beaten up. He felt very angry when it was happening. He felt angry afterwards. In fact that's mostly what he felt all the time. Sometimes he turned that anger on himself. He thought of suicide quite a lot. Though he thought about how to do it, he hadn't tried yet.

        What do you think now?

Key concepts

+ Behind every anger there is a hurt or loss.

+ Hurt, fear, loss and shame are forms of powerlessness.

+ More information changes what we think about others. Making judgements can be risky.

Here are some other questions to think about:

- Who are the angry people in the story: Tim, his father, his mother or the cops?

- Who are the powerless people in the story: Tim, his father, his mother, his girlfriend or the cops?

- What was the result of their actions in each case of anger: 'power with', 'power assist', 'power over'?

- What's the chain of abuse in this story?

- Why do you think Tim's father beat him up?

- Why do you think the cops were angry and abusive?

- What would you do if you were Robyn?

- Has anyone here got the right to be abusive?

- What needs to happen now in this true story?

- Do you know anyone with a problem like Tim and his father? Name him/her.

- Do you need to do something about him/her?

- How did your thoughts and feelings change as you got more information?

We live in a society that often fails and misunderstands adolescents. Part of the problem is how to give increasing power, freedom and responsibility, as people move from being children to adults. Some adolescents have to take it if it is not given. Whatever happens, there are some basic rights that citizens are entitled to. You can ask for them and can expect them.

Key concepts

♦ All people need and are entitled to respect (parents and adolescents).

♦ Abuse is never OK.

♦ You are entitled to respect and attention.

♦ You need to ensure you give the same back.

New power and the possibility of revenge

Increasing adolescent power also means there may be some old powerlessness from the past that needs to be talked about again.

When children don't have needs met or, even worse, are hurt or neglected, these things don't go away. They may be put in a 'shadowy cupboard' for another day because they are problems and hurts which parents may not want to discuss because they don't like how they handled them. They may even deny them because they know that they were not fair. When the adolescent gains more power and some of that may be physicality, size, language, relationship expertise, friends, independent perspective, external support, then there may be a calling up of old issues. Wounds from the past may be reopened now there is more power to deal with them. This can be very uncomfortable for caregivers and parents. And even worse than reopening the cold case for a new look at guilt, shame and mistakes, is when the child, now a young adult, decides it's payback time. Retribution, reciprocity and revenge double the pain and create big bad gaps in relationships. Put crudely, now the young adult has some power it may be time for the parent to be punished, passively or actively.

Adolescence may however be an opportunity for new understanding, opening of eyes as to hurt, and opening eyes of adolescents as to the strife and stress of the parent at the time of the past incident. It may then also become a time of forgiveness and maturity and a forging of new relationships that look forward or strive for better models. Positive changes can take place.

Example: the danger of payback from childhood wounds

Warren was so sick of being 'whacked' by his dad as he grew up that he vowed one day when he was big enough, he would get him back. At age 14 when his dad was drunk he gave him a payback hiding. His dad never touched him again.

Counselling and parenting in new power relationships

Formal 'clean-outs' can be undertaken with counsellors managing the process, or by parents who are prepared to listen openly. It may not always be the parent who is doing the listening. Hurt parents may the seek time and place to talk about past hurts they have experienced from destruction, shaming, name-calling, manipulation and hurtful acts. Both parties need to 'be big' in their listening and have the ability to listen with discipline and *not be reactive*. For this reason it's often better managed by a third party.

Power and hurt

Hurt may lie in the back of a child's minds and foster a mistrusting view of the world when ideally they should feel happy and confident in their place of belonging. When a child or adolescent can't trust the people where their security and safety comes from, they are at a clear disadvantage in the world.

The child may adopt a pattern of hiding their best and trusting self in order to survive.

The storage of hurts for children are foundational for their lives whereas, with a sound secure start, undamaged adults can store later hurts better, knowing always that there is a known safer place and some secure power to handle it.

Children haven't had the power to change things. It's the parent's job to just know what's going on and fix things. It's often not safe for a child to speak up and declare the hurt. They may be squashed or hurt even further by parents or teachers who don't want to be criticised or admit that they got it wrong.

In adolescence, power balances and dynamics change and any stored formative hurts from childhood declare themselves and the adolescent often demands penance from caregivers. Resentments that have been harboured for years may be spoken and brought out into the open. Children who have been hit and abused may open up the box of old hurts and let you have it. This may be in the form of rebellion, damage to things, insults and accusations, verbal abuse, destructive behaviour or even physical abuse. People who have been hit often dream of the day when they can hit back and payback for the hurt of years ago.

It's possible the adolescent doesn't even know why s/he is doing it, and parents may be mystified.

Unpacking the past may surprise parents who ask, 'What did I do?' and say, 'I can't even remember that.' They may have excused and rationalised a mistake long ago so that they could live with it. It requires a lot of reflecting, self-searching and honesty to deal with this challenge.

Adolescents can't always help parents with the actual incidents so 'When?', 'Who was there?' or 'What did I say?' are avoidant and devalue adolescents' efforts to express times when they have felt shamed or belittled. Generally if a person says they felt disrespected the task is to release them from that experience, not to put up a minimising defence. There's no excuse for abuse, but there's also no excuse for parents not trying to fix the past, because children may pass this on to their own children. Now is the time to reflect, ask questions and acknowledge pain for old mistakes and things that parents or adolescents may wish they could have done differently. Any encounter with hurts and regrets need to be done in a meaningful way, and the offending party should show deep regret for the pain caused even though there may be 'another story'.

These may be small or unimportant incidents, like the time that a parent forgot to pick them up and left them waiting in the dark, or the time that they failed to turn up to a prize-giving or sports event, or hit their father, or even things that aren't true like 'I was an unwanted baby.' The ideas and memories that the adolescent holds may be quite unlike those held by the parents. The important thing is for parents not to rubbish or dismiss their memory or viewpoint, and to listen carefully and understand it. The parent or adolescent listener may have to listen two or three times to the same thing before they can empathise with the hurt.

Clearing resentment (and anger) and letting go

The authors have facilitated sessions of clearing resentments. These can bring immediate compassion, understanding and apology. However, very often they need several sessions as the compassion and new honesty are adjusted for, shocks for both parties are recovered from, anger is dissipated and an emotional clearing takes place. It may start a process that takes years but the important thing is that new information is shared, and the process is started.

The process

There are some key elements for counsellors, helpers, parents and adolescents:

1. Fostering the courage to 'come out' with things that parents or adolescents have been holding on to. Issues that one may have been suppressing or that one may believe are dead and past may emerge with an emotional charge. These need to be spoken of in an environment of managed listening with two willing parties.

2. Managed listening best takes place where one person has the right to speak for as long as they need to fully cover the incident or hurtful time. A strict environment of *no speaking* is needed as guilty or shamed listeners may try to reduce their discomfort. The discomfort in itself is a useful defusing of the urge for payback or retribution so it's important that the speaker witnesses the discomfort and the listener experiences a small degree of powerlessness while they sit in that discomfort. There are no interruptions, 'buts', stand-overs, retaliations, 'yes buts' – just pure listening. The speaker defines the hurt not the listener. If the speaker says that they felt shamed, hurt, afraid then that's what happened and that's what needs to be dealt with, not what the listener 'meant' to do. They must listen carefully to what the speaker has to say and acknowledge without excuses or reasons that they have spoken.

3. The listener relays what they have heard without explanations, denials, rationalisations, minimising, or counter-blaming or tit-for-tatting. No 'yes buts' and 'what I really meant' statements. They do not try to make excuses. There are no 'accidents' or denials.

4.   The listener then has the opportunity to apologise for the hurt, shame, sadness, neglect, selfishness, lack of awareness, and pain that they have caused. They speak with *remorse* not resentment. They speak as if they are clear that they will *never do that again*. They may offer compensation or ways of changing things so things are *made better*. It's the quality of the discomfort and apology that dissipates the desire for revenge. If you are the listener, *do not apologise too soon*. It will seem as if you are just avoiding the discomfort and that's then about you not listening again and thinking of yourself.

5.   The speaker has the chance to respond. This may be a clear and immediate acceptance and letting go of the incident, or it may be a suspicious look and acknowledgement, or it may at that time be a non-acceptance of the apology which the speaker has the right to do. The letting go process may take years but it is likely that it is started in some way through this process.

The authors recommend that one person has a chance to speak and that the return process not take place immediately so as to reduce the chance of tit-for-tat dynamics.

The other person can be the speaker next week or next session.

A session could also begin with the apologist starting first with something that has been bothering them (that they committed) that needs to be lifted from their conscience. Even if the adolescent says, 'Gee, I don't remember you doing that, Mum,' there has been a clearing taking place.

Power equalising

The process builds a new relationship based more on new equality and a fairness of treatment in the past. It sets up a new process of respect and communication for further hurts and misunderstanding. It does not mean parents lose all their power. It may mean that the adolescent is still *not* allowed to 'come home later' or 'drink alcohol' or 'have more money'. It *does* mean there is an arena of listening where deals can be struck as the adolescent grows older and needs more freedom.

'Yes I heard that you hated it when I left you with Auntie Jackie and went away for two weeks. That left you feeling alone and abandoned by me and you thought that I would never come back. I was only thinking of myself and I needed to be thinking of you. I feel sad about the whole thing and have thought about it many times. It shouldn't have happened. I feel bad that this has hurt you for so long.'

Or:

'So I've just heard that you were very hurt and angry when we made you get rid of your dog. I'm shocked because I didn't know that. You just hated us for that. It was your best friend and you felt alone and unloved and you had no one to have fun with. I didn't realise that it hurt so much. Now I realise it was important to you as I went through the break-up with your dad. I guess we were just thinking selfishly of ourselves as parents. It shouldn't have happened and you need to know that we would never do that again.'

CHAPTER 2

The Development of Adolescence and Anger in Society

Same needs, different worlds

Every generation of parents despairs of the 'new youth of today'. Today the media highlights those pressures with the prevalence of violence, electronic freedom, and pressure to consume 'brands'. Twenty years ago the concerns were risky sex and drugs. Most parents have a tendency to look back with longing to our youth through 'rose-coloured spectacles' and a sense that it was safer or better. In reality there are issues that are common to all generations: money, sexual safety, risky behaviour, broken hearts, fearful secrets, drugs, violence and being exploited.

If violence is more prevalent amongst adolescents and young adults, what is it about this time in history that might make many young people feel angry and choose violence? Is there more to be angry about? Is violence a more acceptable option? Most adolescents have grown up without hitting and corporal punishment so personal experience has changed and may be different from their parents.

Maybe young people have not experienced physical violence but have received emotional and psychological hurt that was deliberate or was caused by neglect and ignorance. It may be a matter of time before there is a 'giving out what they got' when they were smaller. Some of the problem of emotional or psychological violence is that it's not obvious even to the child and less so to the parent. But the hurt is there and tells the new adolescent to not trust, be wary, and even hit first. There is an attitude of mistrust and payback generated. Anyone who has worked with violent youths or adults knows that these people have in fact received too much violence already in their lives.

Too much discipline and too little discipline can be equally damaging.

Many do not know where they live, or who they live with, let alone where they stand.

The boundaries for behaviour are no longer as black and white as they were even 20 years ago. Parents may give their children one set of rules and values but films and videos present something quite different. Parents may also unconsciously behave with different values also. A classic is swearing.

'Where did she learn that foul language from?' says Mum and swears at her adolescent child for being so vulgar.

Consumerism and the propagandising of brands through sophisticated psychological techniques on fragile developing young minds verges on blatant exploitation and brain-washing. The fragility is stressed by the need for approval amongst peers. Fragile developing esteem is dented and may depend on 'looks' rather than other personal attributes.

For a teenager unsure of his or her identity and self-worth, expensive clothing and other possessions say, 'This is who I am. I am a person who can buy these jeans, this sweater, this car, therefore I'm OK.' It is no coincidence that labelled clothing features so highly among our teenagers' prized possessions at a time in history when so many adults and teenagers lack meaningful attachments and allegiances. They can at least be identified from a desire tag on their jeans or a patch on their sneakers.

In some small way they now 'belong' through possessions. They 'belong' to the Big Tick symbolised by the Nike logo and at least for a moment they are desirable and accepted.

We need to encourage children and adolescents to think critically about the choices they are offered. This is not easy. For all their apparent sophistication, most adolescents are trusting, naive, vulnerable and needy.

For the child from an impoverished home or a critical environment there are limited choices: forever yearn after these things and live with disappointment and resentment, steal them, or find a job and earn the money to buy them. Whatever they do, while they are doing that they are spending less time studying or developing gifts and skills that will increase later opportunities.

A grounded and secure identity with strong values and boundaries and a social network that values people is a big asset when forming new adults. Many young people are not so fortunate and they may seek immediate money rather than studying to get a job that gives more satisfaction and later reward.

Example: needing to work

Jemma is 17 and is in her penultimate year at high school. Jemma lives with her mother and stepfather. She is the younger of her mother's two children and has a stepbrother and sister. Jemma works three nights a week at a local fast food restaurant. With the money she earns she buys her own clothes. Her stepfather says he should not have to supply clothing for children who are not his and Jemma's mother has an ongoing fight with her ex-husband over child support. Normally Jemma works a six-hour shift, but during holidays she works full time.

She wants to go to a tertiary institution when she finishes school and to get there she will need a car because of poor public transport in her part of the city. Often when Jemma is working in the holidays she is asked to work extra hours, sometimes even a double shift.

Jemma hates this. She worries that she will fall asleep on her feet and not be able to deal with emergency situations that sometimes occur from working with hot fat. She often tells her boss that she does not want to work these long hours, but he tells her that if she does not like it she can leave.

Jemma knows that jobs are hard to come by and her friends in similar work tell similar stories, so Jemma keeps going. She does not join a union because she knows that those who do are given little work or bad shift times and all the rotten jobs.

Jemma has an employment contract, but her boss keeps this locked in his office with the contracts of other employees. Again, if she does not like this she can leave. Her boss is acting illegally and Jemma knows this, but she does not have the money, the knowledge, or life skills to take him to court.

When we retain our young people in such working conditions is it any wonder that many of them become angry and desperate? When they have no money from parents we can imagine their feelings of unworthiness amongst others and their anger. When they can't get a job but are told they need brands to feel good can we wonder why they may steal to get what others have.

Teenagers may also lack a cohesive family structure. Children are now as likely to live in a lone-parent or blended family as in the traditional nuclear family. In the past parents were forced to stay on in abusive and violent relationships through financial constraints and many children suffered. Today it easier for parents to end a difficult relationship. While some children are therefore better off, all children suffer loss and grief when their parents' relationship ends. It can mean the loss of their home, their other parent, their bedroom, their school friends, their school, their clubs and after-school interests, familiar neighbours and sometimes contact with relatives: grandparents, aunts, uncles, cousins and a parent.

The child needs to grieve each loss with support and validation of his or her feelings. Unfortunately the people most needed to offer this support are often wrapped up in their own grief. The worst part is when separated parents fight, ridicule and 'payback' each other; this hurts kids more than ex-partners. Grief is often dealt with quite understandably through anger displays. These are things worth feeling angry about.

A history of adolescence

Adolescence as a concept is really only about 70 years old. Before that childhood went up to 13 or 14 and then young adulthood started as the child suddenly took on an apprenticeship and worked. The strange middle years, from puberty to earning a wage, have come into being and have been called adolescence.

Gail Sheehy (1996) writes about the elastic nature of the human life span. Our children are displaying typical adolescent behaviour and physical development earlier. The average age for puberty is several years younger now, perhaps 12, than it was 100 years ago. Young people are caught in suspended childhood called 'adolescence', mainly due to education needs, and economic circumstances that keep them dependent on their parents. 'Adulthood' may not be reached until the late twenties or even thirties.

Adolescence is an invention of the education system. When our great grandparents went into apprenticeships they were given:

- A useful task for the community, for example, builder, cook, printer, bricklayer, dressmaker

- Money for their labour

- Training through practical experience and hands-on learning

- One or two older persons to mentor them for a period of years with teaching, guidance and protection

- Respect by the community for their contribution

- Initiation by older people

- Occupational structures to work within

Today young men and women don't usually leave school until between 16 and 22 years of age. They remain dependent on their parents, caught in a place of false childhood because of their needs for support. In that situation they get little of the above and even when they do finally leave school, they may not be able to get a job. That is worth feeling angry about. This, coupled with the 'busyness' of adults, leaves our young people feeling neglected and anonymous within the community. That is also worth feeling angry about. The need for parents to control what happens in their house and the dependency of the adult children also leaves the adolescent hungry for freedom and power, a sense of importance and purpose. That is worth feeling angry about.

Powerlessness is often a feature of adolescence. Young people can be ambivalent about becoming adults and shouldering adult responsibilities but they still have a need and drive to be noticed and appreciated for their developing capabilities and maturity. Their fears and ambivalence need to be recognised and respected.

In other ages and cultures, 13–16-year-old men and women would be initiated into an adult community and given a place of importance with support and encouragement from their elders. Instead, many of our young people are exploited by advertising, used as cheap labour, given no free training, no place to go for youth activities, minimal time from busy parents and little commitment for their welfare from the community. Adolescents face a dim future of student debt and grave uncertainties about their job prospects. This is all worth feeling angry about.

It is little wonder they experience high levels of stress, unworthiness, anger, depression and suicide as they try to claim support, recognition and power in a community that tends to deny them these.

Parents too have stress, discomfort and anger. They have work, social and advertising pressures. Many didn't expect the deal where they would have to support their children for so long. Neither did they expect so much anger from children that they were making so many sacrifices for. Many respond to the anger with anger.

The way through anger is by listening and this means both parents and adolescents. If, as a parent, you didn't learn to listen to your children when they were smaller, you can't automatically expect them to talk to you now. Learning to listen to the hurt behind anger takes patience and commitment. Most parents love their children enough to do that.

Adolescence has become a time of power tussles. The art of parenting is the handing over of power to the forming adult at a pace that leaves them secure, respected and dignified. Giving power away before time or failing to be attentive, leads to lostness and a lack of direction. Holding onto power and controlling in a way that fails to build good, strong, independent adults, creates controlled and resentful young people who need to rebel.

While adolescents have many reasons to feel angry, these are not an excuse for violence. Why do some respond with violence while most mature into concerned responsible citizens with good boundaries?

Perhaps the difference lies in the early responses of their intimate caregivers. Children who have received loving responsive parenting tend to develop stronger internal structures and a sense of worth, but perhaps there is more. One of the challenges of the future will be to discover what it is that makes some people more resilient than others to the 'slings and arrows of outrageous fortune'.

A person with good self-esteem will probably not take out their anger on the world but parents facing the stress of poverty, isolation and lack of support are not as well equipped to provide the strong parenting that their children need. Working long hours and having little time for quality relating left over may add to the problem rather than solve it. Unless we break this cycle we face a bleak future.

Someone once described the times and stages of our lives like stacked coins. When one coin is pushed askew, the whole stack is affected. For some of our young people the coin stack is askew in many places and may tumble down.

Some blame youth violence on TV, no discipline, fatherlessness, or just spinelessness, or wanting everything for nothing. We believe there is no one simple answer and no one simple solution. Violent solutions and strong reactions have been linked to violent media. Unregulated behaviour has been linked to poor parenting and stress due to consumer demands.

The bill for poor attention to children and young people has arrived in our letterbox and if we don't start to pay it off, the interest will accrue. In the following chapters we hope we can offer some possible solutions.

Key concepts

- Our children are growing up in a society that is different and untested. We need to pay attention to their real needs and meet them.

- Our community needs to take positive responsibility for our adolescents.

The roles and primary functions of parents

The functions listed here are not a rule but the lists show how the primary functions of parents are often divided. They are the result of conditioning, culture, genetics and nature. However, bear in mind that roles change, and you have the power to choose how you want to be.

You can discuss these functions, decide who is doing them, what's been done well and what needs more attention.

- Tick off the functions you have.
- Do you need to expand your functions?
- Are there some you as a parent share?
- Are some reversed?
- If parents aren't doing them, who is, or could?

Fathers

- ❑ Comforting, soothing children
- ❑ Teaching skills, strong limits and boundaries for sons, strength for son to idealise
- ❑ Stable force for the daughter when she is angry with her mother
- ❑ Supporting mother
- ❑ Being a real, available presence and an example for daughter when she forms adult relationships
- ❑ Limit setter and back up for mother in her limit setting, particularly with sons
- ❑ Link to outdoors and adventure

- ❑ Advocate for mother with children and listener to children's concerns and feelings
- ❑ Curbing of children's angry reactions to safe limits
- ❑ Valuing and affirming of daughter's developing sexuality within safe, clear boundaries
- ❑ Mentor, particularly for son
- ❑ Holder of values
- ❑ Holder of boundaries
- ❑ Risk-taker
- ❑ Safety guardian
- ❑ Gateway to the institutional world

✓

Mothers

- ❑ Comforting
- ❑ Feeding, soothing, holding
- ❑ Skill teaching
- ❑ Role model for daughters, affirming value of daughter
- ❑ Valuing son's masculinity, affirming strength of son
- ❑ Stable force for son when he is angry with father
- ❑ To provide a role model for sons
- ❑ Future relationships
- ❑ Limit setter

- ❑ Advocate for father while listening to children's concerns and feelings
- ❑ Valuing and affirming son's developing sexuality within safe, clear boundaries
- ❑ Mentor, particularly for daughter
- ❑ Teacher of nurture and healthy emotion
- ❑ Manager of family relationship
- ❑ Promoter of values
- ❑ Emotional guardian
- ❑ Gateway to relational world

CHAPTER 3

Anger Between Generations

Improving understanding between parents and teenagers

Parents often believe that they were better behaved and harder working and that they had it worse and appreciated more.

'We lived in a cardboard box in the middle of the road.'

'You were lucky to have a cardboard box. We lived in a hole in the ground.'

(Monty Python)

It is easy for a parent to feel resentful at the sight of a teenager sprawling across the sofa absorbed in yet another TV programme when you have just come home from a hard day at work to face housework and cooking. It is particularly hard to take if that teenager then grumbles and moans when asked to peel the potatoes or clean up. This is food for anger and resentment.

When the parents of teenagers get together they may gripe:

'When I was their age I wouldn't dream of refusing my parents.'

'When I was their age I had to work every holiday. My parents made me.'

'When I was their age I kept my room tidy/mowed the lawn.'

Today's youth have many advantages which their parents did not. Most have had more open relationships with their parents than in the past. There is technology available to them that their parents could not have dreamed of. Despite obesity, this generation is apparently better fed and taller than ever before.

✓

Exercise: generational differences

What advantages do your teenagers have that you did not? List them here:

. . . .

. . . .

. . . .

. . . .

. . . .

What disadvantages do your teenagers have that you did not have to deal with? List them here:

. . . .

. . . .

. . . .

. . . .

Do your lists tell you anything about the anger that exists between the two generations in your family?

. . . .

. . . .

. . . .

. . . .

Example from parenting group

When our parenting group was discussing this topic, Paul interrupted: 'I don't think kids should be able to talk back to their parents. If I had done that my father would have taken his belt off to me.'

'That happened to me too,' added Nicole, 'Now I can't stand up for myself at all anywhere, even though my father has been dead for 20 years.'

'Yeah, the same in my family,' Dan agreed. 'And look what it did to me. I can't handle my anger and it's cost me my marriage and my kids. I don't want my kids to be scared of me. I just wish I could find a better way, but it's really hard when you don't know anything different.'

Some parents experienced a painful adolescence and childhood. Often they have made a vow to give their children a better life than they knew. Sonia was such a parent:

Example: working through old anger

Sonia had been the eldest child in her family. Her father, an alcoholic, was either morose and withdrawn from a hangover, bad tempered from wanting a drink or drunk and violent. Sonia's mother was too busy keeping the family and the home intact to be responsive to her children. She too feared her husband's violence.

Sonia was determined to provide a good home for her own children. 'Our house was always such a mess. Mum used to give up in despair. I felt too ashamed to bring friends home. I don't want that for my kids. But now they are teenagers they leave such a mess around and I get so angry! They don't seem to care. I tell them off. I shout at them. I even try to bribe them. Nothing works.'

Sonia had latched on to one thing about her own early life that had been important to her: a clean house. She had lost sight of other more important things that had been missing, such as courtesy, caring and good communication.

Sonia realised that when her children were uncaring and slack they reminded her of her own mother. She realised how angry she was that her mother had given up on not only the housework but on her children too.

When Sonia was able to work through her anger towards her parents she was less angry at her children and was able to talk to them differently. Over time they became less sullen and more responsive to Sonia. 'I don't think their rooms are any tidier but I am less concerned about it. I get on their backs about more important things like not drinking and driving and they seem to be taking notice of me more.'

Parents holding on to resentment from their own childhood or adolescence may affect their relationships with their teenagers. They lack the 'software' to go past certain stages or incidents in their children's lives. They need to do things much more consciously and may need help to reflect on their past experiences.

....

Exercise: letting go of anger

Here are some suggestions for parents on letting go of any anger or 'faulty recordings' which are being carried from the past:

- Write a letter to the person they are angry with. They should not send the letter as getting personal perspectives heard is usually a different set of skills to straight expression. Some people find it helpful to write a letter every day until the energy has gone out of it

- See a counsellor or psychotherapist if they haven't already done so

- Talk to a trusted friend

- Talk to their older adolescent children (17–20-year-olds)

On the past point, be wary about how this is done: there is scope for the process to turn adolescents against their relatives, and parents may understandably be concerned about burdening them with their problems. Advise them to stick to the facts and how they felt at the time rather than blaming or asking the adolescent for help – it should be clear to the child that they are not expected to do anything for the parent. The parent may just want them to listen to something that will help both parent and child to understand things better.

Example: understanding anger

Tom recalls that he felt relieved when his mother told him about her own mother who was always sick and needed her children to look after her. He had not understood why his mother was always so angry whenever he became ill. Tom had thought he must be weak and bad and got sick of her demands.

Adolescents live more in the 'here and now'. Quite simply they have less history and life is a new exploration. Wisdom is still building up and feelings are fresh.

Sharing some family history may give teenagers insights into family patterns they themselves may want to change. This might also be an opportunity for them to understand that listening is helpful if either person has something important to share.

....

Exercise: memories and past fears

As a parent, can you remember your own teenage years? Can you remember what you were afraid of?

Alicia made this list:

People would look at me and notice the spots on my face

People would look at me and think I looked fat

People would look at me

The other kids would notice that my clothes were different

Boys wouldn't be attracted to me

Everybody else would have a boyfriend except me

I didn't have as much sexual experience as everyone else and I was scared that they would all find out

I might make a mistake

People would look at me

I would never grow up and be OK

My parents might make me leave home before I was ready

People would look at me

Paul made this list:

Not as much money as others

People thinking my parents were dorks

Not having a car

Still being a virgin

Being found masturbating

Not having a girlfriend

Exercise: comparing fear lists

- Adolescents: make a list of your fears.

- Parents: what do you imagine your son or daughter's fear list would contain?

- In what ways is the adolescent's list and the parent's list of the adolescent the same?

- In what ways are you different?

Example from parenting group

'My life was tough,' said Maralyn, 'Why should I fall over myself to make things any easier for my kids?'

The rest of the group looked shocked and began protesting.

'Can any of you honestly say that you have never thought that?'

A few people nodded.

'So why should you make things easier for your kids?'

'So that they don't have to make as many mistakes as I did,' Maralyn replied.

'Because I care about them,' said Paul.

'Because I would like to make a difference in the world.'

'Because I want to have good relationships with my kids when they are grown up.'

'Because I want to enjoy my grandchildren if I ever have any.'

'Because I don't enjoy living with abuse.'

....

Exercise: reflecting on family relationships

Parents:

- Why are you making a commitment to relate better to your children?

- What will your children be like when they are your age?

- Will they have made the same mistakes as you have?

- Will they be exhibiting the old family patterns?

- What do you want to give to your children?

- Imagine yourself at your eightieth birthday party: the family is standing around. Delicious food and drink are on the table. There is laughter amid the chink of cutlery on china. One of your children gets up to make a speech. She talks about your contribution to her life. What would you like her to say?

Key concepts

- Understanding and knowing ourselves helps us know and live with our children.

- Fixing it with our own parents greatly helps our parenting of our own children.

CHAPTER 4

Communication

Holding families and building relationships

'She doesn't listen.'

'He just grunts at me.'

'I might as well talk to myself.'

'I could be on another planet for all the notice he takes of me.'

These are frequent complaints from parents of teenagers. They are a good reason for a parent to feel angry. Anger is a motivator for change so the question to go with it is 'What are you going to do about it?'

Example from parenting group

Andrea reported to our group that she had been so fed up with being treated as a non-person-taxi-driver that she stopped the car and confronted her teenage passengers about this.

'They stared at me as if to say, "Who do you think you are?"' she said.

Teenagers look less to their parents for answers and more for service. That is the nature of supporting a young adult who for millennia has been treated as a working person in the community.

But we need to live together and young people also need a familiar wise person to listen to them in times of trouble.

'That's what is so hard to take,' said Andrea, 'It is a one-sided relationship. Give and take, but I do all the giving and they do all the taking. Do I have to just put up with this?'

Parenting still demands dignity though the child/youth may be in an extended transition. Teaching children to maintain respect is still socialising them for a world where they need respect for work hierarchies and authority systems like the law. The real world will not allow them to get away with this and they will be badly equipped if they do not respect others. If they are to go beyond adolescent development they will need to face reality. Demanding respect and backing each other up as parents is important. Absolute consistency is needed.

'Every time I have to tell my kids something I know they are not going to like,' said Andrew, 'I have to steel myself to cope with their negative reactions. I don't like it when people don't like me, especially my kids. I think I'm scared of their anger.'

Andrew realised that he had felt the same way as a child. His father was a withdrawn, stern, cold man who bottled his anger until he could hold it in no longer and then he would explode. Andrew was still afraid that people would explode with anger as his father had done.

Andrew found that he avoided communicating with his sons on anything but a superficial level because he was afraid.

If parents can overcome their difficulties and learn to communicate with their children when they are young, children are more likely to have a good relationship with them in adult life.

When Andrea came to terms with her fear she discovered that her sons saw her as stern and withdrawn, someone who bottled her anger until she exploded as she had done that night in the car when she felt she was being taken for granted.

The most effective way of avoiding both these scenarios is to communicate positively and powerfully and 'train the puppy when it is young'. Early effective regulation, appreciation and communication is the best prevention.

Reasserting standards, rules and protocols

If a foundation of respectful communication has not been laid and kept consistent then re-establishing respectful standards and communication can be achieved but is harder for both parties.

This has further been complicated by the suspended dependence of young adults on parents in order to get a good education. Powerful, assertive, consequence-based kindness is required alongside respectful listening. The areas that are hardest are maintaining empathy and being tough at the same time. One is often seen to exclude the other. A cracking down on the rules implies that the parent hasn't been consistent before that.

Two things are needed: firstly, the confession of previous inconsistency as the fault of the parent with the result that it's confusing for the adolescent, and, secondly, the parent must now keep the promise of future consistency. Negotiation of a new contract is preferable but it's hard to withdraw power so sometimes it has to be claimed, especially where the safety and well-being of the adolescent or other members of the household are concerned.

Sometimes a temporary removal of the adolescent to another family home where a clean start is a possibility can change old patterns. A return to the parental home is later made with the same firm establishment of rules with rewards and consequences being agreed to before re-entry. While the adolescent's part in this contract is compliance, the parent's part of the contract is absolute consistency. Boys and men particularly respect a quite black-and-white consistency.

I recall an adolescent who experienced this 'new home' approach, hating it at first because it was withdrawing some power that previously had allowed the adolescent to be chaotic, deeply disrespectful and disruptive of the entire family life. He referred to his parents as having 'become Nazis'. What the authors also knew was that he was in payback mode to the whole world for sexual abuse he had received from a nearby farmer when he was younger and more powerless. He chose not to disclose this to his parents but the authors were able to assist him with therapy unknown to them. However, the 'bad behaviour' was still not excusable and needed to be managed. I met him ten years later training to be a church social worker.

Remembering the positive

To use the title of a well-known book on communicating with children, good communication has been called *Talking So That Teens Will Listen and Listening So That Teens Will Talk* (Faber and Mazlish 2006). Having the notice from page 54 ('Talking so that kids will listen') pinned up on the fridge has helped many families. It is a reminder for adults and their children that good communication is really important.

Parents should listen to young children so that they still want to talk to you when they are adolescents. Why would an adolescent suddenly want to talk to a parent if the history has been that parents are always too busy, not there or uninterested?

· ·

Exercise: listening and empathy

Here is a conversation between a father and his 15-year-old son. Invite a parent to finish the conversation in a way that will be helpful to them both.

> Parent: 'You feel angry when I remind you about your messy room because you don't want to tidy it. Is that right?'

> Adolescent: 'No, I feel like a stupid kid when you tell me because I never seem to get anything right.'

> Parent: 'You feel upset sometimes because you get criticised a lot at home. Is that it?'

> Adolescent: 'Yeah. Well, and at school. I just can't understand what the teacher's saying.'

> Parent: 'So you can't cope with the school work and you feel stupid and then you come home and I go on about your messy room and it's like you can't get it right here either.'

> Adolescent:

> Parent:

Parents: imagine that you are the 15-year-old son in the example above.

· Would that be a satisfactory ending for you?

· Will you be any better about your messy room?

- Do you feel heard by your father?

- Will you go to him again if you have a problem?

....

Exercise: listening and empathy 2

Here is the start of another scenario.

> Parents: continue the conversation below so that the teenager feels heard and you as the parent feel comfortable with the outcome.
>
> Adolescent: 'I need a new top to wear to Anya's party.'
>
> Parent: 'Who is Anya? Have I met her?'
>
> Adolescent: 'Of course, Dad. You remember her father. He used to coach my gym team at primary school.'
>
> Parent: 'Will Anya's dad be at home when this party is happening?'
>
> Adolescent: 'Oh Dad! Really! So do you think I can get a new top?'
>
> Parent:
>
> Adolescent:
>
> Parent:

Put yourself in the position of the adolescent.

- What is the parent afraid of? Do you feel Dad has heard the request?

- What was Dad's real concern that he has not voiced?

- How could he say it in a more direct statement?

Listening so that kids will talk

Some useful questions for both parents and adolescents to consider are:

- Do you know someone who is a good listener?

- How do you know they are listening to you?

- What do they do?

One of our parenting groups came up with this list for talking to adolescents (or anyone):

- Make eye contact.

- Don't interrupt to talk about yourself.

- Don't give advice.

- Don't compete to tell a more impressive story than them.

- Make encouraging noises to help them talk some more (e.g. 'Uh huh', 'Wow', 'Mmmm').

- Make a comment to show some understanding of how they feel (empathy).

- Sit beside them.

- Let them see by the expression on your face that you care.

- Don't judge them or criticise them or tell them what they 'should' have done and so make them 'feel wrong'.

- Don't try to stop someone who is starting to cry. Some people may say, 'Don't get upset.' It's usually the listener that can't handle the crying and vulnerability and feels uncomfortable and wants the speaker to stop being upset.

- Stay calm so they know you can cope. Stay silent if you need to.

- Say 'I expect you felt angry' or 'Now I understand why you might feel angry' so that they feel OK telling you about their anger.

- Care about them and show it.

Parents: add other particular items specific to your case.

> *Listening makes all the difference.*
> *If you don't listen,*
> *don't expect adolescents to talk to you.*

Talking so that kids will listen

- Face your child when talking to her/him.

- Stop what you are doing and look at her/him if you really want her/him to hear.

- Put yourself at equal height. (This is not easy for some, especially mothers of teenage sons. You may need to ask your son to sit down with you.)

- Say, 'I need to talk to you.'

- Lower the tone of your voice. Women are often not listened to because they speak in high tones, particularly when they get angry.

- Reduce the number of words when talking to boys. Boys may use as little as a third of the words that girls/women use. Often they get a defence running and this causes them to switch off when listening to anything which they may characterise as 'blah blah blah' (too many words). This defeats your objective.

- Speak quietly. People 'switch off' if we shout at them. You might feel like yelling but if you want to be heard, don't shout. The listener's defences lock you out.

- Make eye contact if possible and if culturally appropriate. 'Look at me when I talk to you' results in either shaming or defiance.

- Sound as certain as you can (taking a deep breath can help, so can standing with both feet firmly on the floor).

- If you have something important to say, then say so. 'Let's sit down for a moment. I have something important to say to you.'

- Give your teenager a right of reply and listen.

- If you have something important to say use an 'I' statements and the four-part phrase: 'I feel...when...because...I would like...' (see 'Basic communication – the four-part phrase' handout in Chapter 18). For example, '*I feel* angry *when* food is left in your room *because* it smells. *I would like* you to clean the food out of your room every day.'

- Put yourself and your teenager on the same side of a problem. '*We* seem to have a problem here. I want to walk past your room without seeing so much mess and smelling horrible smells of rotting food. What are *we* going to do about this?'

Exercise: negotiation

Two boys had been brought before the principal for being verbally abusive to a teacher.

One boy said sullenly, 'We wouldn't have spoken to Mr Y like that.'

'Why not?' asked the principal.

'Because he doesn't let you get away with things. And he's fair. And besides he listens to you. Mr Z didn't want to know. I tried to tell him. He never listens.'

Apparently Mr Z had roared at the boy for not completing his homework. The boy concerned had been working five hours a night for the past week because his parents were trying to pay off the repair bill on their car. The boy felt trapped. He had to choose between making the teacher angry or disappointing his parents.

Young people often face such dilemmas. They may also have just neglected to do their homework. How would you know?

• Is there a way that a young person who is genuinely trying to meet deadlines can negotiate a fair settlement?

• Are you more like Mr Y or Mr Z in your treatment of young people in your care?

Read more on negotiation in Chapter 6.

The payoff

• You know you did it right when they listen to you in return.

• There may be a time when the parent hears their son or daughter being a good listener to someone else.

• One day the person being really heard and supported might be your grandchild.

> **Key concepts**
>
> ‹ Healthy relationships require you to communicate well.
>
> ‹ Good communication involves talking and listening well.
>
> ‹ You need to listen to feelings.
>
> ‹ 'I' statements promote responsibility and stop blaming.
>
> ‹ Feelings may sometimes be uncomfortable but they are important.

Relational situations

Most families have reduced the time and situations where talking can take place. There are three main reasons for this:

1.   The increased influence of the peer group reduces family interaction

2.   The increase of TV viewing time reduces personal discussion time

3.   The increased working hours of parents also reduces personal discussion time

A shift of focus from the family to community members outside the family has always been an important part of being regarded as an adult. However in traditional societies adults from the community were more involved and tended to take over from parents as guides. Smaller communities (as opposed to cities) tended to keep the family in relationship with the young adult.

1. The increased influence of the peer group

The peer group is now increasingly important and may replace family interaction. Families may need encouragement to do things together that meet the needs of all members. Parents need to learn about modern music and adolescents need to share in housework. Negotiated shared time is important. Even under some forbearance the adolescent even gets that they are wanted and cared about. Additionally it's important to have something to rebel about rather than have total unguided freedom. Rebellion is in itself formative and teaches negotiation around power.

2. Increased screen time (DVD entertainment, video games, internet and TV)

Screen time has increased steadily over the last two decades and has become more individuated due to the more individual nature of internet and game activity. Many children and adolescents have screen time in seclusion of their bedrooms. This obviously reduces family interaction. The authors have considerable concern about the effect of violent interactions and models of violent solution-seeking to problems. The authors suggest careful management of screen time through watchdog software that limits what is viewed and the hours of viewing, and adds passwords for some TV channels. This requires monitoring. Parents are often the ones watching and may need to reduce hours to increase family interaction. The authors suggest we consciously bring back family meal times and have at least one family meal (with the TV off) per week. Families that eat together are engaging in an age-old ritual of sharing not just food but good will and support.

3. *Working parents*

Previous generations often had a parent at home who could start conversations at the time at which the child or adolescent felt the stress they needed to talk about. Dealing with the immediacy meant that there was a more authentic and urgent conversation rather than the adolescent waiting for hours to talk or talking first to a peer who has less knowledge of the world and its resources. The authors suggest having good mobile phone links between parents and adolescents and dealing with those connections as a priority. Good 'clean-outs' at the end of each day, picking up on moods, and 'keeping the doors open' are all important in reducing the effect of not having parents readily available.

Family meal times

Andy decided that problems were building in his family and that bringing back family meal times might help. 'I took a deep breath and waited for the protests that I knew would come,' he said.

'I started by saying that one day a week we would eat together and I told them it was because we were not talking to each other until we were really angry about something. Having a meal together would give us time to talk.

I don't know how it happened, but after a while we were eating together half the week. On some days we have the TV going but I notice that more often than not no one's listening to it. It's just background. Now it has become automatic that we set the table and eat together. The kids found it hard at first when their friends came around. My son explained it as, "Dad comes from the West Coast and that's what they do there." I guess that made me the weird one, not him. I just know we get on so much better as a family now.

I think we should have an International Eat Together Day. It could help to make a more peaceful world.'

Families that eat together:

- Talk together

- Spend time together

- Solve problems together

- Feel connected

- Help each other feel important and worthwhile

- Develop family rituals that aid connection

- Develop good communication skills

- Tell stories that aid connection

- Learn social skills

- Learn co-operation

- Listen

- Have fun together

- Have arguments but have an opportunity to resolve their differences

CHAPTER 5

Adolescence
The Transition Event

Introduction to adolescence

Adolescence is the time of transition between childhood and adulthood. The adolescent moves from childhood dependence to adult independence. We have however chosen to extend that transitional period from an abrupt switchover somewhere between 12 and 15 to somewhere between 10 and 22.

Earlier physiological changes and extended education have generated the increased transition time.

The independent adult world is a foreign country, and, like any new arrival in a strange place, it takes a while to learn the ropes for the new role and sometimes we make mistakes, especially if we have little guidance.

In that space of time they must cross the bridge and on the other side have an idea of who they are when they get there. Adolescence is a transition time when we can consolidate what we have learnt so far, take some time to grow and learn about the complexities of the adult world before we need to step into it. It gives us time to gather ourselves together and move gradually forward into what is becoming a more and more complex adult world.

There are tasks involved in this development of identity.

Task 1: Deciding who you are not

The obvious place to start is with parents. They are two people from a different age and stage. As today's teenagers they must leave the past behind. They are not that age. The place they have to live is the present. They have never really known their parents as adolescents so their current age is all they have. They are not that stage.

Example from parenting group

'She was such a great kid. Why did she have to change?'

Anya heaved a sigh and said these words one night at a parenting group. Most of the group agreed with her. Anya was asked what sort of adult her daughter would have been if she had stepped straight into adulthood at age ten. Could she imagine a ten-year-old adult? What would be lacking in a ten-year-old that would be required to function in the adult world?

The group came up with these ideas:

- The ability to handle money

- The ability to make decisions

- The ability to relate to other adults

- The ability to negotiate and communicate

- Knowledge about the world and the ability to cope with crises

- Skills and knowledge to earn a living

- Confidence to cope alone without adult help

- The ability to right themselves after failure

- Confidence and good feelings about themselves as a person

- The feeling that they are acceptable to other adults

- More height and physical presence

- Ability and knowledge to keep themselves safe

Anya thought about her own daughter: 'She does everything that I wouldn't do. I'm tidy. She's messy. I like to dress well. She wears these horrible black clothes. I'm clean. She doesn't shower every day now.'

Others in the group reported the same thing. One father was aware that his daughter was reacting against her very clever successful older sister. 'Everything Mere is, Sondra is the opposite,' he said.

Task 2: Deciding who you are

Once we have decided who we are not, we need to decide who we are. This usually involves a search for identity that may span music, dress, friends, school, occupation and hobby, activity, sport, culture, values, religion, beliefs, skills, cars, hairstyle and anything that we have some attachment to.

Most importantly during this time adolescents gather friends around them. It's much more comfortable to have friends around us when we enter a foreign land. Friends are usually an early part of the identity search and continual referencing to and from them is a platform for other identification. They are likely to be of similar age, ethnicity, geographic location, education background and class. We are attracted to those who are like us. Sometimes our friends are the only people around who want us and sometimes they are even chosen in order to defy parents and even pay back parents. 'My gang gives me what they didn't!'

'I'm so angry with my parents sometimes I think of going home with a friend and telling them that we are in a gay relationship (when we are not).'

Parents may go through a period of *grief* at the loss of 'my little boy' or of *jealousy*.

'I watch my daughter say goodbye to her friend at the gate,' said Kara, 'and then five minutes later they are talking on the phone. Can't they bear to be away from each other for a moment? I wish she could do that with me.'

Professionals are warranted in checking out such emotions as complicating factors in a parent–adolescent relationship. Often it's about the parent not having their own relational needs met.

Good communication and relationship, and acceptance of autonomy by parents, may however allow collaboration and relief from the pressures of identity and inclusion.

Example from my own experience

We were visiting friends for dinner. I was talking to our host in the kitchen when his adolescent son came in. Jason was 15, but very tall and well built for his age. He looked 18 at least.

'Dad, Jamie and Zac are at the door,' he said, 'They want to know if I can go to Mark's party.'

'I guess so,' said his dad, 'You've been there before and it's been OK.'

Jason looked down at his feet.

'Dad, I don't want to go. They've got these girls with them. They're about 20. I can't handle it. Can't you say I can't go?'

'Ah, well now,' said his dad. 'I had been thinking that you and I might go fishing tomorrow. If you want to go we will need to be up by 6 o'clock.'

Jason looked relieved.

I heard him go out to the front door.

'Sorry guys. I can't go. Got to be up early to go fishing tomorrow. Parents, you know! They said no.'

'Yeah. Parents!' said his friends. Jason closed the door.

Sometimes, particularly at the outset of adolescence, the limits need to be set by the parent.

Adolescents can seem so grown up and sophisticated at times we can easily forget how young, vulnerable and scared they can be. They need the safety of our limits. But they need limits that are flexible and will grow with them as they learn to cope.

This may create anger, friction and resentment. For example, after being told she cannot go to a rock festival, one daughter reacted as follows:

'I hate you Mum [*sobbing*]. When you are old I will put you in a home and never come to see you.'

Powerlessness

Being physically an adult and being able to father or give birth to children gives a powerful sense of adulthood. Being old enough to drive a car, vote or go to war also reminds adults of their responsibilities and power.

But as an adolescent we may be asked to stay in the same bedroom we have had for the last 12 years, dress in a child's uniform, live on pocket money and ask if we can use the car. A sense of injustice and powerlessness is likely to be present as these states encounter contradiction. With powerlessness comes the emotion of anger. Having powerful romantic or sexual feelings for another person and then getting rejected leaves a space for powerlessness that a parent may never know of but which they may get a taste of indirectly.

The continual shifts in power and opportunity and the wonder of new opportunity deliver a very changeable world for an adolescent. It's the first time for so many things and they all have a big impact because they are the first time. Parents remember the songs of our adolescence and young adulthood better than any other age. That's why supermarkets measure the demographic of their customers, and then play the music and songs that they experienced during their youth. That gives strong familiarity and a sense of well-being that gets transformed into better sales.

Each new step of life has first-time fear and trepidation that can have a knife-edge result of either the power of mastery or powerlessness of non-success. The continual dicing with newness means powerlessness is a common feeling. Some feeling of anger is often the first response. Old people are usually very slow to anger. They don't feel so powerless because they have been there many times before.

Being selfish and self-centred

Children need to let go of their parents. Their parents need to let go of them and also hang on to them to keep them safe on the journey. The process of separation is risky and bold. It's important for the young person not to think of parents so much but to think of self as defined as separate and different. Understandably the young person becomes very self-focused.

One of the most frequent complaints about teenagers in parenting groups is that they are 'selfish'. Their needs are often put before others and they may seem in a 'fight mode' or independence struggle to get free. Reduced empathy for parents and others is necessary otherwise they become caught in thinking of the parent's feelings rather than their own feelings and opportunities and these are the key to independence. There are adults who 'never got free' and remain unpartnered and living with their parents because they could not bring themselves to upset their parents. A young man needs to be able to hurt his mother's feelings, not out of viciousness but as part of the task of separating from the bonds with mother and moving to relationships with partners his own age. If he can't do this he remains forever in some way neutered in relationships and not able to stand equally in relationship with a woman in partnership. Many women observe how frustrated they feel that their male partners can't stand up to their mothers. Generally these women are contesting for the power rather than the man having established himself as independent, respected and equal.

Self-centred, risk-taking, self-asserting; they need to show 'I can manage on my own!' but such a bold step brings fear and trepidation and rightly so as they can't fully do that.

The self-centredness is a pushing away of parental control and direction in a world that extends adolescence and dependence into late teens and twenties and even beyond. Telling adolescents of the effect this self-centred behaviour has on parents keeps them in touch with intergenerational relationships. They may not change, but the telling at least preserves the parents' dignity and self-respect. There will be a day when the parent hears the teenager say, 'How was your day, Dad?' or 'Thanks for washing my shirt.'

One dad commented:

'I hang on to the thought that one day my son will buy me a beer.'

Adults have other points at which they define themselves by self-centred behaviour, out of necessity, either feeling they have lost some sense of who they are or feeling they need to redefine themselves. Recovering from a marriage break-up is a more obvious one. Encountering 'empty nest syndrome' (all children having left home) is another.

A parent reacting very strongly to being treated as non-existent might ask whether perhaps this has been a life-long experience. Perhaps they have always been treated like a doormat?

The section of this book on self-assertion and limit-setting may be useful to those redefining and refinding themselves (see Chapter 9).

Mothers and daughters

A girl whose relationship with her mother has been tenuous may seek more dependency with her mother and at the same time be resentful about this, which may lead to displays of anger. Girls at this age normally need to loosen ties to their mother. However, as with any separation, there is anxiety, so the young girl often seeks older girls or young women to idealise. A girl may be drawn to more powerful or attractive girls whose status seems to enhance them. These peer relationships include aspects of loyalty, treachery, betrayal, sharing of secrets (often about boys and sexuality) and the need to belong.

Mothers and sons

In his early life it is usually the mother of a young boy who provides him with the nurturing and emotional tenderness he needs, but as time goes on he is drawn away from the feminine bond and towards a masculine bond usually with his father. In her book, *Between Mothers and Sons*, Evelyn Bassoff writes about how this pull is beautifully portrayed in the book *Bambi*. When a small Bambi sees his father, he is overcome with terror and wonderment; his once all-sustaining, all-powerful mother seems suddenly different and he himself feels small when confronted with his own gender. 'From this time on,' writes Bassoff, 'the little deer is no longer content to be like his mother or to dwell exclusively in the feminine. Instead he is increasingly fascinated with the great elk who represents the primal, masculine nature' (Bassoff 1995).

Boys tend to idealise fathers between the ages of 7 and 12. Unfortunately for many of our sons today being raised in single-parent (usually mother) families, there is less chance to identify with the masculine and the young boy becomes preoccupied with distant, unreal, male figures on the TV, movie screen or the sports field. He may fail to be affirmed by a man. As a young male in early adolescence becomes more aware of his own sexuality he may find himself disturbed by thoughts of his mother as a sexual being and may push her away. The mother needs to accept the shift of interest to young women and quietly grieve the distance without ceasing to encourage him to demand respect for himself.

The complexity of the mother–son relationship at this time can cause friction and acting out on the part of the teenager. Thirteen-, 14- and 15-year-old boys may seem to change from 'nice boys' to 'bad boys'. They may become obnoxious, dirty, loud and rebellious as part of the process of separation and individuation from their mothers. 'Mummy's boys' don't develop into strong independent men. They are too concerned with adapting themselves to what Mum wants and fail to develop a sense of identity and a real self. This leads to dependency in later relationships with women. Such dependency may lead to insecure attempts to control the female partner and this is a major dynamic in male partner violence. These men have a fearful dependency on women in an age when women seek increased independence. Destructive attempts to control are a symptom of a man shallow in his masculinity and probably without good male friends.

The task is to see that a young man stays respectful but more separate. Dads need to say, 'Don't talk to your Mum like that', thereby modelling respect. This is just as important in separated families. Fathers are still very important. The father who speaks disparagingly of his ex-partner is modelling behaviour that his son may copy in his own adult relationships.

The presence of Mum is vitally important in a son's life. Apart from gaining the strong models of nurture and care, mums teach sons how to relate to women and thus train them for future relationships. Mothers for their part have to deal with the fact that they are not the only women in their son's life any more. They may grieve this loss. Attempts to hold on and control may be met with anger and defiance or worse still compliance.

Fathers and daughters

While mothers are vital for same-gender models and affirmation for daughters, fathers are important too for a sense of security, order and protection. Additionally, a loving dad teaches how to have a trusting, respectful, fearless and fun relationship with peer males and men generally. Some of this practising to relate to men is evident in early adolescence when girls may seem to act flirtatiously. At a parenting group Wayne reports that at this stage his daughter gave him a photo of herself in a love heart frame to keep on his bedside table when she was living away in her mother's house.

It takes a mature and trustworthy dad to notice and affirm his daughter and allow her to be sure that she does not have to be sexual to be loved for who she is. According to Ellis (2003), the rate of teenage pregnancy is higher for unfathered daughters.

Dads are also good for checking the safety of their daughters and saying some of the hard things that need to be said about sex. While daughters may protest, they also hear (without letting you know) that Dad loves and cares about them. Some dads feel jealous of their daughter's interest in young men. A mature dad will retain a balance in this. 'You're not going out in that dress. It's too revealing!' could be replaced with: 'You are giving out some powerful sexual messages in that dress. Is that what you are wanting? How safe do you think you will be?'

Daughters need to know that dads love them. Daughters may feel angry and short-changed if Dad hasn't been there for them and also told them how important they are to them. They need to know that their dad is strong and not a pushover and they need to love and push against them at the same time.

Steve, a separated dad, reports:

'My daughter was acting up badly until I let her know the pain I felt at being separated from her and the fact that her pain was my pain. When she saw that I could shed tears for her she was transformed and much more sensible over boyfriends and more powerful in her relationships with them.'

Fathers and sons

Dads are vital for boys. Most boys are getting too much of Mum and not enough of Dad. A boy needs to experience a positive model and it's vital to his self-esteem to be affirmed by the most important man in his life – Dad. Failure to get male affirmation leaves him liable to dependency on women and unable to develop good, strong relationships with men.

By adolescence the main fathering work should be done and the boy should have the grounding needed for a positive masculinity and responsible manhood. Sons will then be seeking the teaching, company and assistance of other men in the community. Adolescent boys will soon be working and playing alongside them. If a boy has had a negative, uninvolved or absent dad, then he may well be angry towards authority figures and mistrust men.

Often single mums unjustly cop this anger and wonder what happened to their 'nice boy'. Their response may be to say, 'You're just like your father.' This is the worst thing a mother or other family member could say. Dad is usually a strong model whether Mum likes it or not. If you imply that Dad's bad, then he thinks, 'If I'm like him then I must be bad too.' Such fragile boys need to be told that they are good. Their anger and resentment needs to be understood. They will in time form their own opinion about their dad.

Many boys who haven't seen much of Dad may need to go and stay with him and find out more about him. Uncles and male mentors can help where a Dad is not there.

Courneau (1991) and McCann (1999) demonstrate that boys who experience interest and affirmation from Dad or another male mentor tend to do better in school, get on better with men, form better relationships with women, are less likely to attempt suicide, have less depression and better mental health, have fewer problems with the law and have better self-worth and sense of their future.

It takes a mature Dad to not go into competition with the son and win fights or keep him down. If we remember that behind every anger there is a hurt, we would do well to ask, 'Am I part of that hurt?' and 'How can I help the healing?' Fathers need to notice their sons and tell them that they're proud of them and love them. This is a vital and important task for fathers.

Who am I?

Young adolescents are often experiencing feelings they do not like and, like adults, will find ways of avoiding these feelings. Some of these ways can be destructive and dangerous to the young person. In the search to know who they are, children need to rebel, to push against their parents. It can be confusing and scary to push against something that is not resilient and robust. One young man described it this way: 'Pushing up against my father was like running full tilt at a five-barred gate only to find the gate was unlatched and falling flat on my face. I was so angry at him.'

Rebelling can be scary and so the adolescent may find himself rebelling and then conforming. Conforming is not easy either. How can he ever know whether he has got it right or is good enough? And then is this who he is? Is this what he really wants to do?

Example: role confusion and negative transference

Patrick recalled his teenage years: 'Like my dad I had played football since I was little and I was really good at it. I won trophies. When my dad left us, people kept telling me, "You're the man of the family now. You have to look after your mum."

I tried really hard but Mum always seemed so angry with me. I always seemed to get everything wrong. When I think about it now I realise she was probably angry with Dad and I just happened to be the nearest male to take it out on. I got really fed up with trying after a while. I gave up on the football too. I often felt upset about that but it didn't seem like me anymore and I didn't play so well after Dad left.'

15–17-year-olds

Young people in this age group are continuing their development of a good sense of self. They still have needs for love, attention, security, boundaries and space in which to grow and explore. However, by this time they need more space beyond the confines of the family. They need recognition of their status as young adults. If treated well they are likely to respond favourably to special responsibilities such as learning to drive the family car, alcohol adventures, sexual experiences, clothing demands, late nights and first big romances. Boundaries and responsibilities need to be given with trust and respectful boundaries and limitations.

Not being able to venture to new challenges will damage peer respect and create resentment and rebellion. However a history of care and trust is the foundation to build on. The young person will gain a positive self-image and sense of self-worth from this experience.

In this middle phase adolescents are continuing to seek a sense of identity and searching for new ways of being, behaving and looking.

From 17 to independence

From age seventeen to the end of school the young person has a contradiction of being older but still at school with the added pressure of needing to do well so that they may either be able to get a job or go to university. The youth may have a steady partner and often sex will feature so they may have even more tension from a relationship and from looking for peer acceptance. In those circumstances it's easy to be angry and reactive with those you love because you know they will still love you even though you treat them badly, especially if your parents have some dependency on you. Leaving school for a job or university has the stress of a new world and new pressure. Being an adult while taking advantage of cheap accommodation from parents and maybe needing them to pay fees as well is not easy.

Example: being both dependent child and independent adult

Markus, 18, was an only child and the son of parents who were both ministers. He was to all appearances the model child and of course they were very proud of him. In counselling Markus revealed more of himself than his parents knew.

'I had to be the perfect child. Not just for my parents but for the church people. They wanted their kids to play with me so goodness rubbed off onto their kid. I've been having brief gay encounters for two years. My mother found out and I promised that I wouldn't do it again and that I wasn't gay. My dad doesn't know. I'm not telling anyone till I finish university. I'm not stupid. I have to be liked and a model guy for two more years because I can't afford to be thrown out of home for shaming them and being bad.' He was very angry that he could not be himself at the age of 18. He showed it through being argumentative and stomping round the house.

Growing past adoration and contempt

We can often draw strength and enhance our sense of self-worth from parents, but as we ourselves mature we gain other comparisons and also, by competing with parents, we separate from them. The years of 13–21 are that competition time when parents, especially fathers, fall off their pedestal. Adolescents see and gain their own opinion of parents' weaknesses and faults.

Example: doubting his father

Paul recalls that he always looked up to his father, admiring his strength and capability. But then Paul's mother left with another man and Paul watched his father become depressed and dejected. Paul reports feeling very frightened without his strong father to look up to. He began to doubt his own abilities and felt very disappointed and let down by his father.

Paul recalls that later in his teens he had a friend he admired. This young man was the captain of his football team, a tall, well-built, handsome young man who always seemed to have the most attractive girlfriends. When this friend's car broke down Paul lent him money towards the large repair bill. As time went by and the bill was never repaid, Paul found himself experiencing the same disappointment and anger he had felt towards his father. This was proof that men were disappointing and fail you.

Males particularly may compete and devalue Dad during this period. They may not want to be seen with parents and suddenly their tiniest faults will be very embarrassing to them.

Example: impressing her friends

Celia's parents were not too concerned about keeping up with the Joneses. The family car was old, not the kind of car that would impress Celia's friends. Each morning Celia's Dad would drop her off near school. Not at school – because she might be seen! During the journey Celia would crouch down low.

When it came time for Celia to learn to drive she was happy to get behind the wheel of the old car.

It was OK for *her* to be seen driving an old heap, but *not her father*.

The realisation of this loss of an idealised other can be hard for a young person to come to terms with if they are feeling insecure themselves. Embarrassment and shame are precursors of anger.

It takes a mature parent to absorb and understand the criticism that flows to them during these years. Parents will be treated as embarrassing, incompetent or downright stupid. It's additionally complex when a parent is vulnerable and not feeling strong and competent and at the same time his or her children start 'abandoning' their parents for peers and criticising them for not being ideal.

Sexuality

Young people in their mid-teens experience their sexuality with an intense mixture of excitement, curiosity and expectation. Their sexual involvement may be motivated by a need to belong to the group and be like everyone else as well as a need to be liked and loved. The reality of the experience can be disappointing, particularly if the young person is anxious and lacking in self-esteem, afraid of losing their boyfriend/girlfriend or of becoming pregnant.

Young people of this age are often deeply moved by the intensity of their feelings, not only for a boyfriend or girlfriend but also for the planet, the environment, for peace and for God. It is a time of intense idealism and groups or cults may easily influence a young person who lacks a solid family foundation. They can be equally drawn to community service and artistic endeavours such as musical composition, poetry writing and other creative arts. They may ask the questions: 'What is the meaning of Life? Why am I here? What's the point of it all?'

Because of this new emotional depth the loss of a relationship or significant other can be devastating and a young person will need the support of a mentor, parent, older sibling, cousin, family friend or counsellor to help them through the experience until they come to realise that they can cope with these strong emotions and that grief will ease with time. Young people who experience loss at this time may be disturbed to find that they become affected again by former unresolved losses. Their fear and anger may seem strong, overwhelming and outside their control. Those close to them may feel helpless to assist and recoil at the anger and sniping that they may receive.

Music

The newness and excitement of a world being experienced for the first time is not confined to sex, relationships and increased power. Music has that special capacity to express all of these. Every generation remembers with particular meaning the music and songs that were around when they were going through adolescence. Their specialness means that the music of other generations is just not quite as good or moving. Remember that adolescent music is still as powerful to them as yours was to you.

Adolescents will use their music to declare themselves and a new identity. Playing music loudly may be part of anger, payback, rebellion and declaration.

We advise parents to be careful to not 'trash' adolescent music. Anger at adolescent music is usually not at the music but at the independence and defiance that it represents. Claiming styles of music develops identity: metal, rap, harmony, grunge, hip-hop and reggae. We suggest parents take a mild interest but don't get too enthusiastic as it spoils adolescents' separation efforts and may be more about the parent wanting to be liked. As with so many aspects of adolescence young people need their parents to be parents: parents who are interested, caring and friendly, but not friends.

18–20-year-olds

This can be a time of great conflict for a young person who is, in many ways, now an adult with an adult body (perhaps bigger and taller than his or her parents), able to vote and maybe a taxpayer. Yet many are still financially dependent on their parents.

Living away from the family will most likely be beyond the means of even those who are working and more so for those who are studying. In addition the young person must cope with the ambivalence of yearning to be autonomous while also being fearful of managing alone in the adult world.

If the interests and path of the child is the same or similar to the parent the young person may need to stretch beyond the parent's achievements and take on dare-devil pursuits as a way of making a strong statement about her or himself. Male siblings may increase competition with each other. If a parent is seem as a 'loser' by the adolescent then strong efforts to be better than my father/mother may become much more evident. There is a certain anger in this that may pass either with their achievement or with maturity of values.

Fast driving and risk-taking may provide the young person with the feeling of power sought. Drugs and alcohol may help to temporarily dull emotional pain.

An understanding adult who is willing to listen can help with more positive ways of coping.

In late adolescence young people are also moving into more adult functioning. They may begin to feel on more equal terms with their parents, even able and willing at times to mix with their parents' friends and associate in an adult way, to the surprise of their parents who may have become accustomed to their offspring treating everyone over 30 with sullen disdain.

	Milestones	Effects on young person	Effects on adults	Ideas for coping
Early adolescence	Hormonal and body changes Rebellious, defiant behaviour, deliberate disagreement Friends becoming more important Drive to belong to peer group Black-and-white thinking, fixed ideas, dogmatic	Moodiness, possible growth in aggressiveness Robust physicality (especially boys) Power plays in relationships (especially girls) Rudeness, demand for freedom Identifies with friends and need to have 'right' clothes Seems intolerant and unable to compromise Seeking adult support outside the family Social world broadens	Surliness is hard to live with Struggle to maintain balance between good safe boundaries and relationship with teenager 'Everybody else's mother/ father...' unfavourable comparisons between own parents and selected 'other' parents Clash with authority figures at school and home as child complains of unfairness Parent may feel rejected or a failure	Tell yourself, 'This is normal' and develop a thick skin Make clear statements about what is not acceptable Focus on setting limits for undesirable behaviour Stay united as parents; be consistent Avoid undue attention to moodiness and rebelliousness Set limits for what is important and endorse consequences for behaviour Respect their choice of friends, music Use negotiation strategies to resolve home or school conflict; be willing to listen to both sides of a conflict and choose to stay out of the conflict

	Milestones	Effects on young person	Effects on adults	Ideas for coping
Middle adolescence	Less self-absorbed and increased ability to compromise Boundary testing and risk-taking Personal morality and ideals growing Experimenting with clothes, hair Growth of strong emotions and sexual feelings Adventurous socially and physically	More tolerant and able to accept others' opinions (sometimes) May experiment with cigarettes, drugs, alcohol, sex and piercings May question and reject family values Changes their 'look', stronger group identification May be secretive Short relationships until 16 then 'love' (usually) Rejecting safety precautions Believes self to be immortal Tests boundaries Strong challenging of father (boys) Testing/flaunting sexuality (girls)	Child a little easier to live with or even more rebellious Encounter with concerned police or youth worker New assessment of limits Parents may be distressed when their values are rejected Parents may fear that a 'look' may be permanent Parents may fear for child's safety Parents fear for child's safety but 'fussing' antagonises the young person	Show appreciation of maturation Role-model safe behaviour and good self-care Set firm but flexible limits that allow for growth Discuss consequences of behaviour (use what/how open-ended questions) Be prepared to listen; remember, we all change and grow Ask yourself, 'What is the worst that can happen if he or she wears this?' Show willingness to listen to problems; give information about safe sex, etc. Don't use 'put-downs' Be consistent

Late adolescence				
	Idealism developing	Looking for social and political causes, idealism	Parental distress at rejection of values	Listen and ask open-ended questions; be open-minded, drop in information, news items, etc.
	On course to financial and emotional independence	Anxiety about the future leads to angry outbursts and fragile self-esteem	Letting go, sometimes in despair	Encourage discussion; make contracts for desired behaviour, stay in communication
	More stable and enduring sexual relationships formed	Spending more time and attention on sexual partner	Conflict arising from teenagers who are emotionally independent but financially dependent	Show appreciation for responsible behaviour
	Feeling of being an adult and on more equal terms with parent figures	May have experiences, insights and ideas which he or she thinks parents lack	Remaining power used in attempt to keep control	Engage the support of a trusted mentor who can offer support objectively
	Moving towards independence and self-reliance	Wants to leave home and be independent	Parents fear for early serious commitment and neglect of studies	Find ways that young people can contribute to the household and show you value this
	Able to thank others, especially parents, occasionally or think more empathically		Parents may resent teenagers' condescending behaviour	Give responsibilities that recognise maturation, recognise and celebrate achievements
			Adjustment needed by parent to child leaving home and becoming autonomous	Recognise own achievements as parents
				Trust the earlier parenting that you did to bear fruits

Summary

- Anger is an integral part of adolescence. How it is expressed and handled makes a big difference to the process.

- Adolescence is divided into three phases, with different developmental tasks to complete in each phase.

- In adolescence young people change physically, sexually, cognitively, socially, emotionally and psychologically.

- These often dramatic changes can be hard for the young person to accommodate.

- Adolescence is a transition time for adjustment, consolidation, learning new skills, learning how to relate to peers and gaining a sense of identity.

- A young person's feelings and fantasies may seem to be too much for them to contain so it is common for them to 'act out' these inner experiences.

- The peer group is very important to an adolescent as he or she moves away from parents towards autonomy.

Key concepts

- Anger is an integral part of adolescence due to the changes, hurts, sensitivity, fragility and losses taking place.

- A positive experience with the same-sex parent and plenty of affirmation from them is essential to good identity and self-esteem.

- Be patient, keep cool. Don't meet anger with anger.

- Keep consistency in boundaries.

CHAPTER 6

Negotiating and Problem Solving

Example from parenting group

Carol and Steve had been called to talk with the dean at their daughter's school.

'She's been truanting again. We thought we had solved that problem. We felt so embarrassed. We felt like we were the ones who had been misbehaving. We felt so helpless. How can we stop her?'

Others in the group shared their own experiences of feeling helpless to change what their children were doing: a daughter who continued to visit a house where her mother knew drugs were used, a son whose room was never clean and the smell of rotten food and dirty clothes was beginning to permeate the house, a 14-year-old who stayed out well beyond the reasonable curfew set by her parents.

As a group we set up a plan to deal with these situations and offer support and encouragement.

As Carol and Steve said, 'We always seem to be nagging and punishing and it gets us nowhere.'

Negotiating the way to adulthood

Most new parents of adolescents need some coaching in discussing, negotiating and contracting with adolescents. Professional helpers can model and coach this.

A ten-year-old has nearly all his or her boundaries and freedom decided by parents and that is good for providing structure and security. Parents have the power so there is more of a presumption that the result will satisfy the parent.

A 21-year-old has nearly all boundaries and freedom defined by him/herself and that is good for responsible adulthood. The new adult has the power so there is more of a presumption that the result will satisfy the young adult.

In between there is a lot of negotiating for power going on all the time. It is the task of an adolescent to push the boundaries and win power from parents. It's the parent's job to hold boundaries. This action says, 'I care about you' and it gives order and security to the young life.

Working with parents often means working with too much control or not enough control. Assisting parents to evaluate the control level and also possibly their own fears and reactions is best done by generating strong reflective techniques and encouraging friend and family systems to self-moderate.

It is the parents' responsibility to let that power be negotiated from the parent to the child in small amounts appropriate to age. If parents keep all the power, they kill the autonomy of the child. If they give it all away too soon (or can't be bothered) then the child grows without structure, order and security. This can lead to an adult life without order or goals and with feelings of anxiety and insecurity and low resilience. Water in a glass has form. Spilt on the table it runs all over the place. Parents at first provide the container. With good-enough parenting a young person grows to contain him/herself.

- Negotiation of power is continually needed.

- Negotiation involves thinking, talking and trading.

Thinking

Sometimes parents can exacerbate a problem by the way they think about it. For example, 'She is only doing it to wind me up' is a negative assumption suggesting a relationship based on opposition rather than understanding. The adolescent may have another reason for the behaviour and the adult does well to keep open to that 'other' reason which is probably more to do with a vulnerability that needs protection.

- Negative life assumptions reflect the parent's life and model negative responses to the child.

- Assuming 'bad' establishes a 'life position' for both persons.

- An examination of such life positions with the parent about their own life is often worthwhile.

Negative positions

'You have to defend yourself by first strike in life.'

'They are always trying to see how far they can push me.'

'They are never happy until they get me upset.'

'They're just out to get me.'

Carrying resentments about a child damages life-long relationships. Ask the parent and the child to list such resentments and cognitively and emotionally work for release from them through testing the reality of them.

Balancing memories with reality

'He's always truanting.'

'She's staying out late on week nights.'

'He has to have dirt on his shirt.'

'She always shamed me as a mother, like when she dyed her hair purple.'

All of these are absolutes that are not true. They may have happened once or many times but not 'always' as implied. Negative moments need to be balanced with positive ones:

'I felt so proud of her when she wrote that poem for her dying grandmother.'

'I was surprised when he protected his little brother from that bully.'

Speaking for yourself

The use of 'I' statements helps the parent to separate from the child and speak more personally. We avoid building resentment in another by not speaking for them but acknowledging their separate experience.

We encourage parents to use 'I' statements:

'I have so much trouble with your short skirts because I care about your safety.'

'I feel annoyed when…' NOT 'You make me angry when …'

Use:

'I want…'

'I feel…'

'I like…'

'I need…'

'I notice that…'

'I'm aware that…'

'I believe…'

'I feel…when…because…I would like…'

Avoiding judgements and parental commands

We work with parents to identify 'Red Light' words that accuse, demand and are judgemental – such as: 'should', 'ought', 'must', 'have to', 'got to', 'or else', and name-calling like 'lazy', 'stupid', 'thoughtless', 'selfish'. Using these words will increase resentment and decrease co-operation.

Trading

Sometimes we just have to go rigidly by the rules and sometimes other situations allow us to negotiate and trade. The western supermarket prices the apples at £2.50 a kilogram so that's what it sells for. In Asia you usually bargain. The law of the land says that we must register a motor vehicle for a set fee. Purchase of the motor vehicle may however be an up-and-down negotiation of a 'reasonable offer'. Children brought up in a rigid rules environment are less able to trade, bargain and come to a compromise. If children grow with an 'obey-or-else' philosophy or a 'be good or I won't love you' philosophy or a 'be good and don't disappoint me' philosophy they never learn to negotiate from a place of feeling unconditionally loved and therefore confident and reasonable. They learn to be passive and passive people are usually burying their aggression until such time as the 'valve on the pressure cooker' blows and they can hold their anger no longer.

Example: the trouble with being passive

Pita described just such a problem. 'I can't even make a phone call to change an appointment. I'm afraid the person might be angry with me, I guess the same way my father was angry when I crossed him in any way. So what do I do? I just don't show up for the appointment and then of course people are even angrier with me.'

Or, if people can't get what they want openly, they may go underground and get it in sneaky ways, or develop another persona and live a double life.

'I have just found out that Terry has another world I didn't know about. I couldn't believe it. I don't want to believe it. I feel so deceived. That's not my good boy.'

We are doing our children a favour if we model negotiating skills and open dialogue to them. Children need to be taught to trade and talk openly about how they are feeling and what they are wanting.

1.   State the problem: 'We have a problem. You leave dirty dishes in your room. I would like to talk about it.'

2.   Use an 'I' statement in the form of a four-part phrase: '*I feel* angry/ frustrated *when* there's dirty dishes in your room *because* it brings ants around. *I would like* you to remember to put them in the dishwasher.'

3.   Give the results if your teenager changes his behaviour: 'Hey! If we get this sorted we will have more dishes to use, no ants and I will be a much happier mother and probably more willing to help you out with things you need.'

4.   Let the teenager talk. If you receive no response, offer some encouragement: 'Your turn.' 'What do you think?' 'I want to hear what you think about this.' Listen and be prepared to trade.

5.   State your fears: 'I am worried that if we don't resolve this I will keep nagging you and you get angry with me and we will have a bad relationship, and I don't want that.'

6.   State what you are willing to do: 'I am willing to provide the food for your snacks. You either eat them or dispose of the remains. How's that sound?'

7.   State what you are not willing to do and again what you are willing to do: 'I won't clean up after you but I will buy the snacks.'

8.   If you don't have a satisfactory response say: 'I can see this is something you don't want to commit yourself to right now. I want to know by… at…'

Have the list with you as you talk if you want. You can explain by saying, 'I am still learning to do this because our relationship is important to me.'

Here is another example of what you might say:

1.   We have a problem. You are staying out all night and I am getting worried and we end up fighting each other. I am guessing that you don't like this any more than I do and that you don't like talking about it.

2.   I feel worried when you don't come home at night because there are so many ways that you could be harmed and I want to protect you as much as I can. I want you to stick to the curfew time we agree on. Then let me know if for some reason you are going to be late.

3.   If you do this I will be a lot more relaxed and easier to be with, you will be safer and we will both be clearer about the boundaries around here. I think I will also be more willing to help you out. It's because I care, not because I like to control.

4.   Your turn… What do you think about this…? (Listen genuinely and be prepared to trade.)

5.   I'm worried that you will get in with bad company. I am worried that you might start taking drugs. People whose parents don't care about them often get together and do harmful things. I do care about you.

6.   I am willing to come and pick you up if you are somewhere dangerous. I am willing for you to stay out until 11.30pm on weekends and until 10pm on one night during the week. I am willing for your friends to come here on…

7.   I won't let you stay out all night but I will let you stay out at weekends and during the week on one night, as I said.

8.   I can see it's hard for you to decide right now but I want to know by tomorrow night at teatime. I'll be waiting to talk with you some more then. This discussion is incomplete.

Activity for parents

Write your own possible scenario here and then practise it with a friend or partner.

1.

2.

3.

4.

5.

6.

7.

8.

9.

10.

Labelling

Labelling is the basis of stigmatising, discrimination, scape-goating and avoiding looking at the real reasons why a person may have problems with another. Parents have sometimes developed negative ideas about their teenager that might get in the way of them negotiating with him/her. They may have already labelled a young person (he's a loser, she never gets anything right, he's trouble).

We need to remember that labels stick. A parent may first need to remove such a label so that they can communicate effectively with their son or daughter.

Here are some questions you could ask when adolescents are quickly reactive in communication, particularly to labels:

- How much of this is my attitude, not theirs?

- What good things am I missing?

- How would I like to be labelled with that word?

- Is there something historical that I need to drop?

- Have I created their behaviour by continuously repeating that label?

These are essential questions to ask about a conflict that seems to be stuck around a particular issue:

- What is my need?

- What is their need?

- Do I want this to work for both of us?

- What opportunities can this situation bring?

- What is it like to be in their shoes?

- What are they trying to say?

- Do they know I am listening?

- What do I want to change?

- How will I tell them this without blaming or attacking?

- Am I using power appropriately?

- Are they using power appropriately?

- What am I feeling?

- Am I blaming them for my feelings?

- Will telling them how I feel help the situation?

- Is resentment being caused by:

  - Something in my past that still hurts?

  - Something I dislike in them because I haven't accepted it in myself?

Negotiating

Here are some questions to ask yourself before starting to negotiate:

- How can I make this a fair deal with both people winning?

- What can I give to them?

- What can they give to me?

- What points would I want included in an agreement?

- Do we need mediation from a third person?

- Who could that be?

(Adapted from Cornelius and Faire 1989)

Key concepts

- Growing up is a process of negotiating power from parents to adolescents.

- People who can negotiate can retain their own power and also give away power.

- Don't release stored anger in destructive ways.

- Negotiating involves thinking, talking and trading.

- Negotiating is a learned skill and needs practice.

- We need to remove labels from our children in order to negotiate with them as they become adults.

- Clear boundaries give shape and security to young lives.

- Too much control, or too little control, generates anger.

CHAPTER 7

Anger, Shame, Blame and Games

Adults coping with their own anger

Example: breaking new ground

Lorna calls herself a pioneer. She's breaking new ground in her family.

Lorna's father was a violent alcoholic. Her mother was passive and did not protect herself or her children from him as an abusive man. A friend of her father sexually abused Lorna herself. When Lorna looked back over her family history she realised that she came from a long line of violent or passive people. For a long time she found this hard to accept.

'I had no one to be proud of in my family,' she said. But Lorna made a decision when her children were quite small that things were going to be different for her children. When her own husband began to hit her she remembered how often she had wished that her mother would leave her violent father and Lorna decided to end her relationship.

Knowing how important it was for her children to have access to their father, Lorna worked hard to see that these arrangements worked well. She was an enthusiastic participant in our parenting group trying out communication skills and reporting back to us. Years later she arrived at a course for parenting adolescents to learn some more. Her own adolescent years had been turbulent so she wanted to 'be there' for her children.

The last time I saw Lorna she introduced, with pride, her two sons now in late adolescence.

Lorna had proved that it is possible to heal families.

Example: owning their part in the problem

Raelene and Phil came from a similar background to Lorna. They arrived at a Parenting Adolescents group together, although they were about to end their relationship. They were already living apart. Phil was sharing a house with two other men and because there were drugs and alcohol in the house and no room for the children (two boys and two girls) the children were living with Raelene. The children aged ten and up were already acting out.

A daughter was taking drugs and skipping school. The boys were hitting their mother. Phil left the course after two sessions saying it was not doing him any good. He had the same complaint about his anger management group. Raelene managed to attend for most of the course but she wanted to use the group as somewhere that she could complain about her children. She negatively labelled her sons as 'just like their old man', said that the police never helped her, and that if the school had been tougher her children would have been OK. She had adopted a victim position and was blaming others.

On one occasion near the end of the course, Raelene was tearful.

'If I had realised this a few years ago,' she said, 'things might not have got this bad. Now I feel it's absolutely hopeless.'

I was thinking the same thing. Her children had been so damaged by their life experiences and Raelene herself was traumatised and exhausted.

Fortunately a number of people in community organisations got behind Raelene and her children. A church group took three of the children on a camp while the fourth spent a week with his father and emerged from the experience a little closer to his father and no worse for the experience, to Raelene's relief.

Phil returned to his anger management group with his eldest son.

Raelene went to a respite centre for a week and began one-to-one therapy, which she still attends.

A year later this vulnerable family still have their problems, but they are not as close to the edge as they were before. Raelene and Phil stopped blaming everyone and began to own their part in the problem.

If we want to stop the cycle of violence in families we need to do more as a community to offer support to each member and provide opportunities for individual members to heal from their trauma.

In some countries, free or low-cost counselling or psychotherapy is available and can be accessed for a period of time. It's difficult and unjust for this help not to be available to people who have been disadvantaged because of their childhood history and economic opportunities. Living from day to day may require too much effort to have the needed extra energy for examining wounds, starting new behaviours, and giving more to others. Supportive communities and care from extended families are proving essential to support other forms of therapy and change assistance.

If we really want to break the cycle we need to make psychotherapy available for those who have experienced violence. We now know that witnessing verbal and physical violence as children interferes with brain development as well as psychological development (see Perry 1997, 2008; Anda *et al.* 2006; Frodl *et al.* 2010). We know that children learn what they live in their families.

Merely punishing those who are violent will not change their patterns of behaviour. For those who have been traumatised so young, teaching them new ways to behave will not be enough either. Such people will respond better to individual or small-group therapy where they can experience the warmth and empathy that was missing from their lives, express their sadness, hurt and anger, know the safe boundaries of a healthy relationship, build meaningful attachments, make sense of their trauma and find new ways of relating to others from experience.

Community organisations that provide support, groups, courses, accommodation, respite care, counselling and group work for children from violent homes deserve all the financial help and political advocacy we can give them. Instead of howling in protest at violent crime we need to start putting our hands in our pockets as a society and 'forking out' to provide valuable resources that will change the situation.

Differences in male and female anger

In the past there has been a powerful social contract between men and women around emotions. Very generally men get to do the anger and women get to do all the more vulnerable emotions. We train and reward boys for being able to access anger and stick up for themselves. We teach them to be brave and courageous and deny pain. This leaves boys and men converting many emotions to anger very quickly and girls doing the sadness, joy, hurt, grief, depression, worry and happiness, but often not the anger. Men get to be angry rather than cry and women get to cry rather than be angry. This leads to men and boys acting 'out' and girls and women often acting 'in'. 'Acting out' behaviour is easy to notice. We need to be careful that we also notice the quieter expression. Things have changed of course. Decades of feminism have taught women that it's OK to feel angry and messages have been given to men that it's OK to cry, but gender differences remain remarkably strong. For this reason we need to look behind the anger to find the hurt that boys are suffering and for girls we need to look for repressed anger and a 'turning in' that leads to depression. Both are indicators that something is wrong.

In our work with anger we notice that there is a certain type and stage of adolescent boy who is brought to counselling or therapy. Ninety per cent of the time he doesn't live with his birth father and he's very angry with him. He reports that his relationship with his mother is good, though she might not. She's often sick of his acting out and his abuse. When we mention his father there is an immediate response of anger, resentment and ridicule. Fathers have a lot to do with boys and male anger. The family therapist Steve Biddulph (see Biddulph 2008) refers to the common diagnosis ADD (attention deficit disorder) as Absent Dad Disorder.

When a boy is growing up it is important that he gets affirmation from his father in order to feel good about himself as a man. He can get affirmation from a woman but if it only comes from a woman it may leave him dependent on females for his self-esteem – something that is dangerous and a contribution to him possibly feeling the need to control her later on. To feel good about being a man, a boy needs affirmation from a good man. If he doesn't get it, he has a right to feel angry and cheated. He also needs to feel that he has had the attention of a man through the first 14 years of his life (see Blackenhorn 1995; Corneau 1991; Lamb 2003; McCann 1999). The lack of this involvement and attention leaves a hole or wound and he may choose to use drugs or alcohol to deal with it in his teen years.

Many boys have been abused by their parents. From men that abuse is more likely to be physical and from women verbal and emotional. This is never forgotten unless action is taken to heal it. We recommend therapeutic processes to address this.

Overt displays of male anger from young men may even be attractive to young women who may perceive and interpret it as indicating the ability to protect them and a family.

Unmanaged anger in men or women may, however, be turned on the family.

Here's a checklist of suggestions that may moderate some of the parent/ adolescent dynamics around anger, shaming, blaming and games.

- Who are you angry at?

- What did those people/person do to you?

- What would you like to say to them?

- What are you doing with your anger?

- Do you blot it out with alcohol, nicotine, or other drugs?

- Do you displace your anger, take it out on someone else?

- Do you displace your anger on to one particular child?

- When did you start being very angry with that child?

- Are you 'bottling' your anger?

- When do you let the anger out?

- Are you unconsciously encouraging one particular child or person to express the family anger for everyone else?

- Do you sulk?

- Do you use anger to cover up hidden hurt?

- Do you become depressed with suppressed anger?

- Do you have repeated angry conversations or fantasies in your head but rarely have real ones?

The need for an anger vocabulary

Anger is an emotional 'word family' that covers many words from minor anger (frustrated, annoyed, bothered and irritated) through to major anger (enraged, furious, ferocious, irate, fuming and livid). Having many words for anger allows a person to give a more detailed and accurate description of how they feel. Using one swear word for all anger is very limiting and yet this is all that some people have – just one swear word.

If you are a counsellor or other professional, a useful exercise to do with a group or a client is to make a list and see how many anger words they get.

Be clear that sad words like 'depressed' and 'bad' and anxiety words like 'worried', don't belong in the anger family. Doing a verbal check with the client is also useful.

Words like 'vengeful', 'bitter', 'resentful' are 'stale' anger words associated with revenge and payback. Words like 'envious' and 'jealous' describe a mix between anger and insecurity.

See 'The anger scale' in Chapter 16 for an exercise on words for degrees of anger.

What 'games' are played around anger?

Eric Berne, the father of Transactional Analysis, wrote about psychological game-playing. A game is an interaction in which nothing is resolved and where the same pattern keeps happening over and over again. You may find yourself thinking: 'Here we go again!' At the end of a game both people usually end up feeling bad.

The people involved in a psychological drama game often find themselves taking one of three roles, Persecutor, Rescuer or Victim, and a dance begins wherein they move between these roles. Anger is an emotion that is often involved in someone's uproar, repression (sulking) or displacement (persecuting).

Example: playing games

Phil would stop off at his favourite pub for a few drinks on his way home from work.

Raelene would go straight home from work and begin to bring in the washing and cook the tea.

When Phil had not arrived home Raelene would put his tea in the microwave ready to heat up for him when he arrived home (Rescuer).

Phil would arrive home late and tipsy and yell at Raelene because he was hungry and expected food (Persecutor).

Raelene would get upset. She had had housework to do after work and she had done her best. The tea was ready to be heated (Victim). She would heat up the meal for him (Rescuer).

And slam it down on the table yelling at him for doing this yet again (Persecutor).

Phil would try to make her feel better by offering to make a cup of tea (Rescuer) or complain that she was the most bad-tempered woman he knew and why did he have to put up with someone like her (Victim)?

They both felt bad and it would be played out two or three times a week without any reflection on the fact that it wasn't working for either of them.

Games leave us feeling dissatisfied and uncomfortable. They never resolve the problem and they are a sure-fire way of avoiding intimacy in relationships. Have clients examine their exchanges for similar games. Encourage a reflective practice that has a look at the pattern and then helps to free people from the pattern and its roles.

Some coaching steps that may assist the client

1. Be aware of the games being played. Is there blaming, manipulation and helplessness involved? It's likely there is a game to detect.

2. Be aware of feelings, and notice changes when things happen. Try to predict feelings and manoeuvres then imagine freeze-framing the scene.

3. Next, find ways of avoiding and replacing the Persecutor, Rescuer, Victim roles. What will cause an unexpected break? A compliment, silence, laughter, showing appreciation. The key is usually being conscious of the play and then taking *responsibility* for oneself and acting away from control, helping or payback, rather than acting into it.

Try these:

- *Persecutor:* consult with others, ask what they want and need, say what you need.

- *Victim:* take responsibility for your situation, act to change and don't expect others to act for you.

- *Rescuer:* Empower others by supporting them to help themselves. Ask them how you can help and (very important) whether they want your help.

Or:

- Give an unexpected response that is quite different from the one usually given.

- Stop exaggerating strengths and weaknesses.

- Give and receive positive recognition to and from the other person more often.

- Try to find time for things enjoyed and for sharing and being with others.

- Stop doing things for others that they can do for themselves.

- Stop criticising those who don't need it.

- Stop acting helpless and dependent. Stand on your own two feet.

✓

Exercise: Angry game-playing on the family tree

Fill in the family tree and ask yourself some questions to help you get a picture of your family and the ways they misused anger.

- What did each person do for a living?

- Who is dead and how did they die?

- Which people are alike in their patterns of behaviour and relating to others?

- Who usually took the roles of victim, persecutor, and rescuer?

- Who are you similar to?

- Is alcohol or addiction involved?

- Who got left out, marginalised or scapegoated?

- How did each person handle his or her anger? Bottling, sulking, uproar, expressing…?

- What can you learn from these people?

- What are your children learning from their parents right now?

- Who got to feel righteous or superior?

- Which people do not get on well together?

- Think about why that happens.

- Who do your children resemble in personality and anger expression?

- How does that affect you?

- What would be a good word to describe the way each person seemed to you (e.g. sad, depressed, angry, kind, dreamy, practical, intellectual, miserly)?

- What did each person contribute to your family?

- Is there anyone on the tree you are feeling angry towards?

The anger rules

The anger rules have been used successfully by the authors as a foundational belief-set about anger and have been especially useful with children. Teachers and families put them on the wall as a reminder. We encourage adults to have them on a card in their pocket. Children may know them by rote and call them back to adults.

> **Remember the anger rules**
>
> Anger is OK, but:
>
> > Don't hurt yourself
> >
> > Don't hurt others
> >
> > Don't hurt property
> >
> > Do talk about it

You may like to refer to Chapters 16 and 17 and use 'The anger scale' and the 'Triggers' worksheets.

> **Food for thought**
>
> Most parents need exactly what they think their kids need.

Suggestions for the caregiver for when the teenager feels angry

- Use wind-down not wind-up behaviour: for example, lower your voice, speak calmly and slowly and tell your teenager you are willing to listen (See Escalators and De-escalators in Chapter 17).

- Listen (see Chapter 4 on communication).

- If he or she is becoming violent or threatening say firmly: 'STOP! I am going to listen to you right now.'

- Suggest a walk outside in the cool air.

- Anyone who is frequently exhibiting threatening or frightening behaviour or hurting people has a problem. It might be enough just to talk about it one to one. If you cannot be the listener find someone else who will. Young people may begin, in adolescence, to act out their anger about abuse earlier in their lives. An adult with good communication skills can assist the young person to disclose this and seek help.

- Boys need fathers (Blackenhorn 1995; Corneau 1991; Lamb 2003; McCann 1999). If for some reason a boy has not had good fathering someone needs to help him form a relationship with his father or with a father substitute. In one-to-one counselling he may have the opportunity to have his anger about his father heard.

Example: dealing with anger at school

In a UK school in a very poor area the principal of this school had an office that was more like a sitting room. He kept a tin of biscuits and a kettle for making cocoa and made a point of seeing a certain number of children each day to discuss their progress and problems. The child would sit in one of the old comfortable armchairs on either side of the fire.

Every morning this man would wait by the front door of the school and greet each child. If a child arrived looking angry he would draw him/her aside for a quiet word and make a time to see the child later. In this way many problems of violence were avoided and children from troubled homes found a listening ear and the chance to experience a different parent figure to model themselves on.

It is a pity that principals in primary schools today are probably too overworked with administrative tasks to take on this pastoral role. If children could be attended to earlier they would not arrive at secondary school with so much anger that has not been attended to. If children could have anger attended to at secondary school they might not arrive at jails or hospitals later.

The principle remains that *anger listened to by someone is less likely to be acted out later*.

Summary

- People often fear anger and find ways to avoid it in themselves and others. It is usually squashed down and leaks out in other ways.

- Families play anger games. Break the game cycle.

- Use anger management skills, such as 'The anger scale', Time Out and trigger management (see Chapters 16 and 17).

- Schools can help change patterns of abuse in families.

Key concepts

♦ Stick to the anger rules.

♦ People who are angry need to be heard.

♦ Help adolescents with their anger now.

CHAPTER 8

Helping Adolescents with their Anger

Anger at mothers and fathers

The most common people for adolescents to feel angry with are parents as they are the people who have power and control over their lives. The business of growing up means a transferring of that power to the adolescent as they take the responsibility for their lives. It's normal for an adolescent to feel angry with people they have to wrest power from.

This includes teachers, employers, police and any authority figure. That doesn't have to mean abuse or even conflict. It simply means negotiating more power as you grow.

Sometimes people feel angry and don't know why. It's useful to know why you feel angry so that you can do something about it. Here are some ideas about why adolescents feel angry – you could ask the parent to tick examples that they think apply to their child.

Some common reasons adolescents feel angry with either mother or father

- ❑ Failing to set boundaries
- ❑ Setting too many boundaries
- ❑ Failing to respect my (adolescent's) boundaries
- ❑ Not allowing me to become my own person
- ❑ Treating me differently from my brothers or sisters
- ❑ Not listening to me
- ❑ Embarrassing me
- ❑ Shaming me
- ❑ Not supplying the things I really need
- ❑ Bribing me
- ❑ Manipulating me
- ❑ Turning others against me
- ❑ Not touching me lovingly
- ❑ Failing to protect me as a child from danger
- ❑ Failing to be interested in me
- ❑ Using me as a companion
- ❑ Using me to replace my mother or my father
- ❑ Being a wimp
- ❑ Having a mental breakdown
- ❑ Being too religious
- ❑ Moving home away from where I really want to live
- ❑ Selling, hurting or getting rid of a pet
- ❑ Leaving me hungry
- ❑ Being rude in public
- ❑ Making me do things that parents wanted to do themselves or missed out on
- ❑ Pushing for success too much
- ❑ Expecting me to be the same as Mum or Dad or my brother or sister
- ❑ Expecting me to do/be more than I am capable of
- ❑ Not loving me
- ❑ Making me eat certain foods
- ❑ Keeping an untidy house
- ❑ Laughing at me
- ❑ Committing suicide
- ❑ Getting a new partner (step-parent)
- ❑ Making me feel guilty when it's not really my fault
- ❑ Overpowering me with their opinion
- ❑ Giving me things to make up for something they have failed to do
- ❑ Not spending time with me
- ❑ Giving me too much responsibility
- ❑ Stopping me from having fun
- ❑ Trying to control friendships
- ❑ Blaming me for things that happened
- ❑ Trying to control my sexuality
- ❑ Not giving me enough space

- ☐ Abandoning me at some time in my life
- ☐ Having an old car or house
- ☐ Making me wear old or used clothing
- ☐ Gambling too much
- ☐ Getting married
- ☐ Not getting married
- ☐ Sexual abuse
- ☐ Physical abuse, hitting me
- ☐ Putting me down
- ☐ Not being how I think adults should be
- ☐ Rubbishing things that are important to me like my music, dress, friends
- ☐ Not supporting my study
- ☐ Making money from me
- ☐ Making public scenes
- ☐ Not letting me watch my things on TV
- ☐ Not respecting me
- ☐ Being nosy – reading my private writings
- ☐ Forgetting me
- ☐ Leaving home
- ☐ Drinking too much alcohol
- ☐ Doing drugs
- ☐ Talking too loud
- ☐ Not letting me speak
- ☐ Always being too busy for me
- ☐ Teasing
- ☐ Unfairness
- ☐ Setting too hard tasks
- ☐ Not trusting me

- ☐ Accusing me of things that I didn't do
- ☐ Put-downs
- ☐ Taking over things I'm doing
- ☐ Lack of love
- ☐ Parents splitting up
- ☐ Parents fighting
- ☐ One parent treating another parent badly
- ☐ One or both parent not being or acting 'normal'
- ☐ Parents over-reacting or dumping on me
- ☐ One parent putting down another
- ☐ Not having things that other families have
- ☐ Parents on the phone when they are 'with' you
- ☐ Adults always being right
- ☐ Parents working too hard
- ☐ Parents always talking to someone else
- ☐ Separated parents fighting
- ☐ Parent having new emotional attachment
- ☐ Not treating me as well as my peers
- ☐ New baby
- ☐ New person in the house who takes my place
- ☐ Scared of forthcoming event
- ☐ My bedroom taken over
- ☐ My space invaded
- ☐ Having to wait for an adult in order to do something
- ☐ Not having a steady home

✓

- ❑ Having to live away from home
- ❑ Sent to boarding school
- ❑ Being left waiting
- ❑ Feeling abandoned or forgotten by parents
- ❑ Inconsistent parents
- ❑ Conflicting messages from parents
- ❑ Parents talking about splitting up
- ❑ Being angry for a parent
- ❑ Being used in parents' battles and games
- ❑ Making me do things inappropriate to my experience or culture
- ❑ Being called names
- ❑ Being bullied
- ❑ Big changes to my life
- ❑ Not feeling loved
- ❑ Feeling unwanted by parents
- ❑ Adoption
- ❑ No Mum or no Dad
- ❑ Any parent(s) not being there
- ❑ Parent's new lover
- ❑ Being treated as younger than I really am
- ❑ Being criticised
- ❑ Being left out
- ❑ Being lied to
- ❑ Not being told what's happening
- ❑ Feeling unreasonably controlled

- ❑ False accusations
- ❑ Being hurt deliberately
- ❑ Being ordered
- ❑ Being made to beg for something
- ❑ Being 'grassed on'
- ❑ Broken promises
- ❑ Being told that I did something on purpose when I didn't
- ❑ Things stolen
- ❑ Not being able to say what it is that hurts me
- ❑ Going somewhere I hate
- ❑ Being tricked
- ❑ Being left out
- ❑ Hungry, cold or thirsty
- ❑ Not being consulted
- ❑ Disappointments
- ❑ Losing a competition
- ❑ Being cheated
- ❑ Moving home
- ❑ Things moved
- ❑ Things stolen
- ❑ Reduced freedom
- ❑ Someone dies or goes away
- ❑ Pet dies or hurt by others

The most common reasons given for anger at mothers and fathers

At mothers

Not standing up to father

Treating father with disrespect, ridicule

Hitting father

Not letting me see Dad

Making it difficult to see Dad

Saying 'Just like your father'

Getting upset and creating insecurity

Controlling me for my safety

Leaving me

Interfering with relationship with father

Manipulation

No Mum around

Leaving Dad

Shouting at Dad

Putting Dad down

Doing other things while talking to me

Putting girlfriends/boyfriends down

Putting up with abuse

At fathers

Not standing up to mother

Treating mother with disrespect, ridicule, or name-calling

Driving dangerously

Hitting my mother

Leaving Mum

Me having to take Dad's place

Shouting at Mum

Forgetting my birthday

Not paying for things I need

Not complimenting and affirming me

Leaving me

Not protecting my mother

Being unsuccessful at work

Not earning enough money

Having an old car

Going to jail

No Dad around

Treating stepchildren as more important than own children

Controlling things that were 'given' to me

Being too dominant

Being wimpy

Angry sons and daughters

Growing into an independent and positive young man or woman is harder in our culture which has made the nuclear family the growing-up place for our young adults, instead of villages, communities and wider families.

The problem with boys and men being dependent on women

For many boys in our culture, their relationship with their father is often not close, with disastrous consequences later on. Either Mum and Dad get on well, but Dad doesn't get on with the son, or Mum doesn't get on with Dad and replaces the father with her son making him the 'Little Man' creating a situation where Dad feels excluded. This often happens to stepfathers too. Ideally there should be a strong three-way relationship that is pretty equal all round.

At about 14 the son gets a huge hit of testosterone and his body becomes awkward and hairy. He separates from his mother particularly as he now sees himself making his way into manhood. It's necessary to push mother away and become independent. This is sometimes done by looking and acting ugly, being rebellious and obnoxious and wanting more freedom. If there are no strong father links there is a rather empty space to grow into. This often results in the 'Lost Boy', or young men who have poor structure and discipline and aren't sure where they are going in life.

A boy with good father links can transfer them into a positive community of men. Lost boys are fearful and stay relating to their peers, often angry at being cheated out of father affirmation.

Because they have been close to their mothers and dependent on them for support and self-esteem, they transfer that need to their partners and wives who may enjoy looking after them at first but then get sick of them and their dependency and want someone more whole. The under-fathered man may then get fearful and try to control or hold on to the woman he relies on. This can have disastrous consequences. The way out of this is for fathers to take their fathering seriously and have strong positive relationships with their sons. Mothers need to not treat them like their 'Little Man' and not play the son off against father or devalue the father even though she may no longer like him. Fathers who have split up with their partners need to be extra diligent in their duties to children and hurt mothers must never pass marital wounds on to the son who is confused as his father is his first role model, and he may also get trapped in a protector role for the mother. Sons tend to grow into their father and if fathers are made to be bad, the sons may grow likewise and see themselves negatively.

It's never too late for fathers to step in and build relationships with their sons. Beware that if they are angry with you for not performing they will probably express *more* anger before it gets better. For mothers it's never too late to build a strong relationship with a partner and allow sons to separate from them and the duty they may feel to protect their mother.

It's useful to challenge fathers to model the type of relationship that they might want their son to have with a woman. Sons who have been involved in the father 'play-off game' will be angry at first that they have lost a relational power (or manipulation) but will later enjoy the additional security and freedom to be their age and attach freely to a partner.

Daughters who are father-hungry and man-hating

For many daughters in our culture, fathers are, unfortunately, often not emotionally available or expressive in the family. The mother and the daughter may experience a weak or unconfident father. The daughter may be unable to develop strong, healthy, positive links and respect for him. If the mother also tires of his dependence and lack of emotion he may be dismissed or leave. The daughter may become her 'Mother's Little Helper' and absorb all of her feelings of hurt, disappointment, anger and disrespect. However girls need to separate from their mother too, though not as a gender but as a person. The daughter really needs to have had a positive, affirming father who showed her respect and love that was unconditional. A father also shows her how to relate successfully and respectfully with men. If he has been emotionally unavailable and disrespected she may seek father substitutes in males who are also unavailable or dependent.

Daughters may seek love in sexual ways rather than emotional expression, leading to confusion about how to be affirmed. There is a high rate of fatherlessness amongst teen mothers (Ellis *et al.* 2003).

Daughters not receiving positive attention and love from fathers may carry a mother's anger and transfer this to men and partners. A father may have a sense of the women in the house ganging up on him as the daughter identifies with her same-gender parent and her anger.

Ideally fathers need to work consciously at fathering their daughters in positive and loving ways. It is never too late to do this. Daughters deserve parents who provide a strong three-way relationship which includes openness, trust and affirmation. She can then seek partners from a place of good self-worth and not neediness. Her choices then mean that she is more likely to be respected. She can move away from her parents without feeling as if her parents need her too much. She can also walk with the sense of her father always unconditionally loving and caring for her. She has a standard against which she can measure other men and the confidence of unconditional love.

The anger scale

The anger scale is a scale of one to ten that allows the person to identify degrees of anger. It tunes us into how intensely we are feeling anger. This is an important step in anger identification and sensitivity. Many people can only identify anger as an on/off emotion, and that implies that they are only aware of anger when it is almost at the top of the scale and often too late for their own intervention management skills. If we are more sensitive to how we are feeling then we can respond with alternative behaviour earlier and use our anger safely to help get what it is that we want. We need to be in tune with small angers particularly and deal with them as they arise. If we don't then they are likely to pile up and we become liable to explode over a lot of little things. We need to be able to track the big things so that we know when to take a Time Out and avoid a blowout.

Example: anger building up

Jayne woke up late and was angry at the alarm clock. There was none of her favourite cereal left so she was angry with her brother. She forgot to take her money for her lunch and had to go back home for it. She was angry with herself for this.

She was late to school and the teacher mentioned it. Jayne was angry with her teacher for publicly noticing her. At break her friend asked her why she looked grumpy. Jayne turned on her and swore at her and told her to mind her own business. The friend copped the anger for the alarm clock, the brother, herself and the teacher all at once without knowing what the anger was for.

Example: anger that seems to come out of nowhere

Tim had just been dumped by his girlfriend. She told him that morning at school. He hadn't been able to concentrate at school all day. When he got home he went to his bedroom to hide and think some more about it. His mother came barging in to get his washing. He swore at her and told her to get out. He never did that usually. She was horrified by the attack. She didn't know what was going on.

What was the highest you were on the scale today?

This is one of the best questions to begin a counselling conversation about a person's anger, because it starts with a number which is safe and then it can easily lead to a discussion of an incident from which learning can take place.

If the client says 'one' or 'two' then they may need to be better tuned into their anger because most people find at least a small thing to get angry about even before they get to school or work.

How often are you on an eight or nine?

We need to have a variety of words to express anger, ranging from the worst to the smallest. 'Annoyed' and 'irritated' are words for small angers and 'incensed', 'enraged' and 'furious' are words for big angers.

Use 'The anger scale' handout from Chapter 16, p.174 and write your anger words in the spaces to match the level of anger on the scale. The scale is shown below:

What's happening at each level		Anger word to match
Danger exploding	10	....
Stop stop stop	9	....
Notice anger getting out of control	8	....
Take Time Out now	7	....
Calm down	6	....
Say what you need to	5	....
Let go of small tensions or angers	4	....
Say to yourself, 'I'm OK'	3	....
Notice niggles	2	....
Really relaxed	1	....
	0	

The adolescent anger flow chart
Understanding anger: the anger flow chart

People never feel angry for no reason or, to put it more positively, people always have a reason for feeling angry. If you follow a client's thinking, which may be different from yours, you will always find a good reason. Sometimes the rationale is entirely suspect but it's their thinking and reasoning and if it looks limited, then it's the professional's task to enhance that thinking and thus either reduce the anxiety or assist to create more choices than the ones they believe they have.

It's not only reasonable but it's OK and healthy to *feel* anger. If you look at the anger flow chart you will see anger in the centre. It often feels like it is in the centre but it is useful to think of it as a secondary emotion. There is another emotion that came before anger. That is hurt, loss or fear of a hurt or loss. Generally these are all feelings of powerlessness. (This is at the top of the chart.) It is useful then to ask yourself what is the powerlessness that is behind your client's anger or their parents' anger. Adolescents often are angry about bad experiences they have received in their childhood, hurts from parents, being treated as a child or things or people that they have lost.

Anger needs to be expressed otherwise it festers inside, comes out later or causes ill health and accidents.

On the left of the chart you will see that anger needs to be expressed positively as a feeling. If it is expressed positively in action or talk then there is a sense of relief. If it is expressed negatively there is also a sense of relief, however someone or something else gets hurt. That is not OK because that is abuse. People need to be guided to positive expression and listened to.

Anger flow chart

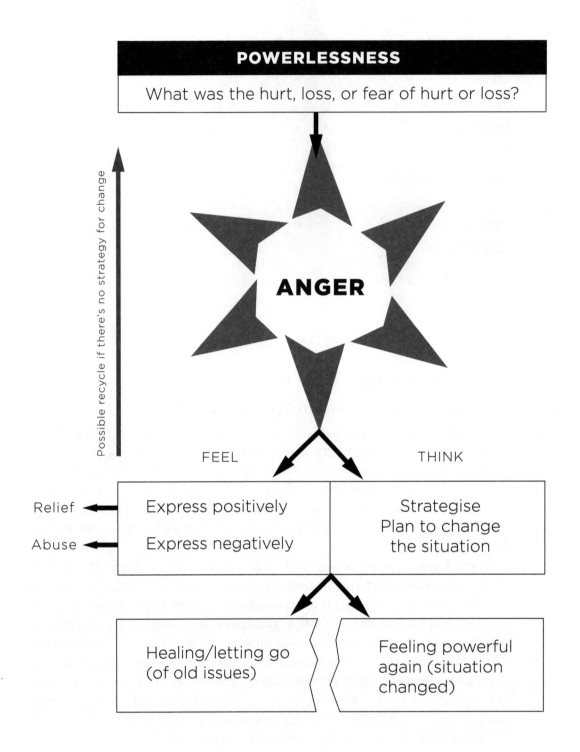

The other thing that we need to do is think. Thinking involves a strategy or plan to change the situation that caused the powerlessness. Failure to have a strategy for change means that the parent or child may at any time re-experience the powerlessness that led to the anger last time. People who have the same thing happen over and over again start to feel hopeless. If the adolescent feels powerless about something in the past or the present then they need to be able to develop the plan that will put it right. The helper can ask simple questions like: What would put this right? What would fix this up? What would help make you friends again? What do you want from the other person? How can I help you to make sure that this doesn't happen again?

Develop a two or three-point plan that if carried out will lead to an adolescent feeling that they can cope with the world. Assist parents to use the same approach if they are feeling powerless. Repeating or duplicating powerlessness just reinforces someone else's behaviour.

Sometimes there is little that a client can do and the skill may just be about learning to let go and let the hurt heal. The powerlessness of death is like that. Deaths of loved ones leave us powerless and they can't be brought back. In such a situation a strategy could be to see a counsellor, find a substitute relationship, write a letter or let go through a healthy grief process.

Take the example of an older son who is angry with everyone. Tracking back to the hurt and the powerlessness may reveal that he is angry with his father for not being there, not affirming him and not even remembering him. He may also be angry that he has to fulfil many of the roles in the family that his father would normally be doing because he is the oldest. That means a loss of his boyhood in some ways. Abusing his mother and teachers is not OK. He needs to express his anger positively either by action, writing or talking. He also needs a strategy which might be to call his father, tell how it is for him, ask another man to talk to his father, ask his mother to relieve him of certain tasks, be supportive of her finding a new partner so that she is less dependent on him, remind his father of when his birthday is, plan a visit to him, see a counsellor, spend more time with an uncle. All of these are options that could be small parts of a larger strategy.

As a practitioner, try tracking an incident of your own anger through the anger flow chart. Make sure that you develop a strategy as many people excuse themselves of the thinking strategy and wonder why the pattern repeats.

Using the flow chart

The anger flow chart is a tool that can be used for any anger incident, large or small. It is best taught by:

1. Taking a client through the flow chart by linking it to a personal incident. There are four key questions that assist this process. The client needs to understand the meaning of each step.

2. Take the client through again with a different incident, encouraging them to supervise their own progress through the incident. Do this with as many incidents as needed for the client to be proficient at managing themselves through the process on paper or screen.

3.   Get the client to recall the four key questions from memory.

4.   Have the client process incidents without any visual cues but from memory.

The steps through the diagram in more detail:

1.   Locate the exploding ANGER sign in the centre.

     Anger is more visible because it is an emotion that is supposed to be noticed. It declares itself and often appears to be wild or uncontrolled (but it is not).

2.   At the top is a box headed POWERLESSNESS.

     Our feelings of powerlessness come from:

     a.   Being hurt either physically or emotionally. Examples:

          ▸   A deliberate wound from a boot during a football match (malevolent physical)

          ▸   A friend calling us a name (malevolent emotional)

          ▸   Not being remembered by a parent on a birthday (non-malevolent emotional)

          ▸   Hitting yourself accidently with a hammer (non-malevolent physical)

     b.   Loss, sadness or grief: losing something or having something taken away from us. Examples:

          ▸   A death – loss of close person, powerlessness over death

          ▸   Sexual abuse – loss of innocence, powerlessness to stop abuse

          ▸   Loss of money – loss of spending, powerlessness over life resources

          ▸   Theft – loss of items and trust, powerlessness over security

          ▸   Breakage – loss of item broken, powerlessness to keep things whole

          ▸   Car breakdown – loss of transport, powerlessness to get somewhere

          ▸   Dishonesty – loss of trust, powerlessness of unreliable information

          ▸   Dad left home – loss of parent, security and love, powerlessness of abandonment

          ▸   Bedroom changed and tidied – loss of privacy, powerless over life

          ▸   Dumped by a girl/boyfriend – loss of friend, lover, powerless over being loved

> ▸ Being bossed – loss of personal choice, powerlessness of no autonomy

    c.   Fear of any of the above before they happen. Examples:

> ▸ Fear of a death happening, sense of powerlessness beforehand
>
> ▸ Fear of being rejected when asking for a date, powerlessness of being unable to predict or control rejection
>
> ▸ Fear of having to sit next to a bully in a car, powerlessness to get home without being thumped

    d.   Shame by an individual or a group. Examples:

> ▸ Being pulled out in front of the school assembly as the failure, powerlessness to be liked and accepted by a group
>
> ▸ Shamed by mother/father in front of family as being badly dressed
>
> ▸ Powerlessness of being rejected as not good enough from someone you want and need affirmation from
>
> ▸ Shamed by boy/girlfriend for not knowing something, powerlessness to make someone like you

Hurt, fear, loss/sadness, shame sit behind all angry incidents. It is our task and the client's task to identify them. Identification of them usually also reduces the intensity of the anger and moves it to a zone of vulnerability that needs to be listened to carefully.

It would be healthy to feel and display some anger over all of the above. It will vary however in how it is displayed, intensity, expression and activity and also possibly delay of expression, all according to the individual, place and intensity.

3.   Locate the FEEL and THINK boxes under the anger symbol.

There are two things that we all need to do with anger in order to honour the emotion and to remain healthy: feel and think.

WE FEEL. We need to positively EXPRESS that feeling in a way that doesn't hurt another person. There are three main ways to express any emotion:

    a.   Physical movement: by moving hands, feet or other parts of the body or by extending that physical movement to an action like slamming a book shut, barging down a corridor, eating faster, clenching a fist, banging a steering wheel, pacing about, walking faster, banging pots and pans.

    b.   Verbally: by using words, sounds/noises at different volumes and meanings. Swearing and screaming come under this category as well as a hiss, yell or raised fast talking.

c.   Body language, especially facial expressions. We may also hunch up, go red in the face, grimace, widen our eyes, purse our lips, breathe faster.

We have a choice of expressing our anger negatively or positively. Whether anger expression is negative or positive depends on the situation and the local rules.

For many, slamming a door is negative and aggressive. Speaking in very cautious and moderate tones may be how anger is expressed when you are speaking to your employer. A person may abandon such moderation however when they express anger to someone who comes from their own family. Usually this is because they expect the other person not to take offence and handle a bit of wrath. However this also is the risky base of much family violence. Negative expression of anger in homes may continue until someone says, 'I used to tolerate this because I loved you but I don't love you any more so I certainly won't tolerate it.'

The client must decide whether they have used positive expression (no one was hurt emotionally or physically) or negative expression. The counsellor or professional can assist in the evaluation of whether it was positive or negative as values and empathy may need tuning.

4.   Move to the THINK box and locate the instruction to STRATEGISE.

The THINK box is the one that some people leave out. At this point it means that you strategise or make a plan to put things right or to take away the powerlessness. If you fail to have a plan and act on it then you risk the same thing happening again maybe in ten minutes or maybe in ten years. If you have too many repeats you end up with a sense of hopelessness and being a victim. Many young people have experienced powerlessness so many times that they feel depressed and useless. The answer is to act. Act to change the situation so that you don't have to feel angry to protect yourself. Too much anger and you get to be known as an angry person and that will make you angrier as you experience the powerlessness of not being loved and affirmed by the world.

Anger is useful for getting you out of trouble. It's no use if you use it to keep you in trouble. The key is to think, have a plan and then change things.

After you have changed things you should feel powerful again over your own life. Remember it's not OK to feel powerful by taking 'power over' others' lives. In the end they get angry and you lose them.

Sometimes what needs to happen is for an old wound or hurt to heal. This too will take away the powerlessness as long as you have taken action for the same thing not to happen again.

> **Key concepts**
>
> ◆ Behind anger is a hurt or loss.
>
> ◆ We have a choice of positive or negative expression.
>
> ◆ Negative expression is abusive.
>
> ◆ The purpose of anger is to put the situation right again.

Try taking something that you are angry or hurt about and tracking it through the anger flow chart. Here are some examples:

Example: help with making a plan

A student is caught smashing up a rubbish bin at school. He's in trouble but the dean is smart enough to ask him what the hurt or loss is. It turns out that he was looking forward to going to Sydney to stay with his Dad for the holidays and days before going his dad rang up and said that he was too busy to have him. He hadn't seen his dad for years and wanted to get to know him again. In fact he'd felt quite abandoned by his dad and as a 14-year-old coming into manhood he wanted his love, pride and approval. He'd already been hurt by his failing to keep in regular contact and felt abandoned by him. He wanted to be noticed by him and told he was an OK guy. The phone call to say that he couldn't come wounded him again in the same place. His powerlessness was his inability to get his Dad's attention and approval.

He was expressing his feeling negatively by abusing property. He could have expressed his anger positively by talking to someone or writing a letter.

He had no strategy or plan to stop himself from being hurt again and so it could still happen again. The dean sent him to the school counsellor who helped develop a plan by calling the father with the boy's permission and helping him to understand his son's needs and disappointments. The father spoke to his son and another close date was arranged. There was still some healing to be done and the father still needed to repair the past but with some coaching the boy could ask for some things for himself and feel powerful again.

Example: talking about the problem

Tania was 16. She was angry because she felt that her girlfriend had stolen her boyfriend. She wasn't speaking to her and was speaking badly of her amongst their friends. Her powerlessness was the hurt that she felt about her boyfriend not wanting to spend a lot of time with her.

She felt hurt at the loss and inability to get the love that she wanted. She was expressing her anger negatively by attacking her girlfriend who she thought had caused the problem. She could have expressed it positively by talking to the boyfriend or girlfriend. She had no strategy to change the situation to heal it or stop it happening.

Fortunately she had a good friend who talked to her and offered to be with her when she spoke to the girlfriend. When she did this she discovered that the girlfriend was happy with her own boyfriend and was just a social friend with her boyfriend. She also started to understand the idea that the boyfriend was free to choose who he spent time with and that it wasn't the fault of the person who he chose to be with. She needed to respect his choices and not treat him like a kid. When she finally talked to her boyfriend about why he chose not to spend so much time with her she found out some things that he wanted changed in the relationship in order to feel happier spending time with her.

That gave them a chance to make the relationship better.

Key concept

+ Behind anger is a hurt or loss.

Exercise: teenagers and anger

Remind yourself of when you were an adolescent… Ask yourself if, as an adolescent, any of the following happened to you. How did it feel?

- You were put down by a teacher or parent in front of other teenagers

- You had parents who split up

- You were promised something and nothing happened

- You felt dumb at school

- Your family didn't have things that other families had

- You had a father who rarely complimented you

- You had a parent who rarely said they loved you

- You had a parent who was an alcoholic

- You had a parent who put the other parent down

- You had a parent who didn't have enough time for you

- You had a parent who controlled you instead of guiding you

- You had to eat food you hated

- You were sexually or physically abused

- You weren't told what was going on

- Your grown-ups thought they were always right

- You had separated parents who fought

- You had a teacher tell you to go away when you tried to tell them something important

- You had a younger brother or sister born

- You were falsely accused of something

- You were treated unfairly in the distribution of something

- You were left out of a group or family happening

- You had to shift home to a new town or suburb

- You had a parent who didn't make it to see you have an important achievement

- You were often told to keep quiet

- You had parents who didn't give firm boundaries and guidance

- Your parents told you not to get angry

- Your parents were too busy to listen to your anger or hurts

- You didn't know why you were hurting

- You were made to go somewhere you hated

- You were betrayed

- You were tricked by an adult

- You were called names by other kids

- You were deliberately hurt

- You had peers who cheated you in games

- Someone or some pet important to you died

- You didn't get your own way

- You were left waiting a long time for a parent

- You weren't allowed to show anger about any of the above

How did you feel?

What did you need in response?

How can this help an adult to relate to and understand your adolescent?

✓

Triggers for parents

Triggers are used by others to set up situations where they can get power over you by getting you upset. They are used as bait. Do not get hooked and lose your power.

Adolescents may try to use some of the following triggers to hook other adolescents and parents:

- Push you to the edge
- Act defiant
- Ask for money/car/to go out
- Mention the parents' separation and maybe blame someone for a break-up
- Delay homework
- Heavy metal posters and provocative music
- Avoid or refuse to do household tasks
- Wreck Mum's or Dad's chances with a new boy/girlfriend

- Buy clothes, spend money
- Act resentful
- Talk/dress dirty
- Not clean up
- Play loud music
- Not speak
- Say things others hate to hear
- Say, 'Make me!' or 'I don't have to'
- Say negative things about a parent's parenting or an adolescent's ability

'Losing it', shouting, ordering or even hitting doesn't help. It may even be exactly what the adolescent wants. It may confirm they're not OK, or it may be that there's a 'gotcha' response to being triggered automatically. The way around this is to:

- Have clear contracts and understanding about what is OK
- Have clear, simple consequences for breaking the boundaries
- Ensure that the boundaries and consequences are guarded consistently and maintained
- Don't act in angry response. Don't react. Don't put adolescents down. Keep cool and understanding, or wait till the 'rush' or angry charge has gone

What to do: self-talk

Say: 'This is a trigger situation.'

Say: 'M wants to get me angry and have power over me.'

Say: 'Who's got the problem? He has.'

Say: 'I'm OK, I'm great, I'm really worthwhile.'

Say: 'I'll walk away' or 'I will ignore this' or 'I'll deal with this later.'

Exercise: working together to help young people manage their anger
For helping staff working in schools and other organisations

Objective

To adopt an effective team approach to help young people manage their anger.

Task

Give staff members a copy of the stories below. After reading them work together in small groups to brainstorm ideas that might assist the young person in the story to gain greater self-esteem and better management of his or her anger.

Ask each staff member to offer a way that they personally can assist the young person when they come into contact with him/her.

Example: Cameron

Cameron always seems to be at the centre of any playground fight. He is always last to start his work and does not complete his tasks. Other children complain that Cameron destroys their work. Cameron has been suspended for swearing at the teachers. The dean has discovered, from talking to Cameron, that Cameron's parents separated four years ago and Cameron's father has not been turning up for access visits. Mother has remarried and the stepfather is violent. Mother appears to be very passive. The stepfather's children now share the family home at weekends and Cameron has lost his place as the oldest son, with older stepsiblings in the house.

Cameron was very upset at leaving his previous home where he had his own bedroom. His dog was recently put down, because Mum said it was too expensive to keep.

Suggestions from a workshop:

- Notice and comment to Cameron whenever he is seen to be on task

- Acknowledge him in the playground, 'Hi Cameron'

- Encourage and enable him to use a 'Time Out' strategy (a calm down place) that he has worked out with his form teacher

- Find a responsible task that he can perform and receive praise for doing

- Give him a care-taking role, such as growing plants

- Ask a senior pupil (or a male member of staff) to be a mentor for Cameron

- Encourage his mother to seek mediation to get his father more involved in access

Your workshop may provide more interventive measures.

Example: Maraline

Maraline is often absent from school and, although there has been previous evidence that that she is a very capable student, Maraline's school work has deteriorated. Her teachers report that Maraline often leads other students in verbal bullying of other girls. Maraline has been caught writing graffiti in the school toilets and was recently suspended for her bullying behaviour.

Maraline's social worker has just reported that she was sexually abused by her stepfather and Maraline is angry because her mother did not protect her from this man. Mother has prevented Maraline from having access to her father for the past three years.

How could staff work as a team to assist Maraline?

Bullying: how adults can help

The child who is bullied faces each day with dread. The child who bullies other children may be doing so for a number of reasons. He or she may have grown up in a home where violence is the only real communication between people. He or she may have been attacked physically, verbally or sexually by a bully. To survive, such a child has learnt to fight back. Having been on the receiving end of abuse, he or she may look for a weaker person to prey on in order to feel powerful for a while. None of these are excuses for bullying behaviour but they may help to understand how to help bullying dynamics.

Which children are vulnerable to bullies?

- The child who is different. 'Different children' are sometimes ostracised by their peers. Their aloneness leaves them vulnerable to those looking for someone to prey on. Their differentness makes them targets.

- The child who does not communicate well. Children who can speak up assertively and express themselves well verbally can be daunting to a bully who is more likely to have poor communication skills.

- A child may have 'victim' body language. Such a child may have been bullied previously, feel unwanted or have experienced trauma, leaving them displaying a sense of inferiority in the world.

- The child who does not connect well with others or has some disability or impairment.

- The child with negative beliefs about him/herself and the world.

Some principles of helping for professionals

- Assist the caregiver to listen to how the child is feeling about being bullied and show them you are trying to understand and that you are on their side. Assist the caregiver to affirm the child as OK and not guilty.

- Assist the caregiver to understand the risks of encouraging the child to fight back. Being caught and penalised as the instigator, losing the fight, escalating the conflict are all risks.

- Assist the caregiver to reassure the child that you are on his or her side and will help him/her find ways of coping.

- Assist the caregiver to get outside help from the school principal or from the dean at the child's school.

- Assist the caregiver to help and train the teenager to feel more confident and able to be assertive. Making short clear statements and masking fear are useful. Teach self-assertive communication and behaviour and know the difference between aggression and assertion. If you help your teenager learn self-assertive behaviour you are giving them a skill for life.

- Assist the caregiver to understand the importance of the child being treated with respect and not put down at home.

- Assist the caregiver to include the adolescent in discussion about the bullying and ask for their ideas and suggestions.

- Assist the caregiver to ensure the adolescent has personal space and privacy for which they have rights and responsibilities.

- Assist the caregiver to teach the adolescent life skills and encourage and praise them for their efforts. An example of this might be when the young person wants to open a bank account. Tell them how to go about it and then leave them to do it themselves.

- Assist the caregiver to appreciate the importance of regular meals together and other occasions when communication is easier. Encourage them to have time alone with their child on a regular basis even if it is just on car journeys or a shopping trip.

Working with a victim

Some of the most effective work on bullying can be done with the victim who may carry some unconscious messages that bullies hook onto as they select suitable people to victimise. Generally we don't support the idea of training in counter aggression though disciplined physical training may increase confidence. We recommend checking through the handout on p.214.

Identifying and working with a bully

It is very hard for a parent to accept that their child is bullying other children. It is almost instinctive for a parent to defend and deny that a child is bullying. There are usually two reasons:

1. They feel guilty already about their parenting and they wish to avoid that feeling by denial. Guilt may come from inadequate time and care with children, the child copying models from home.

2. Loyalty to their kin. It may be considered an insult to the family. Shifting of blame, denial, minimising and rationalising are the four most common defences.

Social workers, caregivers and teachers usually don't warm to bullies and it's easy to resort to simple punishment. This doesn't really deal with the problem of what's happening to the bully. The bully's needs are equal. Usually s/he needs connection to someone who offers warmth and understanding within safe, strong boundaries. These are probably what the bully has lacked and yearns for.

How can you help?

- Don't let the victim's carers get into their own payback.

- Talk to the young person when s/he is not in trouble so that you can relate on a more adult level. The young person is thus more amenable to listening.

- Use a strengths-based approach. Find what they are good at and build on it.

- Tell him/her that you are very concerned and you want to help them find better ways of getting on with people.

- Ask him what he thinks might happen if he or she continues to bully.

- Let the young person know bullying is not acceptable. Say what will happen if it continues. 'You will need to change then, so how can you change now?'

- Help the young person feel connected to his or her school, his or her culture or ethnic group, his or her peers and at least one member of his family. It may be hard for the young person to allow herself/himself to be connected to others in a positive way, because he or she has learnt to be detached.

- Give roles and tasks that will help him/her to feel valuable and worthwhile. Start small. Don't give tasks that are beyond his or her coping ability. Sport is often a physical outlet that appeals to physical bullies and it demands a team approach. Give praise for a task well done. Get the young person involved in activities of a team nature which are monitored by an adult who is firm, wise, fair and has good limit-setting skills.

- Find and appoint a mentor who is trustworthy as well as patient and has good boundaries.

- Help the bully to learn to care for something. Start with plants or objects. Protect animals and small children.

- A persistent bully may need psychotherapy.

- Therapy that involves the family will be of benefit. It is likely that the young person's problem is the family's problem.

- Seek a group programme in your area that teaches anger management with teenagers and offers positive ways of channelling anger.

- An outdoor pursuits course channels anger and energy into survival skills and activities while building the young person's self-esteem. A skilful tutor will assist young people to build good interpersonal relationships as part of a programme, teaching interdependence as well as self-reliance.

- Assist parents to repair and resolve any damage they may have done in their past parenting.

Growing up a winner

There are various attributes of a 'winner'. Getting on with others is one of the most important. Being positive is another. Positive thinking is easy and is the first response for someone who has had positive experiences in the world and has grown to trust that it is a place that helps and provides for one's needs. It's harder for someone who has no reason to think that the world is on their side and has learnt to regard others as a possible danger rather than friend and supporter. However positive thinking can be learned and consciously applied by a continual optimistic analysis that is not necessarily based on reality but on the systematic screening of negative thoughts and assumptions to reduce negativity. This positivity can be set considerably below the reality level but not to the degree that the new position puts the individual at risk of being naive. Assuming no one will take things from your house if you leave the door open and unlocked is naive. Assuming that the thief lingering on the street outside your house has a better side and will respond to encouragement and friendship is not naive. The power of positive assumptions is well documented. Phrases such as 'you get what you give' and 'expect the best and you get the best', have a truth endorsed by psychology. Slightly narcissistic people tend to believe in themselves that little bit more and attract positivity and opportunity. Thinking well of yourself and others 'brings out the best'.

We are attracted to people who are optimistic and people who are hopeful and they tend to have more energy and enthusiasm for life.

How can we assist parents and adolescents to be more positive, optimistic, enthusiastic and attractively happy? Ron Taffel, in *Networker* (September/October 1999), cites ten attributes of children who thrive.

The attributes of winners and how parents can foster these

1. Mood mastery: the ability to soothe the self during intense emotional states in ways that fit a child's particular temperament.

    Parents can help children by: soothing and comforting from babyhood, staying calm themselves, empathising with the child's feelings, staying with a feeling and not avoiding the expression of uncomfortable emotions by another, setting safe limits for the expression of those feelings. They can help each other by being appreciative, noticing the positive, offering help, and applying a sense of humour especially in stressful situations.

2. Respect: being clear about expectations and knowing how to follow through with reasonable consequences when they are not met. Appropriately respecting the wisdom of others.

    Parents can help themselves and children by: respecting the child and their feelings, respecting themselves and their needs, listening and communicating well, respecting others themselves, avoiding labelling, prejudice and stereotyping, setting fair limits and consequences.

3. Expressiveness: being able to talk about the important things, emotional literacy.

    Parents can help by talking with each other and help children by: talking and listening, expressing feelings, listening to feelings, teaching emotional literacy and a feeling vocabulary, tuning in to the particular needs of their child, taking into account the child's personality. Doing the same with each other sets a harmonious and secure environment and models how relationships are done.

4. Passion: acting with interest and enthusiasm and following a cause.

    Parents can help by being interested and enthusiastic about the child and their interests, even if these are different from those of the parent. Parents need to have their own interests and hobbies, express their ideas, beliefs and values and encourage discussion in the family. Passion also means helping the child to deal with disappointment, competitiveness and perfectionism.

5.   Peer smart: being able to relate to others, give and receive guidance, be discriminating about choice of friends and confidantes.

Parents can help by relating to their own children and others (this means discussing and questioning, not just giving instruction). Through the parent listening actively, being respectful, being kind and considerate of the feelings of the child and their circle of friends, the child's judgements and world is endorsed.

Helping the child to problem solve in relationships sets up skills for life.

6.   Focus: being able to stick to a task and complete it, set goals and organise tasks to fulfil goals.

There are two very important skills that will take a child, adolescent or adult everywhere and are core to education, occupation and recreation: staying focused on the task and being able to delay gratification so that larger and longer tasks can be completed.

Parents can assist by showing children how to organise their world, plan for tasks at different levels and stage completion, overcome setbacks, and organise activities and goals that are appropriate to the age and capabilities of the particular child.

Encouragement while tasks are progressing transfers the parent's vision to the adolescent.

7.   Body comfort: being able to accept the way they look and feel in their body, to not be obsessing about one's body, to be avoiding struggles around food and to be avoiding sexual attitudes that affect self-image.

In a world that is increasingly pressured by looks, appearances and the promotion of illusions, parents can do two things: assist in the championing of authentic behaviour and values, and model acting out those values.

Parents can help if they accept their own bodies, affirm how the child looks, value and affirm their choice of clothes, encourage activities that enable the child to enjoy body movement and being in time and space, for example, swimming, gymnastics, dancing, running and relaxing. Singing and music are also opportunities for authentic enjoyment, happiness and spontaneity, things that take people past criticism and judgement (even if they don't like others' choices in music).

8.   Caution: weighing up the impact of actions, valuing self-safety, seeking guidance, setting limits for self and others.

Parents can help by setting safe limits for children from birth and explaining, discussing and expanding the limits as the adolescent grows. Parents still help adolescents learn through consequences and observation of others. Parents still keep adolescents safe and teach safe behaviour. Modelling the sought behaviour reduces values conflicts.

Being open to talking assists adolescents to discuss 'first events' and associated difficulties afterwards.

9.   Team intelligence and belonging to a group: understanding how people live and work together and experiencing this while maintaining a sense of self and identity.

A solid home creates a sense of belonging even when children are grown. It's from belonging and membership that secure adolescents explore their individual world bravely but securely. Even when angrily asserting independence the family that is positive, firm and affirming, encourages sound identity and a place of safety that they can retreat to.

10.   Gratitude: displaying empathy, appreciation, being able to delay gratification, having a healthy appreciation and a personal spiritual dimension.

Parents can help by showing empathy with the emotions and needs of their adolescent even though they may be being pushed away. Empathy is even more of a challenge when some of the actions may be inconsiderate of what the parent is feeling (e.g. fear for safety when late home). Gratitude plays a great part in building empathy as the constant affirmation encourages considerate and positively responsive behaviour in return.

Relationships based on criticism and fear of the withdrawal of love and respect foster guardedness, defensiveness and withholding of information.

Example: unconditional love

A young man was enduring a court trial for murder. Outside the court, the family gathered and vowed to the media that despite his crime they would stand by the young man, offering him unconditional affirmation and support.

That was good and touching but it might well have been that if this young man had received unconditional love from age one to five that he might not be standing where he was.

Summary

- Ask children and adolescents what their bigger hurts and angers are.

- Use effective 'Time Out' (calm down) procedures.

- Track anger using the flow chart.

Key concepts

- People who feel angry need to be heard.

- There is always a good reason for a person to feel angry.

- Behind every anger there is a hurt.

- If you feel angry make sure you have a strategy for changing things.

- Damage can be repaired by listening and empathy.

- Knowing your triggers gives you more control over them.

- Time Out (withdrawal) helps you to keep safe. You need to come back and complete the discussion.

The healthy family checklist

Think about your parenting and family and consider these statements:

- ❑ Healthy families talk to each other. They tell each other when they are angry: 'I feel angry when you don't clean up after a snack, because it makes work for me that I don't deserve. I want you to put away the butter and jam and wipe the bench.'

- ❑ Healthy families listen to each other and show that they care about how others feel

- ❑ Healthy families are not abusive. They recognise that anger is OK but abuse/violence is not OK. Abuse can be physical, emotional, sexual and psychological. It is not OK.

- ❑ Healthy families teach young people to take Time Out (walk away) when they feel they might get out of control.

- ❑ Healthy families encourage each other to talk through angry feelings and not store them so that they burst forth at a later date.

- ❑ Healthy families manage their anger by recognising circumstances that trigger their anger.

- ❑ Healthy families encourage members to find safe ways of expressing anger.

- ❑ Healthy families calm and soothe distressed children so that they learn to calm and soothe themselves in times of stress.

- ❑ Healthy families model and teach the anger rules.

- ❑ Healthy families are good communicators and teach children a 'feeling vocabulary'.

- ❑ Healthy families set boundaries but are flexible and move the boundaries as family members grow.

- ❑ Healthy families respect other's rights to have an opinion, have feelings, have likes and dislikes, make mistakes, set boundaries, choose friends, keep safe and develop to their full potential.

- ❑ Healthy families provide opportunities for members to redeem themselves when a mistake has been made.

- ❑ Healthy families affirm and compliment each other.

- ❑ Healthy families have fun together.

- ❑ Healthy families have a shared spiritual core.

- ❑ Healthy families value service to others.

- ❑ Healthy families foster family-around-the-table time.

- ❑ Healthy families admit to having problems and seek help.

- ❑ Healthy families welcome outsiders without pretending.

✓

- ❑ Healthy families give increasing autonomy to young people.

- ❑ Healthy families don't hold grudges.

- ❑ Healthy families develop trust.

- ❑ Healthy families exhibit a sense of shared responsibility.

- ❑ Healthy families teach a sense of right and wrong.

- ❑ Healthy families express love and caring.

CHAPTER 9

Positive Limit Setting

Setting limits positively

Example from a parenting group: no limits

'I feel so helpless to stop my kids. They walk all over me. What's the use of saying, "You can't do that"? They know they can because I can never stop them,' said Sandra, mother of two sons and one daughter.

'How did your parents set limits for you?' I asked Sandra.

'They didn't,' Sandra replied. 'I had all the freedom in the world. I did what I wanted.'

'What was it like?' I asked.

'Great,' laughed Sandra. 'When the other kids had to go home at a certain time I knew I could go anywhere. All of us who had parents who didn't care, well, we went off into town and hung out together.'

'What was it like to have parents who didn't seem to care?'

Sandra stopped for a moment. The group was quiet.

Sandra reached across to get the tissue box.

'I remember sometimes when we stopped fooling around and I'd just be sitting somewhere there was this empty sinking feeling in my stomach. No belonging. I hated that. But it went away when we started doing something crazy or if I lit a cigarette or something like that. They were just never there. I don't want to be like that for my kids but I don't know what to do about it.'

Two reasons why it may be hard for a parent to set and maintain limits:

1. If our parents have not set good limits for us it is much harder to do it for our own children. The imprint of our parent's behaviour becomes the default setting for our own parenting. If there is no software installed then it has to be done from constant consciousness and vigilance.

2. It's hard to set limits for adolescents as if as parents we have not done that through childhood. Considerable conflict and rebellion is likely because the parent is trying to do so at the very point at which these should start to be broken down. It is possible, but the parent needs to be prepared for some hard work and will need good support from friends, partner, a counsellor, a parent's group, an extended family or another family.

Contracts vs punishments

Some parents when they think of limit setting with children think immediately of punishment. Our prison system with its scores of repeat offenders is evidence that punishment is not effective.

There are few advantages of punishment. Punishment seems fair in a tit-for-tat world but sets up an atmosphere of trying to avoid the punishment rather than stopping the behaviour. The attitude amongst peers may be 'bad luck you got caught' rather than considering the values driving the behaviour. Punishment is an external driver and values-empathy-co-operation is an internal driver.

Other disadvantages of punishment

- It doesn't teach a person the behaviour that you do want, only what you don't want.

- It doesn't encourage responsibility.

- It doesn't encourage good moral development. People don't work out a good personal code of morality and think for themselves.

- If the punishment is physical it teaches violent behaviour and aggressive ways of solving problems.

- It gives a retributive model rather than a contributive model.

- It breeds resentment and payback.

- It tends to remain specific to the offending act rather than transferring to several similar acts.

Most people who were punished can remember the punishment but not why they were punished. Punishing is often a power trip for the punisher.

Contracting

Contracting desired behaviour and consequences beforehand is different. It is not punishment.

Three things are required:

- Communication as to what the desired behaviour is

- The setting of a consequence that is appropriate

- Contract agreement

Communication about what the desired behaviour is

The desired behaviour can be set by the parent but for adolescents where autonomy is developing, a mutual agreement is preferable. It needs also to be associated with a good reason based on empathy for others or safety for self. Reasons are an important part of the adolescent world. Ultimately the adolescent may not agree so a 'power over' response may need to be made but these have limited duration because there's a time when they may say that they choose to ignore the request.

The setting of a consequence that is appropriate

A consequence should also be negotiated and agreed. Often the question: 'What is a fair consequence or penalty if you break this agreement?' is a good start. It's good if it's related, such as drinking and driving means no driving, no clothes in the washing basket means no washing done, using the petrol in the car and not replacing it means reduction in car use. It's got to sound fair. It should be as short term as is possible. Consequences lasting more than a month lose power.

You may need to say: 'Ah ha. Hmmm. That sounds like too much/too little. How about…?'

The parent may also set a positive consequence or reward. Such reinforcement is often more powerful.

Contract agreement

Contracts are adult ways of working in the world. Buying a car, starting a job both require contracts of understanding for both sides. There is a benefit for both parties and the importance of a person keeping their word is central to contracts. Handshakes or a formal repetition of the contract help cement the importance of the agreement. Always insist that the other party stops what they are doing and give full eye contact unless this is culturally offensive. 'So we are agreed. If you break the agreement then…will happen automatically.'

✓

Model contract

I . . . . agree to:

- Tidy my room once a week

- Take out the rubbish

- Empty the dishwasher on Tuesdays and Thursdays

- Cook tea on Monday nights

- If I use the car I will clean it and re-place petrol

We . . . . (Mum and Dad) agree to provide £ . . . . per week allowance, which is to help . . . . with the cost of clothing.

. . . . will meet any other clothing costs from his work at the supermarket.

Signed: . . . .

Signed: . . . .

Signed: . . . .

Date: . . . .

Positive reinforcement

'Catch a person doing good.' Many adults only comment to children and others when things start to go wrong. Notice and comment when things are going right so the behaviour change is positively based and the negative may never happen.

- Remember the five to one rule. If anyone has plenty of positive recognition they can cope better with criticism. Try five good comments to every criticism.

- Many children and adolescents have been so starved of affirmation and compliments that for them bad/critical recognition is at least better than no recognition at all. If we slip into only noticing kids when their behaviour is bad then we are encouraging negative behaviour. Ask yourself, 'Am I giving out five times more positive than negative comments?'

- Offer limited choices: 'You can go to Sara's party where I know her parents will be home or you can go to a movie or ten pin bowling. Which one will you choose?'

- Model and practise good adherence to your own rules, especially Time Out when you are frustrated with adolescents.

- Trust adolescents with responsibility, care, money (to practise handling), power and affirm their good handling of responsibility.

- Trust them. Trust the good work you have already done as a parent.

- Use 'Four levels of muscle with the mouth' assertive communication (see the handout on the following page).

Consistency

The power of agreements, contracts, rules, boundaries and discipline is in consistency. It is about you being true to your word and agreement. If you are inconsistent:

- Adolescents learn they can try you out each and every time

- You don't tell the truth. You don't keep your word. You model breaking your word to your teenager and not surprisingly the adolescent may break their word

- You can't be trusted

- There is a lack of solidness, structure and reliability that will lead to your teenager feeling less secure. Insecurity means living with anxiety

To win back your credibility you will need to keep your word at least six to ten times.

Consistency gives:

- A sense of relief that the world has order

- Trust in you as a parent

- Honesty for all

- The behaviour that you want

- Responsibility for actions

- Reliability – you know a thing is going to happen

Be consistently consistent!

Responsibility

Responsibility denotes trust, co-operation and teamwork, equality, mutuality, realism of life and work ethics.

Some useful participation ideas:

- Being responsible for preparing a meal one night a week. If the cook cleans up on their cooking night they will be more careful with the amount of mess they create in the process.

- Having the responsibility for the grocery shopping. Make up a family shopping list and set the budget. Choose a couple of items as a treat.

- Caring for the family car, for example, checking oil and water, cleaning.

Four levels of muscle with the mouth

Level 1: Give an 'I' statement ('I feel...when you...because...I would like...').

Level 2: Make eye contact if possible. Lower your voice. Slow your voice.

Deepen your voice.

Repeat your four-part 'I' statement.

Pause and add firmly 'I mean it'

Level 3: Make eye contact if possible. Use a low, slow, deep voice. Repeat your 'I' statement.

Now add the consequences if the behaviour does not change. (Only give consequences that you can enforce and where possible fit the undesirable behaviour.) You may negotiate the consequence at this point (hopefully you will have already negotiated the consequences before this point so they will not come as a surprise to the young person).

Level 4: Remind the person of what you have wanted them to do or change using a low, slow, deep voice and then carry out the agreed consequences.

Here is an example:

Level 1: 'I feel angry when the petrol in the car is not replaced after you have used it, because it often means that I have to stop for petrol on my way to work when I am in a hurry. I want you to replace the petrol you use.'

Level 2: 'I feel angry when the petrol in the car isn't replaced after you have used it, because it often means that I have to stop for petrol on my way to work when I am in a hurry. I want you to replace the petrol you use. This is only fair. I insist that you do this if you are going to use my car.'

Level 3: 'I feel angry when the petrol in the car isn't replaced after you have used it, because it often means that I have to stop for petrol on my way to work when I am in a hurry. I want you to replace the petrol you use.'

'What would be an appropriate consequence if you don't?'

[Response]

'OK, so the next time you forget you will not use the car the next week. Do you agree to that? OK, we have a deal.'

Level 4: 'You forgot to replace the petrol you used. You remember the deal we had. This means that this week you will need to find another way of getting to your football practice because you will not have the use of the car. That was our deal so that's how it is.'

Now write out your own problem and how you will tackle it with your teenager:

Level 1: _____

_____

_____

Level 2: _____

_____

_____

Level 3: _____

_____

_____

Level 4: _____

_____

_____

Exercise: questions for parents on setting limits

For parents of pre-teens:

- How are you setting limits for your child at present?

- Will you still be able to use this method when your child is 16?

- If not, you will need to change your methods so why not change now?

For all teens:

- Did your parents or teachers use any of the following when setting limits for you when you were young: advising, preaching, judging, criticising, violence, blackmail, verbal abuse, bribery or other manipulations?

- How did you feel?

- What effect did this have on your behaviour?

- How do you feel now?

- How did it affect your relationship with your parents and teachers?

The parent needs to use their self-empathy to empathise with the adolescent they are dealing with.

Key concepts

- People learn by experiencing the consequences of their behaviour.

- Positive attention is much more effective than negative attention or punishment.

- Be very consistent.

- Children are more co-operative if they share in decision making about their behaviour.

- Fairness and a willingness to listen will encourage co-operation.

- Short, clear, firm communication is best.

CHAPTER 10

When Parents Separate

Good reasons for feeling angry

The separation of parents gives many reasons for a child to feel angry. Anger is an understandable element of loss and no matter how much a parent or child gains by a separation, for the child:

- Their stable secure world is disrupted

- Parents have been fighting and their emotions and needs given lower priority

- They may have been pressured to take sides

- Their welfare is reduced and poverty may even be a result of income going to support two houses

There may be anger at possible losses of:

- A familiar neighbourhood or a school

- Familiar rituals and security

- Friendships, contacts with a family member or even grandparents and other family members

- A loved room or home and possessions

- Control of one's time and broken dreams and ideas of the future

- An ideal family and the balance that may have brought

There are many more issues and they are all good reasons for feeling angry.

Beneath the anger may be hurt, sadness and fear. Males are most likely to mask these vulnerable emotions with anger. Parents may be happy to be free of a hurtful relationship but children need the opportunity to grieve and have their grief accepted and recognised. It might not be wise to continue a relationship but even a bad relationship needs a period of mourning to end satisfactorily.

Children first and foremost want parents who love one another, have resolved their problems and model good relating. If that is not possible then it may be best to separate.

Children need parents who act like responsible adults, not angry children.

Children have the need and the right to be parented by adults.

Parents might decide to stay together 'for the sake of the children'. If the relationship is abusive this might not be wise. Children do not want to feel that their parents endured pain for their sake particularly if they are reminded of this for ever after.

Generally it's not the divorce that most affects children, it's the destructive relationships they endure prior to the divorce and after the separation.

Katy put it this way:

> 'I hated all those years when Mum and Dad were together. They were always fighting. I was on edge all the time. When would they start hitting each other? Would one of them leave this time? Would they both leave and then who would take care of me? I was really upset when they did split but in a way it was a relief. Finally it had happened. I didn't have to worry about it anymore.'

Kelly said this after the break-up:

> 'I could handle the break-up. Most of my friends have separated parents. It was the fighting and trying to use me and my brother to payback, spy and be on their side that hurt. Why split if you can't live in peace after? What's the point? They may have just as well stayed in the same house fighting.'

What helps to make a clean break?

Adjusting to living in two homes can be fraught with the remnants of the hurt and disagreement of the parents. Children deserve a more peaceful settlement and adjustment to change.

Here are some suggestions for recently separated parents:

- Try to avoid calling one place home and the other Dad's house or Mum's house. This means that children have to divide their loyalties and themselves to accommodate their parents' needs.

- Help children to have their own special places in both houses even if it is only a cupboard or some shelves and a bed.

- Adolescents are developing their own lives and peers are very important. Enhance your relationship with them by taking this into account when planning visitation arrangements.

- A parent shouldn't talk about the other parent in a derogatory fashion, not to the adolescent nor to others in front of your adolescent. You may hate your ex-partner vehemently but your children should be free to love a parent if that is how they feel.

- Children who hear a parent being denigrated must walk on eggshells. They do not want to upset either parent. They feel squeezed by forced loyalties.

- Children should not have to carry their parents' pain.

- Adolescents and children should not have to act as a go-between, messenger or a spy. It is an insidious position. For example:

  'Tell your father to get that girlfriend out of the house or I'll be stopping child support.'

  'Tell your mother if she doesn't pay up I'm taking her to court.'

  'Tell your mother, while she has trips away I can't afford to pay her.'

  'Who was there?'

- Teenagers who are forced to carry such responsibility carry with it great pain and distress and may be overly responsible for comforting one parent or younger peers.

- An adolescent needs an opportunity to talk out his or her anger. If a counsellor is unaffordable, find a trusted family friend or an older cousin.

- Getting the adolescent to talk freely may take courage because they might want to complain about the parent. That's OK because it's their business and it usually begins to dissolve when they talk. Communication lines need to be kept open and care taken to watch out for signs of depression when feelings of sadness and hurt have not been talked out and resolved.

- Seek professional help for all parties if necessary.

It's naive to expect children to like a new partner. They will still have loyalties to their own mother and father. Children need time to adjust to their parents' new relationships. Empathy and patience on the part of a new partner will help. Adolescents with a growing awareness of their own sexuality may find that the idea of Mum or Dad having a sexual relationship, particularly with a new partner, is disturbing and embarrassing. We recall a client, a young 13-year-old, who loved his dad and hated the idea of the break-up, being torn, anguished and desperate when he heard his mother being sexually active with the new man through his bedroom wall.

We, when working with potential step-parents often tell them, 'Understand this: his or her children are young and fragile and dependent. The (natural) parent that you are in love with must always put the children first. This is right and good. That means that you are number two. If you can't handle that then don't move in.' To the natural parent we say, 'Frequent change of partners causes insecurity, damages the parent/child bond and can leave children vulnerable to abuse. Don't take a new partner into your home until you are sure that it is going to last. Check out any new partner before allowing them into your home and don't leave them alone with your children until the children are happy about that.' Young adolescent girls with developing sexual attractiveness and the need for an affirming father figure are particularly susceptible to possible abusive behaviour.

It's important to listen not only to what a child might be saying but also listen to his or her feelings and actions. There is always a reason for what children do and if they are seeking our attention there is a reason why they are doing this. Helpers can practise communication skills with the parent before practising on the children. Sometimes being a parent is like being a 'feelings detective'. They may not be able to state their feelings and the parent may need to work it out for them.

If at all possible children need to know both parents. If a girl does not know her father she has a choice: she can either imagine he is a monster or a prince on a shining white charger. Neither will be reality nor a good basis for establishing healthy adult relationships. Children need the same-sex parent to help them develop positive affirmed identities and they need the opposite-sex parent to know how to relate to the other half of the world and form relationships.

Some children have never known one parent or the parent may have left when the child was very young. It is often in adolescence that the turmoil about this comes to the surface as the young person is acquiring a sense of identity. The care-giving parent may find it painful to talk about the departed parent in a balanced way but for the sake of the child's developing self it is important that the child has a rounded view of their absent parent. For example:

'Yes, I am angry that your mother left, but I think you would have enjoyed her sense of humour.'

'That's sad, but let me show you some photos of the good times.'

'Yes, we were once in love.'

We all have a need to know where we come from.

Summary

- Children need time and opportunity to grieve the loss of their parents' relationship.

- Parents should not use their children to get at, or payback, the ex-partner.

- Contact with both parents is important.

Key concepts

- Children have a right to their own feelings, space and possessions.

- Parents' anger at each other should not involve the children.

- Children have a right to feel hurt and angry at parents who can't get along.

- Children hate it when separated parents fight.

CHAPTER 11

When Parenting an Adolescent Feels Like an Impossible Task

Many parents reach a point where they feel desperation. This is due to:

- Coping skills that were good for a child not being good enough for an adolescent

- Inadequate resources and too much pressure (often to carry alone)

- Rejection by a child because of an inappropriate former role as a support person

- The child moving into payback mode as an adolescent

Extreme measures will be needed to contain a young person and keep everyone safe. Parents in these circumstances need support in many forms to bring their family through traumatic times or a major shift in tactics. If, as a society, we do not have help available, we should not be surprised at the rise in crime statistics. Desperate parents need support and encouragement to go into the community to access assistance. You as the professional helper may perform either role – referral agent or professional helper.

Support available

When assisting parents the following support may be helpful for a time, long enough to generate the energy to position a change.

- Find a family member or friend who will agree to have the young person for a few months until he or she has calmed down. Often he or she will not act out the same when away from the family who were the scene of the childhood trauma. This method has been used in other cultures and times to deal with very difficult youngsters. Don't have him/her back until you have a new contract with consequences signed by your teenager. Do not be weak, and expect some verbal abuse.

- Tough Love is a parents' organisation that operates in some countries. It supports parents to set strong limits for difficult adolescents. Parents may need someone to call on when the going gets really tough and other parents to affirm them for their efforts.

- Some men's organisations provide a mentoring service for adolescent males. This can be particularly valuable for young males who have lacked positive fathering experiences.

- The parent may consult the child's school guidance counsellor or dean – although unfortunately many young people are suspended from school and such a service is not available to them.

- Some support organisations run camps or other adventure activities for young people. Outdoor activities may give a young person an opportunity for success in a different arena and create a time for mature reflection.

- A local police youth officer may have some ideas. The police sometimes run camps and other activities for young people.

- Cultural organisations may enable a young person to gain a better sense of identity and self-worth (see Chapter 13).

- A counsellor or professional helper may help the parent and the adolescent to communicate and express remorse, regrets and sorrow for the circumstances that have led up to the current situation.

- If any party is being physically attacked it is usual policy to contact a local family court and the police.

Example: reaching an agreement

Tom chose to write a letter to his son, which he had delivered by a family member. In the letter he expressed his sorrow and regrets for the childhood this troubled boy had lived through and asked him to meet him in a public place, the local mall, to talk. To his surprise his son turned up and some agreement was reached about his violence in the home and alternative living arrangements. For the moment disaster has been avoided and Tom is able to focus on his other equally troubled children.

The parent may be encouraged to seek therapy for themselves. Living with unresolved trauma experiences can make parenting of adolescents much more difficult.

Look at the section in Chapter 7 on games in families. Is any party in the victim role? It is understandable that someone who has been a victim would take on this role and be stuck in it.

Address any of the following by reframing beliefs such as:

- It's hopeless

- Nothing works for me

- It's no good trying

- I'm a loser

- If it wasn't for …

- Nobody cares what happens to me

All can have positive reframes though these will need coaching.

Example: reframing a belief with a photo

Janice found a photo of her son as a little boy and put it on the fridge.

'What's that doing there?' he demanded when he saw it.

'It's to remind me that you are my son and I love you,' replied Janice calmly.

'I don't know if it has done him any good,' she said. 'He didn't answer, but the other day it fell off when he went to the fridge for a drink and I noticed he was careful to pick it up and put it back where it was. So I suppose it must be important to him that it's there.'

Summary

- Extreme situations call for extreme change.

- Time away from the family may be necessary for a violent or abusive child.

- If adolescents are violent, parents need to take action and seek safety and legal protection.

- Very angry kids are very hurt and scared.

- Very angry kids may take their anger into adult life unless it is dealt with.

- The community is at risk when very angry kids are not attended to.

Key concepts

- Listen to others' feelings. Talk about your own feelings.

- We should never put up with abuse.

- Violence and abuse are a community responsibility.

CHAPTER 12

Special Circumstances

Adolescent anger and special circumstances

The circumstances dealt with in this chapter are not unique to adolescence; however teenagers are less equipped to deal with them. Adverse life incidents seem huge and final. They do not have previous life experiences of coping to fall back on and tell themselves, 'I coped last time – I can cope again' or 'there is a time beyond this bad time because I have been here before'. Often they have not yet developed the adult skill of being able to talk to themselves inside and self-soothe. There is also increasing evidence of incomplete brain development and hyper-reactiveness in abused children and adolescents. Such states predispose a child to reactivity, reduced empathy and social problems (Perry 1997, 2009).

While peers in this challenging stage may be supportive, they often do not have the skills, knowledge and services that an older person may have to help nor the knowledge on how to engage them. Sometimes the peer group that the young person feels anchored to may draw them down: 'If my friends can't cope and are giving up, I can't either.'

In adolescence past hurts and traumas from childhood may resurface and suppressed feelings may seem hard to bear. Young people who have experienced such traumas as loss of a parent, violence and verbal abuse from parent figures or sexual abuse need to be sure that they can rely on caring available adults for support.

Suicide and despair

As we have stated earlier, focus on the present is a feature of our teenage years. The future is sometimes hard to visualise and the young person may believe feelings of loneliness, grief and despair will go on forever. Adults who live and work with teenagers need to be alert to signs that a young person is feeling this way.

Individualistic societies often have high youth suicide rates. While many of us may not be able to change the causes of the young person's despair, we can be vigilant and steer them towards someone who can help them to cope with these strong emotions.

Some signs to be alert for:

- Preoccupation with death in: conversation, music, dark dress, and death-focused cultures such as Goths, gothic rock, deathrock, post-punk, darkwave, and Emo styles, extreme vampirism and cannabalism

- Self-harming: piercings and tattoos that may be self-administered, excessive or facial, scratching, biting, cutting

- Eating disorders: anorexia, bulimia

- Excessive use of drugs and binging of alcohol and mind-altering substances (petrol, pharmaceuticals, and narcotic plants)

- Lack of interest in the future, disillusionment and cynicism

- Loss of interest in normal life pursuits (could also indicate drug use)

- Spending long periods of time in room alone and seeming to have few friends. Social paranoia

- Sudden giving away of possessions as 'presents'

- Sudden brightness, even celebration after long periods of depression (farewell activity)

- Hints like 'What's the use? I might as well give up' or 'You would be better off without me'

- Plans or attempts to have serious accidents are often a shame-free way of a 'back door suicide': 'I hope I have an accident' or 'I imagine myself crashed against that pole'

- Hints may be consciously or unconsciously expressed in writing, poetry, school assignments, private diaries and journals

- Logging on to death/suicide websites for solace, inspiration, excuse validation or even pacts

What can you do?

- Ask outright if you suspect a young person is feeling suicidal. 'I have noticed…and I am guessing that you are feeling very depressed. How depressed are you?' 'Do you ever feel so bad that you might take your life?'

- Ask how often and how much they feel this way: 'That's death talk. Have you been thinking like that for long?'

- Ask them how they intend to do it. If they have already thought of a way, the danger is more acute. Check for stored medication.

- Don't advise or lecture the young person. Listen to how they are feeling.

- Let them know that they can talk to you at any time.

- Work with them to go and seek help. A parent or professional may need to set this up for them. Let them know that you will follow this up: 'After your appointment with the counsellor I'll meet you so that you can let me know how I can help you.' Young people who have already attempted suicide need ongoing support from an adult whose strength they can draw on.

Sexuality

Adolescence is hormonally and socially a time of exploration and vulnerability. Attempts to control sexual behaviour are likely only to be successful if there is a base of love and trust of the parent borne in child years. Even then secrecy and lies are ways of handling overt curiosity and control by parents and caregivers. Sensitive vulnerable emotions are often associated with first encounters of sex and love. First 'deep loves' may bring great joy and meaning to life but breaking up is in proportion and equally devastating.

For girls the quality of their fathering may effect their ability to handle male relationships. Many young girls will do anything to get the love and attention they may have missed out on. Fathers giving unconditional love and care leave an adolescent woman with the strength to handle male interest and affection without feeling that they have to do anything to retain respect and attention.

Pornography, usually from the internet, may be accessed earlier than teen years and what were once sophisticated sexual techniques are easily observed and modelled. About a third of internet traffic is for pornographic activity and this has been criticised for creating greater objectification of human intimacy. Such objectification may be seen as harmful for both sexes in its reduction in the level of expressed intimacy and affection. If the internet is the key source of sex education then parents and professionals may need to be the source of teaching the relational side of sexual behaviour. Parents need to reinforce public health campaigns about safe sex to help keep adolescents safe from STIs (sexually transmitted infections) and unplanned pregnancies.

Contraception though widely available may be avoided as admission of planning and seen as reducing of spontaneity especially if forbidden.

Anger may be common when parental talking and acting becomes seen as control and intrusion. Sometimes respectful intrusion may be necessary and staring into the face of anger is what is needed for good care of vulnerable young adults. There is however a point where the power to influence stops and further engagement needs to be on a hypothetical basis. Anger may become the driver for anti-controlling behaviour.

> Melinda: 'I'm so sick of my parents' moralistic "care" and judgements. I'm thinking of bringing another girl home and pretending to my parents that we are lesbians…just to get at them.'

Third parties such as extended family, counsellors, therapists and mentors, can often be better at giving help and information than parents especially in late adolescence. For younger adolescents a parent may say, 'I need to feel confident that you have the right information. Do you mind if I ask you some questions?'

Many adolescents wonder about their sexuality during the adolescent years. Good information can reduce fears and homophobia. For example, Helen remembers that when she was 13 she became obsessed with one of the prefects at school:

'I couldn't keep my eyes off her. I kept going to all the parts of the school where she was. I thought she was so beautiful and confident. I wanted to be just like her. I did my hair in the same style, but I kept worrying that I was gay because I felt like this. What would the other kids do if they found out? I knew they would tease me. I anguished over it for ages.'

Rates of suicide are higher for gay young men than heterosexual young men.

We live in a partly homophobic society, so for the young person who knows or believes they are homosexual, this can be very difficult. Those who believe homosexuality is wrong can be condemning of potentially gay youth. This can be disastrous if the person concerned is the child's parent or a loved family member. The isolation of such teenage experiences can lead to feelings of despair and ideas of suicide.

Key concepts

* There is an association between anger and parental attempts to control romantic and sexual behaviour.

* Young people need support from a strong adult when in crisis.

* If parents cannot offer this support, they need to find someone, or an organisation, who can.

CHAPTER 13

Being an Adolescent in Two Cultures or Being Different

Adolescents living with two cultures

Many young people have the added challenge of living in two cultures: their home culture and the dominant Western culture. They may enter a new society as immigrants, refugees or simply from a different lifestyle or region. There are huge pressures to conform and be the same as others. Some stories from clients and trainees are told in this chapter.

> Fatima: 'As a young Muslim woman I was teased and ostracised and an object of cruelty because I was different. I was sick of being called a terrorist. I took my headscarf off and life suddenly changed. I never put it back on.'

This means that adolescents must often juggle two sets of values, boundaries and expectations.

In any culture parents are struggling to control their teenager's behaviour and keep them within accepted desirable limits. Parents may fear that they will be judged by their children's behaviour. Everyone has some good reasons for feeling angry. They may depend on styles of parenting and control from their own childhood in a different culture. Without the controls and mediation of the parents' 'old world', these methods can create an environment of control by fear which the teenager then acts out aggressively in the wider world, or turns in on him/herself, leading to depression, anxiety, low self-worth and even suicide.

How parents can help themselves to understand

Professionals may encourage parents to be prepared to ask themselves some searching questions:

- How is the culture different from when I was a child?

- How did my parents set limits and how did it affect me?

- How did I feel?

- How did this affect the way I related back to my parents?

- What struggles has this brought into my life?

- How have these methods helped me to become a self-sufficient, autonomous, confident adult?

- How would I have liked it to be?

- How can I be a pioneer in my family and my cultural group?

- How can I make it easier for my children to live in two cultures?

There is loss and therefore grief for the young person who moves between two cultures, particularly if they feel that they must choose one or the other. A young person may sacrifice the all-important sense of belonging. Urban gangs have grown from the gnawing need to belong when young people feel dispossessed by both cultures. Within their new 'families' they gain a place not given by either their new or old culture.

Anger can be expressed safely by talking, sharing with peers, physical action, social action, and proving oneself in other ways with achievement. More creatively parents can share their confusion and isolation with their children rather than using 'power over' tactics.

We learn what we live, and we live what we learn.

Difficulties that adolescents with two cultures can face

Example: stereotypes

Laura (a young Chinese woman) writes about the struggle to maintain her individuality while staying connected to the family and culture she knows and loves:

> 'People tend to stereotype you without getting to know you. Often a stereotype of an Asian girl is: neat, good at maths, learns the flute or piano, plays tennis or badminton.
>
> I have always strived for individuality. I try to be different. I have played hockey and football and I have learnt to play the trombone. I guess it's because I want people to see me for myself. Being Chinese is a huge part of who I am but not all of it. Being one nationality does not mean that all the people of that nationality are the same.
>
> One frustrating thing for me has been dating. Being Chinese my parents have always been strict. They don't like or allow me to go out with anyone who is not Chinese.
>
> I don't think they are racist but they believe that it is hard to understand or overcome the differences between two cultures. They are scared that I will get hurt.

But sometimes I am attracted to someone who is not Chinese and that is difficult because I don't want to hurt my parents.'

Laura has a right to feel angry with peers, friends, society, parents and family. Her empathy allows her to reduce that with her parents as she sincerely tries to understand them.

Some young people carry from an extended family the expectation that they will succeed for the family. Often money and the hopes of relatives weigh on the young person's shoulders.

Example: mistrust and control

Alasi writes:

> 'I am 16 years old. I am full Samoan and I have been in New Zealand for four years.
>
> Growing up in New Zealand is complex. My parents who were church-going brought me up in Samoa. I was used to the way things were back there and coming over to New Zealand was a hard thing. Growing up here is very stressful and sometimes I feel I want to go back to Samoa.
>
> My guardians don't approve of any of the social things I want to do. I know it is because they care and don't want anything to happen to me, but it is then I wish I were back in Samoa. Ours is a small island and my mum knew where I was because everyone knows everyone else. Over here I am so restricted and it is very frustrating having to tell my friends that I can't go out.'

Alasi has every reason to be angry with the unwelcome control of her 'old culture' over her 'new culture'. Reaching to understand them both reduces the tension and anger.

Customs that are different from one's peers can leave a young person feeling excluded in adolescence. Language difficulties can mean that young people encounter conflict with teachers and impede school progress.

Example: isolation

Diem writes:

> 'I am 18 years old. I have been in New Zealand for six years. When I arrived in New Zealand from Vietnam I found English very, very difficult. The teacher tried to talk to me but I could not understand. I felt very lonely.'

Diem has every right to feel angry with his parents for bringing him to a strange foreign and bullying country. Finding one friend would probably reduce his anger considerably.

Some young people cope with difference by staying with their own cultural group as much as possible.

Example: fear and insecurity

Kwan writes:

> 'I was born in South Korea. Unlike Europe, which is multi-cultural, Korea consists of one race and one language. This gives a sense of security and unity. Having grown up in this very different society, I found myself surrounded by new, different faces, new language and ideas. I was totally lost and frightened because it was like I was deaf and mute at the same time. I have seen many cases of Korean students in Europe who have lost interest in learning English altogether after fruitless attempts to fit into this society. They start to hang around only with Koreans and create their own little Korea in a UK city.'

Kwan is angry with his lack of security, multiple cultures, strangeness, possible racism, lack of communication, and being the 'odd one out'. Good support from bi-cultural peers and adults might relieve some of that. Knowing that it might not always be like that would also help.

Adolescents often fear that they will lose their culture of birth and can carry the anger of relatives, who see them turning away from the old ways. Young people themselves may feel angry at being trapped in the middle.

Example: devaluing and not belonging

Shirley (from Holland) writes:

> 'My parents gave me an English name to escape the teasing I might have from a Cantonese name. All my life people have judged me. My Dutch friends would look and see an Asian. But being Chinese is not just how you look. It goes deeper to your beliefs and way of life. Chinese immigrants would see me and think "pun tong fan", a white Chinese (actually it's much worse, it means a banana: yellow on the outside and white on the inside). It's always been hard in the middle, not Dutch, yet not fully Chinese.
>
> I remember, on a childhood trip to China, I was disapproved of for not addressing everyone as Auntie and Uncle to show warmth and respect. They thought I was rude and ordered me cakes in restaurants. "Here's your white food." I was so mad.'

Good empathy and understanding from observant parents might reduce some of the loneliness of Shirley's dual cultural experiences. Such devaluing in each culture can lead to not feeling like being either rather than feeling a belonging in both cultures.

If there is added pressure to succeed and please parents and the cultural group a young person can feel they have failed themselves and the whole world. It is hard to recover from such damaged self-worth.

Some young people grow up in mixed-race families. When this is handled well children grow with extra flexibility, tolerance and confidence, but if families struggle with this aspect of their lives a young person can feel confused and angry and have low self-worth. Many young people in this situation will resort to running away or running from a sense of shame and a confused identity.

Example: identify and belonging

Olah writes:

> 'I am a young person who has grown up in a split of cultures between a Nigerian father and a European mother, living in the UK. I feel I have missed out on a lot about my African culture on my father's side, because my mother did not agree with me being involved with this. I feel very sad and angry that I never really knew much at all about my African history as I don't look white and people talk to me as if I am an African or Afro-Caribbean. After my parents separated I have learnt about my Nigerian ancestors and heritage. It has always been hard not knowing who I really fit in with, African or English. I sound English until people see my face. The advice I would give to other young people is, no matter what colour or culture you are, the biggest mistake you can make is not knowing who you are and where you are from.'

Olah got into a lot of trouble angrily reacting to racism and being called something he didn't understand. Being proud to be both is based on reasons to feel proud. Instead he had a devaluing of the part of himself that he knew little of.

Key concepts

* Adolescents who live in more than one culture have more challenges to meet and good reasons to feel angry.

* Living in two cultures with supportive adults can be positive in terms of mutual understanding, depth of character and intellectual growth.

* Adults who live and work with adolescents from different cultures need to be aware of the additional challenges these young people face and offer support and understanding.

CHAPTER 14

Self-Care for Adults who Live and Work with Adolescents

Adolescents live on a roller-coaster ride of changing emotions and behaviour. It is not only challenging for them but also for the people who have some responsibility for them. Successful practitioners and especially caregivers need a great deal of tolerance to maintain an understanding environment. Tolerance can be very stressful and maintaining empathy with someone in emotional pain and turmoil can generate vicarious traumatisation that accumulates if you are engaged much of the day with a stressed or upset person. Self-care is important to avoid stress overload and maintain energy and resilience.

Tips for managing your stress as parents

Here are some ideas for parents to manage stress:

- Create your own space off limits to children or adolescents: a corner of the lounge or bedroom, a seat in the garden

- Claim time for yourself: bathroom time, time with friends

- Use water: a shower, or soak in a bath to relax and unwind. Swim

- Treat yourself to things that help you feel cared for, such as clothing, bath care products, music you enjoy

- Use your breathing to relax and calm yourself. If the going gets tough, bring your awareness back to your breathing. Notice your breath entering and leaving your body. Take four to six deep breaths and breathe out very slowly. Breathe through your anger. Take time to focus on your breathing every day

- Take Time Out for meditation or prayer

- Write letters to your children expressing your anger and your fears. Do not send the letters

- Join a group of other adults who also live or work with teenagers

- Talk to people whose children have gone through this stage. It gives you hope

- Use your intimate relationship to offload (if your partner is happy to do that)

- Have a massage. Take turns with your partner or a friend to receive and give massages. Offer a foot soak and massage to a friend or partner and receive one in return

- Accept offers from relatives to let your teenager go and stay for a few days

- Swap teenagers with a trusted friend if your teenager is willing. They are likely to behave in a more adult way in someone else's house

- Avoid clothes shopping with teenagers

- Play a musical instrument

- If you work with teenagers, lobby for more recognition of the need for stress reduction help: fun Time Out, counselling for the workers, group support time, supervision, better pay so you can afford to get help in other aspects of your life, like housework help and lawn mowing. You need weekends to unwind, free from having to rescue or be understanding all the time

PART 2

HELPING ADOLESCENTS

The following pages can be used as discussion points, ideas for counselling sessions, handouts for caregivers of adolescents, and as activities for reflection. They have been allocated a page each for photocopying reasons. You are invited to copy pages with a tick in the corner.

CHAPTER 15

Rights and Responsibilities

Rights of adolescents

Part of the problem is how to give increasing power, freedom and responsibility as people move from being children to adults. Some adolescents have to take it if it is not given. Whatever happens, there are some basic rights that citizens are entitled to. You can ask for them and can expect them.

Rights of adolescents

As an adolescent you are entitled:

1. To have at least three adults who care about you

2. To have a Mum and a Dad who pay attention and give time to you, or a caring adult in their place!

3. To not be abused – verbally, physically, emotionally or sexually, and have property respected

4. To feel angry from time to time

5. To feel safe

6. To have feelings accepted and validated

7. To earn some money

8. To be taught what you need to know

9. To have food, clothes and shelter in order to become independent

10. To be respected as a human being

11. To have a job when you leave school

12. To be listened to

13. To be taught skills not just given information

14. To make mistakes

15. To be responsible for mistakes and put things right

16. To not be exploited by advertisers

17. To be unhappy and have your sadness validated

18. To choose your own optional subjects at school

19. To be happy and have fun

20. To feel scared, unsure and lack confidence

21. To have a community or people who know you and look out for you

22. To have a part of the house that is private to you (e.g. bedroom, garage)

23. To be attracted sexually to others

24. To have good role models

25. To laugh and smile a lot

26. To play your own music

27. To negotiate rules and consequences

28. To know what's happening

29. To any education that you want!

30. To have your birthdays and special days recognised

31. To have spiritual concepts and traditions passed on

32. To have your contribution recognised

33. To grow up

Key concept

♦ All people need and are entitled to respect.

Things I will need to back up my rights

- Both parents to continually make an effort to meet and talk with me about interests and concerns from my perspective

- A place I can lock things in

- Parents who fight CONSTRUCTIVELY and DON'T ABUSE each other

- Adults to help me get ways of earning money

- Parents who listen to me when I'm young so I don't stop talking to them when I'm older

- People who ask what it is we need to know

- Absent fathers or mothers to keep in touch

- Police who are helpful and listen

- Accurate information on drugs and diseases

- Positive, helpful adults who come up to me and pay compliments

- Parents who model how to sort themselves out

- To be taught to 'see through' advertising so I can discriminate

- Adults to recognise that relationships and sex scare us and are often painful

- To have suggestions from wise people about what we need to change, because often we don't know

- To have parents and employers who can handle happy people

- To be given clear ideas about what the rules are, who's in charge and to know we will be fairly treated

- No adults and employers who sexually harass us

- To be told we can do it

- Birthday and Christmas presents

- Step-parents who are gentle and respectful when they join our home

- Adults who give good rules and models for forming sexual relationships

**You are entitled to respect and attention.
You need to ensure you give the same back.**

Responsibilities

With rights and freedom come responsibilities. Try these...

As an adolescent I claim responsibility to: (tick box)

- ❑ Correct things when I make mistakes
- ❑ Keep my word. My word is my commitment and my integrity
- ❑ Clean up after myself and put things back where I got them
- ❑ Look after my own health and not abuse my body
- ❑ Ask for help when I need it
- ❑ Earn the money that I spend
- ❑ Keep sexually safe and healthy
- ❑ Say thanks for things given to, or done for me
- ❑ Not risk my life or the life of others
- ❑ Respect people who may say no to sex, or say no to sex if I wish
- ❑ Drive safely
- ❑ Obey the law
- ❑ Not gossip or cheat friends
- ❑ Stick to what I really believe and not do things just to be liked
- ❑ Not put up with the abuse of others
- ❑ Grow up and expect more freedom as I grow

- ❑ Choose good actions for my age and take responsibility for them
- ❑ Become independent from my mother and my father
- ❑ Grumble about rules, but do it anyway
- ❑ Make the world a better place
- ❑ Affirm people
- ❑ Be positive as much as I am able
- ❑ Stop and reflect about things and develop a spiritual life
- ❑ Look after things, space or privileges given to me
- ❑ Look after things loaned to me, especially cars
- ❑ Pay equal shares with friends and dates
- ❑ Be generous to others, especially the less fortunate
- ❑ Handle difficult people – the world is full of them
- ❑ Love others and show it
- ❑ Allow myself to be loved by others
- ❑ Remember friends and support them when they are down

- ❏ Celebrate my special days and believe in my own self-worth
- ❏ Respect elders for their experience, age and struggle
- ❏ Get the most from school and work, even though that may be hard

- ❏ Not abuse others physically, emotionally, verbally, or their property
- ❏ Know what I am feeling and talk about my anger and hurt

Key concepts

- ◆ With freedom and power comes responsibility.

- ◆ Handling power and freedom requires integrity, empathy and self-worth.

Rules of my bedroom

The following are some rules that you may like to consider for your bedroom.

As you grow older, it is normal to want more say over your life. Usually the first things that you will want more say over are:

♦ Your clothes

♦ Your bedroom

♦ Your time

Think about them. You may want some say over these now and some later. Then go to your parents and negotiate them. Don't expect all, but expect some. Everyone is different so the deal at the end will be different for everyone.

The deal

What I would like to be entitled to:

We all agree: (tick box)

❑ This is my bedroom so I say who can come in and who stays out

❑ I'm entitled to a lock on the door

❑ Others knock before coming in

❑ No one is to go into my cupboards and drawers

❑ I can have a heater in my room when it's cold

❑ I can have friends in my room with the door shut

I promise:

❑ No rotting food in the room

❑ I'll keep the door shut so you can't see my mess

❑ I clean up and tidy up once a week/twice a month or...

❑ No weapons in my room

❑ I'll vacuum clean twice a month or...

❑ I'll put all washing in the basket otherwise it doesn't get done/I'll do my own washing

I agree to:

❑ No smoking, of any kind, inside, at all

❑ I'll read in bed until.../I'll read in bed until I want to

❑ I can paint/wallpaper my room with my choice of colour/wallpaper. Or: Parents paint/wallpaper with their choice of colour/paper

✓

- ❏ I can have my sound system up to...(1–10) when parents are around and to...(1–10) when just my brother/sister is around and to...(1–10) when no one is around

- ❏ I can play any music except...

- ❏ I can play video games in my room...hours a day

- ❏ I can use my computer...hours a day, or until...o'clock

- ❏ I can use the internet...hours a day

- ❏ I can use my phone up until...o'clock at night.

Other options:

- ❏ I can have/not have a TV in my room

- ❏ I can watch TV in my room until...o'clock

- ❏ I can watch any DVD/internet I like

- ❏ I can watch any DVD/internet except material that is...violent, cruel, sexual, pornographic, psycho, supernatural

- ❏ I can play computer/online games except/including

. . . .

. . . .

My own rules are:. . . . .

. . . .

. . . .

My parents' negotiated rules are:. . . . .

. . . .

. . . .

These rules will be revisited on . . . .
(date) to see if they need changing.

Signed: . . . .

Signed: (Parent/s) . . . .

Date: . . . .

✓

Students' problems

Every student is human. Every student has problems.
   Every student is entitled to have problems.
   Think about yourself.

(Tick the box if you think you do/have/are any of these)

☐ Trouble explaining things

☐ Don't like school

☐ Don't listen to the teacher

☐ Money problems

☐ Talk over the top of the teacher

☐ Tough childhood

☐ Tell others what to do

☐ Family problems

☐ Rude to others

☐ Get bossed around

☐ Disrupt

☐ Help individuals

☐ Call people names

☐ Put things in others' language

☐ Disrespect people

☐ Work hard

☐ Easy to respect

☐ Help people when asked

☐ Argue and like to be right

☐ Mean well

☐ Late to class

☐ Laugh a lot

☐ Pick on people

☐ Quite smart really

☐ Distract from the subject

☐ Smile at people

☐ Unhappy

☐ Remember people's names

☐ Not approachable

☐ Sometimes hurt others' feelings

☐ Stressed

☐ Shame people

☐ Angry with life, not students

☐ Respect people

☐ Don't get on with Dad/Mum

☐ Listen to good reasons

☐ Worry what people think of you

☐ Friendly with everyone

☐ Self-esteem problems and need others to like you

☐ Tell good stories

☐ Culturally different from the teacher

On a scale of 1–10, how much is your teacher like you?

Alike   1   2   3   4   5   6   7   8   9   10   Unlike

◆ How can he or she understand you more?

◆ How can you understand the teacher more?

◆ Could you talk to him/her about these pages?

'Problem' teachers

Every teacher is human. Every teacher has problems.
Every teacher is entitled to have problems.
Pick the teacher you have most trouble with.

Name: . . . .

(Tick the boxes you think apply to this teacher)

- ❑ Trouble explaining things
- ❑ Maybe doesn't like school
- ❑ Doesn't listen to me
- ❑ Maybe has money problems
- ❑ Talks over the top of me
- ❑ Maybe had a tough childhood
- ❑ Tells others what to do
- ❑ Maybe has family problems
- ❑ Is rude to others
- ❑ Maybe is being bossed around
- ❑ Disrupts
- ❑ Helps individuals
- ❑ Calls people names
- ❑ Puts things in my language
- ❑ Disrespects people
- ❑ Works hard
- ❑ Is easy to respect
- ❑ Helps people when asked
- ❑ Argues and likes to be right
- ❑ Means well
- ❑ Is late to class
- ❑ Laughs a lot

- ❑ Picks on people
- ❑ Is quite smart really
- ❑ Distracts from the subject
- ❑ Smiles at people
- ❑ Is unhappy
- ❑ Remembers people's names
- ❑ Is not approachable
- ❑ Sometimes hurts others' feelings
- ❑ Maybe is stressed
- ❑ Shames people
- ❑ Maybe is angry with life, not students
- ❑ Respects people
- ❑ Maybe didn't get on with parents
- ❑ Listens to good reasons
- ❑ Worries what people think of him/her
- ❑ Is friendly with everyone
- ❑ Maybe has self-esteem problems and needs to be liked
- ❑ Tells good stories
- ❑ Is culturally different from me

We all come across people who seem difficult to get along with. Teachers are the same. They have good days, bad days and hard times like all students. Sometimes, however, we don't like the things in others that are part of ourselves, like being bossy, nosy or moody. Are you seeing a reflection of yourself? Try the tick list. Dealing with this is a skill for life. Ask: what good thing do I want in the long run? Education? An exam pass? Extra help? A good relationship? Then form a plan to get what you need that means that you deal successfully with teachers without upset.

> **Key concepts**
>
> • Everyone is entitled to have problems.
>
> • All people need and are entitled to respect.
>
> • We are often strangely like the people we have difficulty with.

Genealogy

Having family that goes as far back as anyone can remember is important. They all stand behind you and contribute to who you are. You can draw strength from them. Such strength raises self-esteem and pride. We can then handle anger better.

    Fill in the spaces with what you know and anything about them.

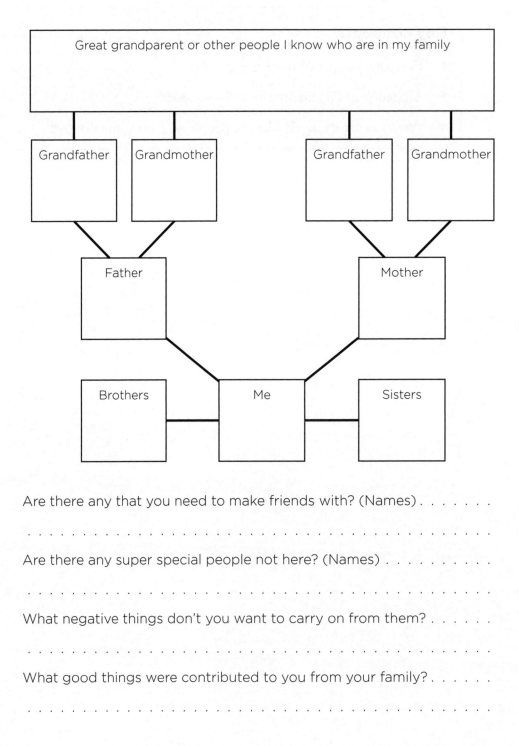

Are there any that you need to make friends with? (Names) . . . .

. . . .

Are there any super special people not here? (Names) . . . .

. . . .

What negative things don't you want to carry on from them? . . . . . .

. . . .

What good things were contributed to you from your family? . . . . . .

. . . .

The importance of your family

Living in the big wide world out there can be difficult. We need all the support and protection that we can get. Families give us:

* A sense of a place to come from – home base, the clubrooms of life, roots

* Mother, father, brother, sister, but are also uncles, aunts, cousins, nieces, nephews, grandfathers, grandmothers, in-laws, second cousins, step-parents, stepbrothers and sisters, the works

We have a right to expect the following from them:

* Unconditional acceptance: no matter what I do I'm still accepted as a person – my family will say, 'OK, even though you're having a hard time out there and you might have got it wrong, we're still here for you and you have a place here'

* To be told the unpleasant things about ourselves that we don't want to hear

So:

1. Don't hurt the people who care. Don't hurt the family and its reputation.

2. You don't get to choose your family so it's full of people that you might not choose as friends, but whom you still need to get on with. They're there to give you variety and to teach you how to get on with all sorts. Be tolerant of the difficult people in your family.

3. What you give out to your family, influences what you get back from them.

4. You're more likely to dump your anger and hurts in your family because they will still care for you.

5. You hope that they will still care for you if you dump your rubbish there so don't hurt them in the process. If you hurt people too much they go away.

6. Listen to them. They tell you things that you never thought of about yourself, good and bad.

7. Don't use them. Respect the family. Don't steal from them, say bad things about them outside the family or use them to hide bad things.

8. Don't accept abuse from anyone in your family – physical, sexual, mental, spiritual or abuse of your property.

9. Love them even if they make mistakes.

10. Don't bring shame on the family. Look after its good name.

11. Ask what you can give to your family.

12.   Help out other family members.

13.   You will always be closer to some than others. But be as close to as many as you can. They need you too.

Do this and your family will be there for you.

Feeling 14 for boys

There are some ages that have more dramatic changes than others. Around 14 there is a huge boost in testosterone in the male body.

If you are 14 here are some things that are normal for you to feel or to happen to you. You are likely to feel or be:

- Clumsy and awkward
- Getting into more trouble
- Being more physical
- Fighting more
- Getting hairy everywhere
- Feeling grumpy
- Being easily distracted
- Unable to think straight
- Being more rowdy and loud
- Wanting privacy
- Getting pimply
- Feeling shame and sensitivity about yourself and your family
- Feeling not as good as others your age
- Hanging out with the guys
- Feeling excited and adventurous

- Wanting more recognition from males outside the family
- Thinking your father is dumb
- Wanting more freedom
- Wondering if you are gay or straight
- Feeling angry about being controlled
- Being hurt easily
- Feeling more aggressive and defiant
- Wanting to have more to do with girls
- Finding girls' bodies attractive
- Having strong sexual thoughts and desires
- Looking at or wanting to look at pornography
- Masturbating

You won't experience all of the above, in fact you may be very different. The important thing is not to feel bad about it. Try to talk to someone about anything that bothers you. We suggest an older male. It's important now that you have a few older men in your life apart from your father and that you can feel OK in their company and even talk to them about things as they come up. Your parents may only see your untidiness and give you a hard time. It's OK to get some distance from your parents but don't abuse them. If you have been hurt or abused as a child you may start to feel angry about it now and have feelings of wanting to pay someone back. Talk to someone, or the person directly if that is safe.

Feeling 16 for girls

At around 16 there are a lot of changes taking place for girls. You hit puberty earlier than boys and spend the years up to 16 dealing with the complexity of having a woman's body and being part of a relational group. At 16 some changes take place that take relationships deeper.

Here are some things that could be what you will go through or you may have already:

- Looking for a meaningful relationship
- Thinking about first sex
- Wanting a partner who is just yours
- Being sensitive about skin and weight
- Feeling attractive
- Friendships are important
- Developing greater understanding for other people
- Having first serious break-ups
- Wanting private space
- Wanting more freedom
- Wondering if you are lesbian or straight
- Being sensitive and hurt easily
- Getting very depressed
- Little things can mean a lot
- Having wonderful highs
- Falling in love for the first time
- Wanting nice clothes and to look beautiful
- Feeling OK at social events
- Feeling shame and sensitivity about yourself and your family
- Feeling not as good as others your age
- Having strong sexual desires
- Considering contraception
- Reading women's literature about sex
- Checking out pornography
- Masturbating

You may feel really angry at how things are or have been, and say things about that for the first time. Be careful about verbal abuse, cutting comments and put-downs. You are likely to feel angry and rebellious about parental control and their concern that you are safe. It's normal for them to feel protective of females but you could reassure them by learning self-defence. Intense high and low feelings make relationships difficult. Don't attack people. Write your feelings down in diaries or poems. Though feelings may seem overwhelming, remember things will always be better as you grow older. You will fall in love even more deeply in the future.

T-shirt message: choose your slogan for a T-shirt

T-shirt slogans often say things about the people who wear them.
What would your T-shirt say to the world if you had a choice of what to put on it? How would you present your personal message about yourself?
Write on the T-shirt below then talk about it with someone.

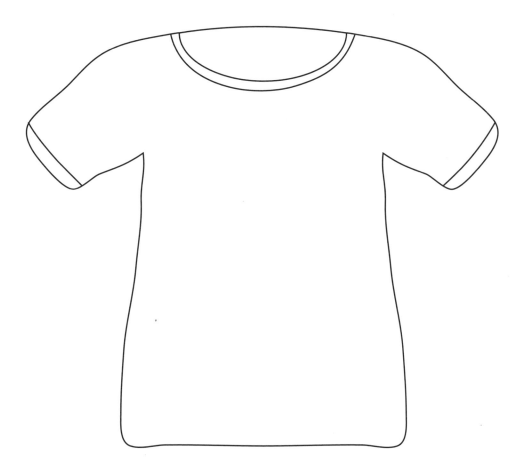

- Does it welcome people or push them away?

- Does it say good things about you?

- Are you happy with it?

- Would you prefer something else?

Draw it again and change it if you want to.

Key concepts

- People treat me according to the message I give out.

- All clothing carries a message.

CHAPTER 16

Ways of Managing Anger for Adolescents

There are a number of exercises, skills and awarenesses that assist in the management of anger and the understanding of origins and repression. We have captured the ones that we have found most useful in our work. Clients are all different and so will find pages here that particularly interest them based on individual personality and also where they are in their mood mastery. Our favourites are the anger scale and trigger work.

Each hand out page may stimulate an hour's discussion and is best taken slowly. Sometimes the adolescent just picks for themselves because they know best what they need, and sometimes the professional needs to engage in guidance.

Early warning signs of feeling anger in your body

People experience anger in different ways. If we know what happens to us when we feel angry we get more time to make choices about what we do. The better we know the warning signals, the better we'll be able to deal with our anger.

They can be divided into:

• Signs and sensations inside the body

• Signs and behaviours outside the body

• Thoughts and words that go on inside the head

Imagine a situation where you the caregiver or you the adolescent were recently angry about something or with someone. See, hear and feel yourself there. Take yourself to the angriest moment then check out the early warning signs in the three categories below. What are the signs that you are feeling? Whenever you feel like this you can choose what you will do. You now have extra time to do something positive.

Body (inside)

Heartbeat:

❑ Fast   ❑ Can hear and feel it

Breathing:

❑ Fast   ❑ In the chest

❑ Heavy   ❑ Deep

❑ Short   ❑ Catch breath

Sweating:

❑ Hot   ❑ Damp

✓

Head tension:

❑ Bursting   ❑ Band of steel

Tense jaw:

❑ Tight   ❑ Rigid

❑ Aching   ❑ Teeth hurt

Stomach:

❑ Knotted   ❑ Exploding

❑ Concrete lump   ❑ Hunger

❑ Churning   ❑ Feel like crying

❑ Fire in me

Scalp rises:

❑ Head tingles   ❑ Hair prickles

Other signs inside my body . . . .

. . . .

. . . .

Body behaviour (outside)
These are things we often do if we're feeling angry.

❑ Ignore others   ❑ Tense laugh

❑ Fold arms   ❑ Narrow eyes

❑ Agitated movement   ❑ Take drugs

❑ Tense toes   ❑ Narrow focus

❑ Withdraw inside self   ❑ Evil eye

❑ Stand up   ❑ See red

❑ Clench fists   ❑ Pretend others aren't there

❑ Twitch   ❑ Stamp

❑ Tighten/purse lips   ❑ Slam doors

❑ Staring eyes – squinting   ❑ Walk out

❑ Tense eyes   ❑ Smoke

❑ Walk away   ❑ Drink alcohol

❑ Say 'Nothing'   ❑ Squirm

❑ Frown   ❑ Slam things down

❑ Kick foot   ❑ Tears in eyes

✓

- ☐ Bang walls
- ☐ Shout

- ☐ Hang head

Thoughts (head)

- ☐ Can't think
- ☐ 'You wait!'
- ☐ 'I'll get you'
- ☐ 'It always happens to me!'
- ☐ 'F___ you!'
- ☐ Messages from mother
- ☐ 'I'll kill my brother/sister!'
- ☐ Messages from father
- ☐ 'I don't give a s___!'
- ☐ Fantasy of violence/revenge

- ☐ 'Bloody mothers/fathers!'
- ☐ Scheming
- ☐ 'I'll smash _____!'
- ☐ 'Here we go again'
- ☐ 'Wanker!'
- ☐ 'Leave me alone'
- ☐ 'I hate brothers/sisters!'
- ☐ 'I'd like to _____ you!'
- ☐ 'That's it!'

Other. . . . .

. . . .

. . . .

Key concept

♦ If we know early signs of anger we have more choice about our actions.

The anger scale

Get to know your levels of anger better. When you can think 'right now I am on a 3 or a 9' then you are getting to know your anger. Then you can do something about it. The lower levels are the hardest to have that instant knowing. The lower you are on the scale when you realise you are angry, the more space you have to choose something different!

Write your anger words in the spaces to match the level of anger on the scale.

What's happening at each level		Anger word to match
Danger exploding	10	. . . .
Stop stop stop	9	. . . .
Notice anger getting out of control	8	. . . .
Take Time Out now	7	. . . .
Calm down	6	. . . .
Say what you need to	5	. . . .
Let go of small tensions or angers	4	. . . .
Say to yourself, 'I'm OK'	3	. . . .
Noticing niggles	2	. . . .
Really relaxed	1	. . . .
	0	

Key concepts

- Everyone gets angry. Anger is OK.
- You need anger to protect and help you.
- What you DO with anger is what matters.
- If we know the early signs of anger we have more choice time.
- The lower you know the more you can choose not to lose.

Anger scripts

Tracking what you learned from your family about expressing anger can be very helpful. You then have a choice about how you do it for yourself instead of copying others without realising.

How does/did your father act when he was angry? . . . .

. . . .

What similarities and patterns do you notice? . . . .

. . . .

How does/did your mother act when she was angry?. . . . .

. . . .

Is this how you want it to be?

❑ YES   ❑ NO

How would you like it to be? . . . .

. . . .

How did they handle conflict? . . . .

. . . .

What will you change to make it how you want it?

I'll stop doing these things: . . . .

. . . .

Was anybody afraid at home? . . . .

. . . .

I'll start doing these things: . . . .

. . . .

What did you learn at home about:

How men are angry?. . . . .

. . . .

Things that I'll find difficult will be: . . . .

. . . .

How women are angry? . . . .

. . . .

✓

Ways I'll overcome the difficulties are:. . . . .

. . . .

Resolving conflict?. . . . .

. . . .

How did you express anger as a child? . . . .

. . . .

The name of someone who will support me in this is: . . . .

. . . .

How do you express anger now?. . . . .

. . . .

Key concepts

 ◆ You can change the things you were taught about anger and abuse.

 ◆ Behind every anger there is a hurt, loss, fear or shame.

Cycle of abuser and loser

If we abuse and disrespect others we are losing relationships and opportunities. Before we can change from loser behaviour we need to know what it is that we are doing wrong.

Mostly when we hurt others we have a period of tension-building beforehand and after hurting someone we have a period of feeling bad about it and maybe trying to make up for it.

Think about the times that you have hurt someone in your family or close to you. Then think about the lead-up to that. If we know the lead-up signs then we can avoid damaging other people.

Tension

Tension has inside signs like breathing, pulse, temperature, sweat, stomach, energy and muscles. Then there are outside signs like fists tightening, feet shifting or wanting to kick, arms raising, jaw tightening, lips pursing, eyes narrowing, hair standing up.

These have already been covered in this chapter (see the 'Early warning signs of feeling anger in your body' handout).

Triggers

Triggers are things that we have sore spots about – like money, times to come home, boyfriend/girlfriend, pimples, names.

What are yours? Write them in the top box of the 'Cycle' diagram on the next page.

Abuse or hurt

Consider the ways you most commonly abuse or hurt someone – physically, verbally, emotionally, socially, with property or sexually.

Write down the details in the 'Abuse' box e.g. punching, swearing, stealing, lies, hiding things and making up gossip.

Regret

Then think of the things you do to make up for what you have done because you regret 'losing it' or hurting a person that much: do jobs for Mum, buy presents, offer to take them out, sweet talk, do what they want. Write those down in the 'Regret' box.

Stopping the cycle

This is a cycle so the more often that you do it the more you may hurt someone and the less you regret it. That's bad for your later life and for your current living. Be good to people that you love and who support you and would probably help you whenever you asked.

The cycle can be stopped by being aware of the tension building and choosing to do something else to release the tension and not hurting anyone. Take Time Out, or start talking so that the tension can be brought down. If you feel regret, then the best thing that you can do is to find a way you can be absolutely sure you will never do the same thing again. Talk to someone about your patterns. Ask your parents to do the exercise too.

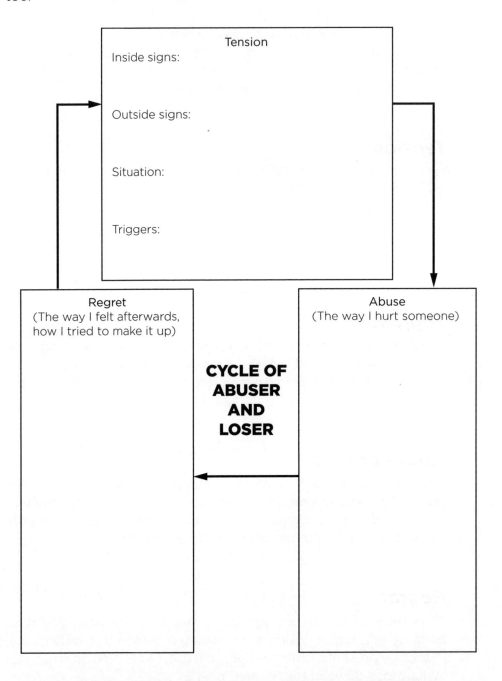

Tension

Inside signs:

Outside signs:

Situation:

Triggers:

CYCLE OF ABUSER AND LOSER

Regret
(The way I felt afterwards, how I tried to make it up)

Abuse
(The way I hurt someone)

Key concepts

- We need to break negative cycles.

- If we know early warning signs of anger then we have more choice.

Tracking loser and winner behaviour

Often we do things without working out if they will get us what we want. The next pages are 'tracking' pages. The first asks you to track a situation where you got angry and lost it, abused someone or just didn't handle the situation well. Write down the sensations and thoughts that were going on in your body so that you can recognise them earlier and have more choice over your actions next time. Notice the words that you used and the actions that you took that 'stuffed it up' and left you with a situation that didn't get what you wanted. Also note the effects that this had on the other people and yourself.

People often lash out in anger and end up hurting others and not getting what they want.

Fill in 'Tracking my loser behaviour' then turn to the opposite page and plan to be a winner by being clear about what the intention is, then working out how you could get the result you want without damaging others.

If we are clear at the beginning about what it is that we want we can often be smarter about getting it. Plan two different ways that you think could work to get a good result.

Get a winner attitude rather than just 'blowing it'.

Choice of a winner: getting what is good for me and good for others.

What do I really want?

Tracking my loser behaviour what happened that left others and/or you feeling bad?

The situation: . . . .

. . . .

. . . .

My signals inside (feelings, sensations): . . . .

. . . .

. . . .

My signals outside (body language, face, hands): . . . .

. . . .

. . . .

My thoughts (fantasy, messages, beliefs): . . . .

. . . .

. . . .

The words I used: . . . .

. . . .

. . . .

The actions I took: . . . .

. . . .

. . . .

Effects on:

    My friend: . . . .

    . . . .

    . . . .

    Me: . . . .

    . . . .

    . . . .

    My parent: . . . .

    . . . .

    . . . .

Alternative actions – list what you could do instead.

The situation: . . . .

. . . .

. . . .

My thoughts: . . . .

. . . .

. . . .

My words: . . . .

. . . .

. . . .

My action: Choice one:. . . . .

. . . .

. . . .

My action: Choice two:. . . . .

. . . .

. . . .

The result:

For me:. . . . .

. . . .

For my friend:. . . . .

. . . .

For my parent: . . . .

. . . .

So what do you really want?
Get it peacefully.
Get the attitude, be a winner!

Key concept

- We can change loser choices into winner choices.

Transferring anger

Transferring anger happens when you are angry with one person and you express it to another who links somehow to the first person. It can happen in several ways:

♦ You transfer the anger from one person to another person who isn't the source of the anger but reminds you of them

♦ You have anger from the past and you carry it through to the present

This can destroy good relationships because no one likes you to get angry with them when they don't deserve it. Dumping anger on people that comes from somewhere else is unfair and really confusing for the other person.

Why does it happen?

1. Because sometimes it isn't safe to express it to the right person. They could be bigger, older and more powerful or you're just afraid that you may get a bad reaction that you can't afford. Mostly we're afraid that people won't like us if we get angry with them. That's not unreasonable because many people just can't handle hearing the anger of others. But usually people can handle our anger much better than we think. They often have more respect for us if we do it without attacking them. They get a sense of our strength.

2. Because we often haven't finished expressing it and what's left gets tangled up in other situations without us realising. It helps to ask the questions 'Is this anger out of proportion to what's happening here? Why am I so angry right now? Do I have some anger that's coming from somewhere else?'

3. Because the other person is not so powerful or they love us and let us get away with dumping on them. It's not OK to transfer anger on to weaker people or those who love us and dump angry feelings on them especially in a way that blames them.

4. Sometimes we don't know what it is that we are angry about. It happened so long ago, like sexual abuse as a kid, or a parent died or left. We're so used to being angry we just live like an angry person. And people get used to us being angry.

The art of not transferring anger is:

♦ To know when we are angry

♦ To express it when it happens instead of later

Or, if you have carried anger from another place or time, explain to people that you are not angry with them but ask if you can have a rage or a complaint session to get rid of some stuff you are carrying that has nothing to do with them.

- ◆ How much anger do you carry?

- ◆ What things from the past are you still angry about?

- ◆ How much anger do you just squash down?

- ◆ What would your friends say you are angry about?

- ◆ Who do you dump on?

- ◆ Who should really hear your anger?

- ◆ Who can you ask permission to unload some anger with? They could be a friend or person who will listen and understand you.

Bottling anger

Twenty years ago if a grandmother said she was bottling she was probably preserving fruit in glass jars. Nowadays when we talk of bottling we are more likely to be talking about repressing our anger. It is one way that people try to cope with angry feelings, by squashing them down and trying to keep the lid on.

Girls are more likely to adopt this coping strategy than boys. Many families may unwittingly encourage boys to act out their anger: 'Boys will be boys' might be said as a boy raves and rages. A girl is more likely to be praised for being quieter and 'good' or given a hard time if she displays anger. An adolescent boy may be boisterous and loud and take out angry feelings on the sports field or behind the wheel of a car. While some girls might act this way it is more common for girls to suppress their anger and appear to be compliant and well behaved.

When Grandmother bottled fruit, one method was the overflow method. She filled the jar with fruit and juice until it was overflowing and then screwed on the lid. Putting on the lid would send the excess juice running down the sides of the jar to form a sticky mess on the bench. As with the fruit juice, too much suppressed anger will escape somehow. It may be expressed less obviously and consciously as sarcasm, nasty comments, spiteful behaviour or bullying of people who appear to be vulnerable. It may even explode with an outburst that seems unnecessary.

Those who store their anger in this way will often gather a gang around them to lash out at others, usually with words. It may be by criticism, put-downs, names, sarcasm or lies. For a while the young person will have a feeling of belonging with others around for support but all too soon members of the group will grow tired of friendships built on anger towards others. They will wonder when they will be the next victim of this overflowing rage and will start to pull away from the group.

People who suppress their anger and then vent it in this way usually become very lonely people.

Example: venting anger

Julia was ten when her parents divorced. The separation was very messy with both parents arguing and fighting. Julia felt powerless, tossed, as she was, between her parents and being forced to hear their angry tirades about each other. In school Julia worked hard to achieve good grades and most teachers were glad to have her in their class. But then they did not see how she mimicked them in the corridors after class and they did not know that she was the author of many of the nasty slogans written on the toilet walls. It was Julia too, who gathered a group of classmates together to wait at the school gates in the morning to tease and taunt Ella who was overweight.

There are other ways of suppressing anger. Some people may suppress their anger so much that they make themselves ill or develop frequent headaches. Others will only let their anger out when they are under the influence of drugs, including alcohol, which can loosen our inhibitions.

Then you get an angry or aggressive drunk. Some can only keep their anger in by smoking dope.

It is also common for people who suppress their anger to use smoking cigarettes to hold in their anger.

Example: anger and smoking

Janie says that when she is just so angry she has a cigarette. 'I draw it down into my lungs with the cigarette smoke and it just stays there. It scares me sometimes,' she says, 'that one day it's all going to come bursting out and then what will happen?'

Soothing and calming anger

Be an Expressor:

1. Find some positive ways to express your anger:

    *   Write in a journal

    *   Draw or paint

    *   Walk or run your anger out

    *   Write unsent letters to the person you are angry with

    *   Talk to someone you trust about your feelings or, even better, if it is appropriate and safe to do so, talk to the person you are angry with.

2. Use 'I' statements (no blaming 'you' statements that will inflame the conflict).

3. If it is possible, talk out your anger with a counsellor.

Example: anger and running

Jackie finds that running helps her to express anger: 'When I am feeling really angry I go out for a run. Running helps me feel strong and powerful. I imagine that the person I am angry with can't help but hear me and pay attention. I pound my anger out with my feet.'

Be a Soother:

1. Breathe your way through the anger. Take a deep breath and exhale very slowly. Picture your angry feelings leaving your body and leaving you feeling peaceful. Do this four or five times.

2. Be kind to yourself. Use positive self-talk: 'I have every right to feel angry. I have been through a lot. Now what shall I do with this feeling?'

3. Adopt some good self-care tactics such as:

    *   hugging a cushion

    *   stroking an animal

    *   talking to a friend

    *   listening to music

    *   dancing.

✓

Find a way to express anger first. This can be as little as talking through your anger in your head or as much as walking out your anger, or writing it out in an unsent letter. Then choose a way to soothe and comfort yourself:

- Practise comforting self-talk. 'I have every right to be angry about this. Now I am going to do something nice for myself.

- Take a shower or bath. Water can be very comforting

- Swim or play pool

- Take a walk and deliberately look for something beautiful or interesting e.g. a raindrop on a leaf, a spider's web, a picture on a wall or in a newspaper or magazine. Study it carefully

- Draw a picture

- Write a poem

- Make a warm drink

- Phone a friend. Or if a friend is not available phone a helpline. Use all your senses. Find something that has a pleasing texture to touch, listen for enjoyable sounds

- Listen to music that you like

- Write in your journal

- Decorate some storage boxes

- Find something good to hold on to like a pillow or a soft toy

Very often deep anger is caused by hidden hurt and rejection. Hurting others does not heal wounds. Care and kindness towards ourselves and asking for help are much more effective.

CHAPTER 17

Managing Triggers, Time Out and Chill Down

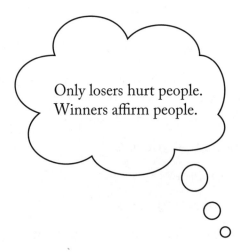

Only losers hurt people.
Winners affirm people.

Triggers

Adolescents, as young people, are forming into adults. They don't have the sureness of themselves that older people should have. It's easy to hurt adolescents and we also hurt each other when we're feeling threatened. Triggers are emotional wounds and vulnerabilities resulting from our past experiences that set us off. They trigger feelings of powerlessness, hurt, fear, confusion or anger. Triggers can be set off consciously or unconsciously. Sometimes they are set off deliberately by others who want to get to us – have power over us.

When people are triggered they often react without thinking. Everyone needs to develop consciousness and awareness of what triggers are so that they can think and choose their actions rather than have just reactions.

.People may also set up situations that trigger others, again consciously or unconsciously, to make them experience powerlessness, hurt, fear, confusion or anger. People do this often to give themselves a sense of power over others. A person may have been experiencing the same feelings they have inflicted and, rather than dealing with their own feelings, they blame the other person. The attitude is, 'If I'm not feeling OK then you can feel bad too, like me.'

If people are to take responsibility for their own thoughts, feelings and behaviours, they need to do the reverse: compliment and affirm others, so that they get positives back.

> Why do we often hurt the ones we love most?
> Because we know they will still love us after, or at least for a while!

Don't be a loser. Know your triggers.

Often people are more conscious of what triggers those closest to them (intimate people, our parents) than they are of what triggers themselves. If they ask their intimate friends to help them identify their triggers, they can learn a lot about getting on with other people.

Triggers are often comments made about an adolescent's:

- self-worth

- parents or family

- friends

- behaviour or ability to work

- girlfriends or boyfriends

- racism

- skills

- minds, intelligence

- looks

- sexuality

Handling triggers

We need to develop skills to remain self-empowered when we are triggered. The keys are:

- Recognise that we are being baited

- Self-talk, 'I'm OK' or 'I can nurture myself' or 'It's their problem'

Then we can respond in a way that:

- Stops conflict (like walk away)

- Affirms the other ('I like you!', 'Be nice to me!')

- Deflects with humour or distraction

- Questions ('Why did you say that?')

✓

Dealing with triggers

Triggers are sore places that are very sensitive and easily hurt. Sometimes others try to upset us and get power over us by deliberately trying to trigger us or 'press our buttons'. We can react without thinking. When we bite the bait we are hooked and lose power.

You could put the following suggestions on a card to be carried in a pocket.

Ways to deal with people trying to trigger you

Step 1 – Begin with the affirmation: 'I'm OK' or 'I nurture myself' or 'I'm a good guy.'

Step 2 – Choose any of these:

- Walk away

- Ignore as if you didn't hear

- Accede – say: 'Could be', 'Think about it', 'Thank you'

- Ask, 'Who's got the problem?'

- Imagine something good happening to the other person

- Ignore

- Imagine a shield protecting you

- Take Time Out

- Anticipate and prepare for possible triggering

- Let go of the 'bait'

- Use your de-stress methods.

Hint for helper

Acknowledge the hurt that takes place when a trigger works. Say how that hurts you as well when that happens to you. Try to track to the original hurt. Offer a way that can stop that hurt – say, 'I know a way that you could stop that hurting' or 'I know a way that you could stop losing power... But I don't know if you're ready for it' or 'I don't know if you could handle it/ do it'. Invite enquiry. Notice and reward successes:

- Breathe deeply and smile

- Ask why they need to do that

- Think 'In the long term what do I want?'

- Use an assertion phrase

Hints on helping to overcome triggers

It seems necessary always to use Step 1 and then proceed with one of the other options. A good activity for helping trigger management is:

a.   Identify the trigger and state that you don't wish to lose power to others this way any more.

Hint

It is useful to use the concept of a hook on a fishing line with the trigger on the end as bait. Biting at the bait means that you will be hooked and lose power. Any retort, negative response, or body language counts as 'hooked'. It is useful for facilitators to play a game of fishing by physically holding an imaginary hook in front of the person's nose. This can be done methodically or spontaneously. A bite gets a 'Gotcha', a No-trigger gets an affirmation and feedback of how it feels to have failed to get them hooked.

---

b.   Check why the trigger triggers, if this is useful.

c.   If it's a verbal put-down, ask 'Is it true?' 'Am I a loser, wanker, braindead, etc?' A helper can assist you, with questions or support, to identify that there is no truth in the statement.

d.   A helper then asks, 'If you're not a loser, and she needs to call you a "loser" for some reason – who's got the problem?' The helper persists until the person states clearly that the other person has the problem. The helper has them repeat again what their self-talk will be if that trigger is used again.

e.   Helper congratulates and affirms them for their decision to keep their personal power.

My hooks (triggers)

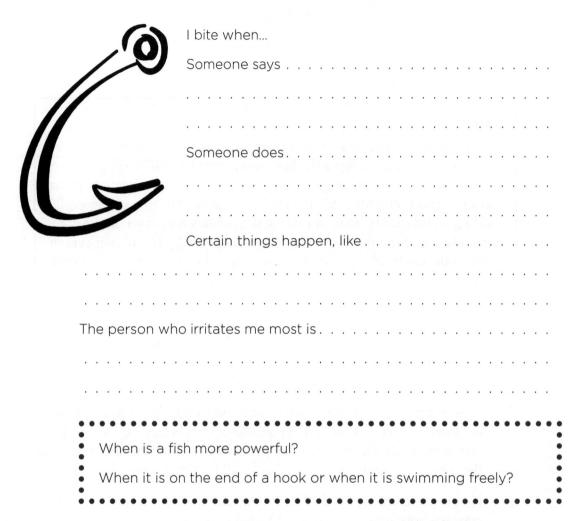

I bite when...

Someone says . . . .

. . . .

. . . .

Someone does . . . .

. . . .

. . . .

Certain things happen, like . . . .

. . . .

. . . .

The person who irritates me most is . . . .

. . . .

. . . .

When is a fish more powerful?

When it is on the end of a hook or when it is swimming freely?

**If you talk back, get smart, put down, insult, swear,
say the same thing back, get rude, give rude signs,
hurt back, control back, then you are hooked!**

**The other person has you on a line. You
aren't in control of you – they are.**

Triggers for adolescents

Triggers are often used by others to set up situations where they can get power over the you by getting you upset. They are used as bait. Don't get hooked and lose your power.

Situations
We can all set up situations that we know irritate other people or that we can get upset about. Sometimes we do this without realising it.

You triggering others
You might try to trigger parents, teachers or other authority figures by:

- Deliberate disobedience
- Stuffing up their social life
- Dressing dirty
- Loud music
- Saying, 'Make me!'
- Putting them down

Losers do that
Instead negotiate a better deal. If you want to come home later, do some bargaining. If you want to change things, talk, tell them and do deals.

Parent triggering you
Sometimes parents try to trigger adolescents. This is unfair. They may say:

- 'You're still a child'
- 'Idiot'
- 'Useless'
- 'Loser'
- 'Lazy'
- 'No-hoper'
- 'Ungrateful'

These are put-downs.
   Other times simple things may trigger you like:

- 'Have you done...'
- 'No, you can't'
- 'Do what you're told'
- 'I told you to...'

What to do: self-talk

Say: 'This is a trigger situation.'

Say: "'M' wants to get me angry and have power over me.'

Say: 'Whose got the problem? He has.'

Say: 'I'm OK, I'm great.'

Say: 'I'll walk away', 'I'll ignore this.'

Do NOT react or lose it.
Follow the instructions above.

Peers verbally triggering you

Friends and brothers and sisters know the easiest and best ways of getting you angry at words. They are experts at it. Some verbal triggers are:

♦ Peers – dumb, thick, loser, you've got no friends, nerd, jerk, teacher's pet, I'm not your friend, wanker, useless, dickhead, you suck, geek

♦ Sexual triggers are usually one of the hardest to resist – prick, dick, jerk, fuckwit, girl, gay, homo, fairy, poof, fag, cocksucker, bum-boy

♦ Racist triggers are big bait – coconut, black, nigger, trash, honkey, white boy, house boy, traitor, Uncle Tom

♦ Family hooks are sure bites for many – your mother's a slut, your family..., your father..., your girlfriend...

Key concepts

♦ Triggers are hurts we react to without thinking.

♦ Being triggered gives my power to others.

♦ Choosing not to be triggered gives us power.

Triggers worksheet

Use this worksheet to examine trigger situations you have had.

The positive action I did choose or could have chosen	
The negative action I responded with (if I did!)	
CHOICE	
My feelings when I was triggered	
My triggers	

Key concept

◆ Choosing not to be triggered gives us power.

Time Out

Choosing Time Out or 'Time In' control of myself

Three steps

Step 1 – 'I am feeling really tense/angry/upset.'

Step 2 – 'I am going to take Time Out for half an hour.'

Step 3 – 'When I come back, I'd like to talk about this some more.'

The purpose of Time Out

♦ To interrupt a situation which, if it continues, could explode and get out of control; to keep everyone safe.

♦ To give you an opportunity to stop stuffing up your life.

♦ To give you an opportunity to work out different ways of behaving.

♦ To work out your feelings and work out what you want.

Preparation for Time Out

♦ Explain Time Out to your family, teacher, friend and anyone else who might need to know so they understand what's happening. (They also might like to try using Time Out.)

♦ Plan how you're going to use the set time you'll have when you use Time Out. Work out a contract or deal with your school, your family or your friends.

♦ Put up a notice somewhere, or put a card in your wallet, reminding you to take Time Out. Remember, it's cool to be in charge of your life.

♦ Make sure everyone understands the deal and what's happening.

♦ School counsellors are there to help.

Using Time Out

♦ When advising someone that you are going to take Time Out, speak calmly and quietly. Avoid speaking in a way that might suggest you are taking Time Out to annoy them.

♦ Don't be hooked back by taunts, names or challenges. Don't stop to discuss it. At first they may try to get you from leaving by baiting you.

♦ Do something physical to burn off adrenalin. Run, play sport, fix something, dig the garden, clean up, walk, mow the lawn, do vacuuming, skateboarding or cycling.

Remember:

♦ Don't drink, take drugs, drive or stay around trouble when taking Time Out.

♦ Taking Time Out puts you in control of your life.

After coming back from Time Out

Don't start talking again until the charge, or rush, has gone. Don't talk where there are spectators. Then make a conscious effort to make a fresh start to solving the problem:

♦ Talk in a different room

♦ Sit down on a chair or on the floor

♦ Talk in a quieter tone and in a lower volume

♦ Leave a pause after the other person has spoken to allow what they have said to sink in

♦ Talk calmly without an 'edge' in your voice or swearing

♦ Ask the other person to tell you what they think you said

♦ Repeat back to the other person what you think they said: 'I'm just checking out...'

If you start feeling angry again, take another Time Out or get a third person to coach you.

✓

Time Out

Time to express, calm down, look after yourself.

The 5 Ds

- DON'T ABUSE VERBALLY OR DAMAGE ANYTHING
- DON'T DRINK OR DO DRUGS
- DON'T HURT YOURSELF
- DON'T USE TIMEOUT TO PAYBACK OTHERS
- DO COME BACK SAFELY TO TALK ABOUT SOLUTIONS

Key concepts

- Time Out is time in charge of yourself.
- After Time Out, come back and fix the problem.

✓

Time Out at home
Adults and adolescents

Basic principles

- That Time Out be a time of safety, expression, calming.

- That the person always be responsible for not abusing people.

- That Time Out without accountability is a cop-out – see box below.

- That the principle of tracking the anger to a cause is applied if possible.

- That abuse should have consequences.

- Time Out is a time for expression, calming, nurturing and thinking about how to improve the situation.

- Time Out is for a set amount of time so that people don't worry.

- Time Out doesn't fix things. It just allows time for you to work out how to do things better.

- Time Out keeps people safe and halts destructive behaviour.

- The person you leave may not like you taking Time Out.

- Don't drink or use drugs during Time Out.

- If you have to drive, drive very carefully.

✓

Steps

- There is an agreement with all the people in the house that Time Out is a house procedure and will be respected.

- Time Out is not a punishment but simply a safe place chosen when tension is too high.

- The adolescent or parent chooses a place that is a Time Out place for him/her. This is often a bedroom, garden or a garage.

- The adolescent/parent chooses to go there when they are unable to handle what is happening or to keep everyone safe.

- They are never interrupted in that time.

- There is a set amount of time agreed upon as a limit (e.g. 30 minutes). The Time Out person can come out before this time is up.

- The Time Out person then goes back to the person that they were sorting things out with and continues to do that in a safe way. If unavailable, a time is made to continue later.

- If it becomes difficult again another Time Out is taken.

Be consistent: Time Out.

Time Out for schools

Basic principles

♦ That 'Time Out' be a time of safety, expression, calming.

♦ That 'Time Out' be a time for thinking about how to improve the situation.

♦ That 'Time Out' be accountable – see steps below.

♦ That the pupil always be responsible for not abusing people.

♦ That 'Time Out' without accountability is a 'cop out'.

♦ That the principle of tracking anger back to a cause be applied where this is possible.

♦ That abuse should have consequences.

Steps

♦ The pupil has specific permission to be a 'Time Out' pupil.

♦ The pupil has 'Time Out' clearly explained.

♦ The pupil has a prearranged signal such as a licence, card, statement or hand sign that can be easily shown to indicate he or she needs 'Time Out'.

♦ The pupil uses this when he or she is fearful of being abusive or disruptive.

♦ The pupil leaves the room with no disruption.

♦ The pupil reports to the principal or ancillary staff member and this is recorded.

♦ The pupil goes to a pre-agreed 'Time Out' place.

♦ The pupil stays there for an agreed amount of time.

♦ The pupil goes back to the classroom teacher with a strategy for improving the situation.

♦ The teacher assists the pupil to track the initial cause of powerlessness.

♦ The teacher may assist the pupil to strategise for change.

Escalators in action
Easy steps to being a loser in relationships

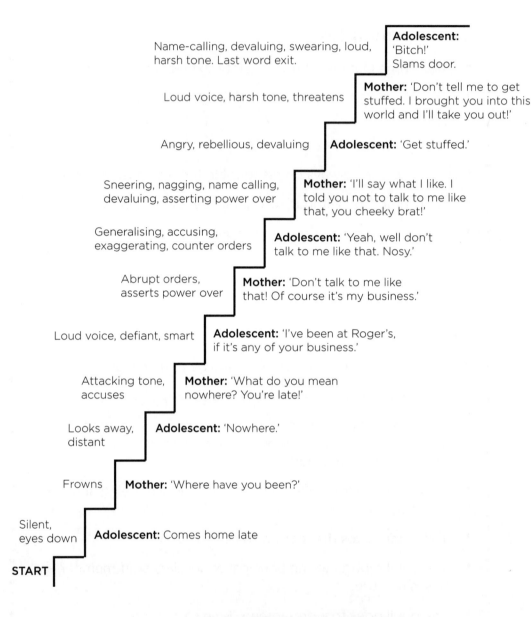

Name-calling, devaluing, swearing, loud, harsh tone. Last word exit.

Adolescent: 'Bitch!' Slams door.

Loud voice, harsh tone, threatens

Mother: 'Don't tell me to get stuffed. I brought you into this world and I'll take you out!'

Angry, rebellious, devaluing

Adolescent: 'Get stuffed.'

Sneering, nagging, name calling, devaluing, asserting power over

Mother: 'I'll say what I like. I told you not to talk to me like that, you cheeky brat!'

Generalising, accusing, exaggerating, counter orders

Adolescent: 'Yeah, well don't talk to me like that. Nosy.'

Abrupt orders, asserts power over

Mother: 'Don't talk to me like that! Of course it's my business.'

Loud voice, defiant, smart

Adolescent: 'I've been at Roger's, if it's any of your business.'

Attacking tone, accuses

Mother: 'What do you mean nowhere? You're late!'

Looks away, distant

Adolescent: 'Nowhere.'

Frowns

Mother: 'Where have you been?'

Silent, eyes down

Adolescent: Comes home late

START

How to wind it up and stuff it up!
What did he really want?
What did she really want?
What did they get?

Key concept

+ Fighting back makes losers.

Adolescent escalators used by parents

Attitude: 'You are not OK, I am right.'
These are behaviours that are guaranteed to inflame a difference of opinion into full-on conflict.

Blaming:
'It's the kid's fault! If it weren't for you kids I'd be...'

Put-downs:
'Dumb bloody kids!' 'Lazy.'

Threatening:
'If you don't shut up I'll smack your head in.' 'I'll kick you out.'

Swearing:
'Piss off!' 'You little shit!' 'What the f___ are you doing!'

Cursing:
'Drop dead, you _____!'

Talking over the top
Not listening, talking louder, talking a long time without stopping, ignoring others' voices.

Sarcasm:
'Sure you're going to do it; the day you do I'll throw a party.'

Insults:
'I'm embarrassed to be seen with you.' 'I'm so ashamed of you.'

Abrupt limit setting:
'That's it!' 'I've had it!' 'I'm finished!' 'Get out!' 'I'm not interested!'

Dragging up the past:
'You did it again!' 'The last time I saw you...'

Stonewalling:
'I don't want to talk!' [*Slams the door.*]

Yes, butting:
'Yes, but what about when you...' 'Yes, but you aren't...'

Manipulating:
'If you love me...' 'What about your poor parents?' 'I need you.'

Demands:
'Do it now.' 'Where is it?'

Criticism:
'Can't you get it right?' 'You know, the trouble with you is...' 'Why do you always...'

Giving advice:
What you should do is...' 'I know best.' 'When I was a child...'

Giving orders:
'Go and get...' 'Do it now!' 'Shut up!'

Accusations:
'You've done it again, haven't you!' 'You did it!' 'Have you stolen...' 'When did you break...'

Exaggerating:
'You always...' 'You never...' 'That's the 100th time.'

'You' statements:
'You put it there...' 'You lost it.'

Global labelling:
'You kids are all the same...'
'Who'd have a boy?'

Vocals:
Groaning, sighing, nagging, whining, harsh tone, mocking, shouting, contemptuous tone, grunting, silence.

Facial expressions:
Rolling eyes, sneering, scowling, grimacing, narrowing eyes, tightening lips, looking away, black looks, disbelief.

Gestures:
Shaking head, pointing a finger, shrugging, obscene gestures, shaking a fist, hands on hips, folding arms, waving away, pointing.

Every time you can choose to do something different.

Parents

Why do these just make it worse?

Why do you do them?

How could you *de-escalate* if someone else was doing it to you?

Parent escalators used by adolescents
Handling personal conflict

Attitude: 'You are not OK, I am right.'

These are behaviours that are guaranteed to inflame a difference of opinion into full-on conflict.

Blaming:
'If you hadn't...' 'My parents didn't...' [*said to friends so parents can hear.*]

Put-downs:
'Parents are so dumb.' 'Dork of a Dad.'

Threatening:
'I'll run away.' 'I'll...'

Swearing:
'Get f___!' 'You suck!' [*any word a parent hates.*]

Cursing:
'Go to hell.' 'Hope you...'

Talking over the top:
Shouting, not listening, talking fast, cutting others off.

Sarcasm:
'Yeah, you're a great Mum!' 'In your dreams!'

Insults:
'Fat slob.' 'I'll get a real father.' 'You're not my mother.'

Abrupt limit setting:
[*Storming out*] 'Never talk to me again.' 'I've had it!'

Dragging up the past:
'I remember when you...' 'What sort of parent would do...?'

Stonewalling:
Not listening. Locking bedroom door.

Yes, butting:
'But not right now.'

Manipulating:
'You don't love me. I won't come unless...'

Criticism:
'You always do something...' 'You need a parenting course.' 'You did it wrong.'

Giving advice:
'You need to do... like X's Dad.' 'Buy this.'

Giving orders:
'Get my tea by 6pm.' 'Do my washing.' 'Take me there.'

Accusations:
'You did it.' 'You mucked it up.' 'You set me up.' 'You want me dead.'

Exaggerating:
'You always...' 'You never...' 'You can't...' 'He's incredibly stupid.'

'You' statements:
'You caused this.' 'You made me...'

Global labeling:
'Why are adults so dumb?' 'Parents!' 'Mothers are useless.'

Vocals:
Whining. Mumbling. Not speaking clearly. Mocking. Angry tones. Contemptuous tones. Groaning.

Facial expressions:
Rolling eyes. Mouthing words. Bad looks. Looking away. Laughing at others. Narrowing eyes.

Gestures:
Fingers. Sneering. Kicking, Throwing. Folding arms.

Demands:
'Where's my...?' 'My washing's not done.'

Comparisons:
'Other parents don't...' 'X's Dad gives him...'

Every time you can choose to do something different.

Adolescents

Why do these just make it worse?

Why do you do them?

How could you *de-escalate* if someone else was doing it to you?

Key concept

♦ You always have a choice.

De-escalators
Handling personal conflict

Attitude: I am OK, you are OK too, be happy, go for the bigger goal. These behaviours will always reduce the intensity of conflict.

Listen:
Don't interrupt. Avoid trying to 'win' – if you 'win' at the expense of someone else, you both lose. Put yourself in their shoes – try to understand what the other person is saying to you.

Reflect:
Show you've heard by repeating back the main part of their message (even if you disagree) before you express your own point of view.

Think:
'I'm OK, you're OK.'

Use 'I' statements:
Give clear statements of your own point of view.

Focus on the good.

Take responsibility for your feelings:
You generate your own feelings. No one else makes you feel anything.

Ask myself:
What's my attitude? Do I feel like payback?

Avoid the hooks:
Let negative responses and abuse flow over you and don't let it 'hook' you.

Take Time Out when you notice you are becoming too angry to think straight.

Wait till the charge or rush goes.

Say something to help the other person feel OK.

Stick to the issue:
Avoid getting sidetracked.

Apologise:
Let go of the need to be 'right'. Don't be afraid to admit your mistakes. Clean apologies are cool!

Be accurate:
Be specific, don't exaggerate, be honest with yourself.

Be open to negotiate:
Go for a win/win solution.

Use gentle tones.
Practise acceptance, forgiveness, generosity of spirit, good humour.

Relax your body, especially shoulders, chest and abdomen.

Slow your breathing:
Breathe through the nose. Use abdominal breathing.

Slow your rate of speech:
Allow pause of three
heartbeats before you reply.

Deepen your voice by relaxing
shoulders, chest and throat.

Focus on reducing the anger of
the other person.

Hands:
Show open hands.

Body language:
Stand or sit equal or lower. Nod
and show you're with them.

**What is the greater good created by de-escalating?
How come you are so cool and likeable?**

Key concept

- If you like yourself, you can handle someone else's problem more easily.

De-escalators in action
Easy steps to dealing with a loser/aggro parent

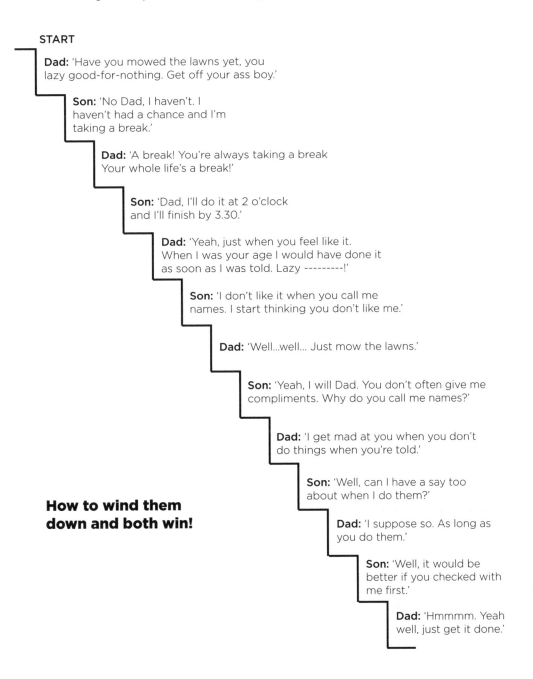

START

Dad: 'Have you mowed the lawns yet, you lazy good-for-nothing. Get off your ass boy.'

Son: 'No Dad, I haven't. I haven't had a chance and I'm taking a break.'

Dad: 'A break! You're always taking a break Your whole life's a break!'

Son: 'Dad, I'll do it at 2 o'clock and I'll finish by 3.30.'

Dad: 'Yeah, just when you feel like it. When I was your age I would have done it as soon as I was told. Lazy ---------!'

Son: 'I don't like it when you call me names. I start thinking you don't like me.'

Dad: 'Well...well... Just mow the lawns.'

Son: 'Yeah, I will Dad. You don't often give me compliments. Why do you call me names?'

Dad: 'I get mad at you when you don't do things when you're told.'

Son: 'Well, can I have a say too about when I do them?'

Dad: 'I suppose so. As long as you do them.'

Son: 'Well, it would be better if you checked with me first.'

Dad: 'Hmmmm. Yeah well, just get it done.'

How to wind them down and both win!

Every loser/aggro adult is different.
Choose the right words for each aggro adult you have to deal with.

Key concept

♦ Some parents have abuse problems.

De-escalating in action
Easy steps to being a winner as a parent

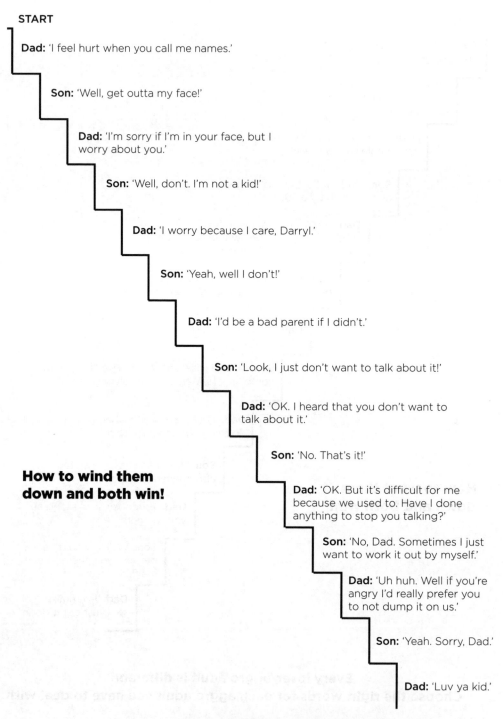

START

Dad: 'I feel hurt when you call me names.'

Son: 'Well, get outta my face!'

Dad: 'I'm sorry if I'm in your face, but I worry about you.'

Son: 'Well, don't. I'm not a kid!'

Dad: 'I worry because I care, Darryl.'

Son: 'Yeah, well I don't!'

Dad: 'I'd be a bad parent if I didn't.'

Son: 'Look, I just don't want to talk about it!'

Dad: 'OK. I heard that you don't want to talk about it.'

Son: 'No. That's it!'

How to wind them down and both win!

Dad: 'OK. But it's difficult for me because we used to. Have I done anything to stop you talking?'

Son: 'No, Dad. Sometimes I just want to work it out by myself.'

Dad: 'Uh huh. Well if you're angry I'd really prefer you to not dump it on us.'

Son: 'Yeah. Sorry, Dad.'

Dad: 'Luv ya kid.'

What are Dad and Darryl going to get from this?
How many winners are there?
What would defuse you?

Staying cool

Cool people can smile

Cool people are liked

Cool people...

Cool people are powerful inside

Cool people don't get HOOKED!

Cool people don't need to fight

Cool people help others to be cool

What can you do when someone...

Wants to get angry

Tries to hook you

Tries to hurt you

Wants power over your feelings

Puts you down

Gets in your face

Provokes a fight

Name calls

Treats you dumb

Plays games with you

Baits you

Triggers you

Teases

What can you do to stay cool? Pick from 'Staying cool' above or write better ones.

Automatic loser button

Some people have a big automatic loser button.
    Others have small ones.
    Some people like to hit your automatic button to make them feel good about themselves.
    If you have a big one, it is easy. If you have a smaller one, it is harder.
    We get bigger buttons from being told in our past that we are no good, being neglected, being abused, being forgotten, feeling unloved.

If you have a large

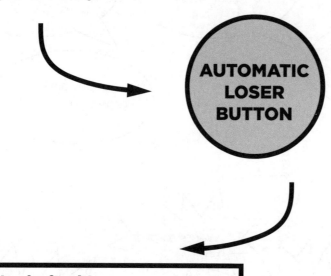

AUTOMATIC LOSER BUTTON

Look after it!
- Don't let it trigger your smart mouth
- Don't let it trigger your fist
- Don't let it trigger your foot
- Don't let it trigger your bad looks
- Don't let it trigger your 'black hole' gut
- Don't let it trigger your anger and hate

Keep cool
- Say: 'I am OK.'
- Say: 'Who has the problem?'
- Say to yourself:
  - 'They have the problem.'
  - 'I can handle this.'
  - 'I am so cool I can let it go past me.'

Big picture – little picture
Will you win a small fight or win the big picture?

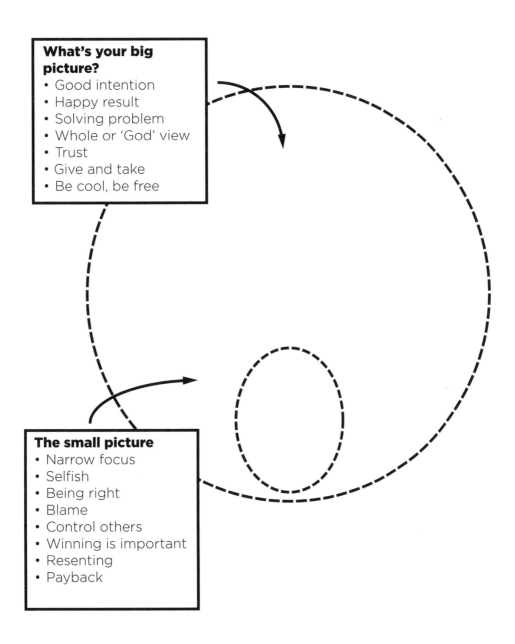

What's your big picture?
- Good intention
- Happy result
- Solving problem
- Whole or 'God' view
- Trust
- Give and take
- Be cool, be free

The small picture
- Narrow focus
- Selfish
- Being right
- Blame
- Control others
- Winning is important
- Resenting
- Payback

Key concept

♦ Small minds live in small pictures.

Are you being bullied?
What can you do?

Bullies are usually angry people who misuse their anger by abusing people who are vulnerable and easier for them to prey on. If you are being bullied you might ask yourself, how is it that bullies see me as vulnerable?

It could be your body posture: Do you look like a victim? Look at yourself in a mirror or shop window. Practise standing tall with your head held high. Imagine you are balancing something on your head as you walk. It will help keep your head up and shoulders back.

Do you avoid eye contact with other people your age? Practise in the mirror again, making eye contact with yourself. It might be hard at first to make eye contact, but it is worth it.

Do you fight back in arguments? People who retaliate show a desperation to win and a fear of losing. Bullies will look for people who are afraid. Use 'I' statements. Speak from your own truth and feel strong: I feel... I believe... I like... I need... I think...

Steady yourself when you feel scared: Focus on your breathing. Feel your breath go in and out. Stand with both feet firmly on the ground. Remind yourself you have a right to your place on the planet.

Try visualisation: Picture the bully in his underpants, or going up in a puff of smoke. Imagine yourself in a suit of armour. It does not have to be heavy metal. It could be a special force field. Your imagination can be a powerful tool.

Use humour: 'You're a geek!' 'No, not Greek, I'm a New Zealander!'

Seem to agree with the abuser (but know in yourself that you know the truth): 'You're a geek!' 'Yeah, I know. Geeks rule the world.' Or 'Yes, you may be right.' (He may also be wrong, you think to yourself.)

Know about being passive, aggressive and assertive and be assertive:

- Passive: I can't. I wish I could. It's not fair. Why can't I? Don't do this to me.

- Aggressive: You're stupid, what would you know? Who cares about you! Idiot!

- Assertive: Thanks for letting me know. I want you to move right now.

Ask questions: 'You're a homo!' 'Really? I didn't know that. So what's a homo anyway?'

Apologise: 'You're a geek!' 'I'm sorry. I didn't know that would bother you so much.'

Be confusing: 'Nobody wants to be with you.' 'My fan club will be along shortly.'

Be grateful: 'You're a dork.' 'Thanks for telling me. I'm working on being a super dork.'

Build a support group: Join with groups and take on roles, for example in the school production. Be a scene mover. You then belong to a group who are more likely to back you up. You will feel stronger as part of the group. Learn to listen to others and how they are feeling. You will have more friends who will back you up.

Write a diary: You then have yourself for a friend.

Talk to the school counsellor.

Get physically fit: You will feel stronger. Try walking, running, swimming, weight training.

Take a self-defence course or do a martial arts class.

Don't believe what a bully is telling you. You know yourself that you are OK.

CHAPTER 18

Communicating Better

Communication takes place in many ways through bodies, expressions volume, tone and words. Here we emphasise the use of words because this is a book but we need to remember that probably the most important thing is how we say things.

For communication there is a giver and a receiver. These things go together, so much of this book is about getting parents to talk and adolescents to listen and adolescents to talk and parents to listen. That's a sort of deal because if one party stops doing one of them, then it all starts to generate misunderstanding and assumptions. Trust safety and respect are important ingredients. Disrespect generates resentment and hurt and attacks generate a need for protection and so safety to speak the truth from vulnerability is very important. Simple structured phrases are a start that can lead to other things. They may feel false and parrot-like at first but soon they grow, integrate into our normal language and come out more personally. We recommend their repeated use and committing them to memory.

Training your adults to communicate

Communicating is so essential for success that you can't afford to get annoyed with yet another person telling you that you need to communicate. If you have resistance to the word 'communication' it may be because you haven't been listened to and it stopped being a useful thing to do. Here are some reasons why adolescents often give up talking:

♦ Parents order or direct and don't consult or explain

♦ They are afraid of your anger or emotions

♦ They are afraid that you may make a bad decision and be at risk

♦ They just don't know how to because no one did with them

♦ They believe that bossing is OK because they were bossed as kids

♦ The world has changed and they don't understand it as well as they used to

♦ They are sorting through their own problems and can't handle anything else

♦ They self-listen: when you say something about yourself they talk about themselves, instead of staying with you

Even the best parents fail to listen sometimes. You can train parents to listen better by saying:

♦ I don't feel heard by you

♦ Can I just repeat myself?

♦ Could you just tell me what you thought I said because I'm not sure that I said it very clearly?

♦ Here's what I thought you said. Is that what you meant?

♦ Can we take turns at talking please?

♦ Please can we have a deal that no one interrupts while the other is speaking?

♦ It's hard to talk with you if I don't feel listened to

♦ Can we do a deal?

♦ Why did you say that just then?

♦ I'd really like you to say something nice about me (or 'Can I have a compliment please?')

- Mum, Dad I need you to not give orders or boss me. Can I have good reasons?

- Thanks for your advice. Do I have a choice?

- I love you, especially when you listen to how I am feeling

As you can see it's a two-way process. Don't expect to be heard if you aren't listening. A test is to check out with the other person as to what you think they said to you. 'Can I just check with you about what you think I said?'

They can then correct it if you have got it wrong. That doesn't mean that you have to agree with it. If the other person knows that they got through to you that's often enough.

Try to understand how the other person feels. Say things like: 'You must feel disappointed, sad, happy, scared or angry.'

Listening will give you true friends, make you popular, be successful at work and get you things at home.

T.R.U.S.T is the essential ingredient. Some key tips are:

1. **T**iming

   Choose the best moment and the best way to talk to people.

2. **R**espect

   Show human respect and equality to people remembering that they feel bad and vulnerable too.

3. **U**nderstanding

   Show concern and empathy. What must it be like to be in their shoes?

4. **S**incerity

   Have integrity and honesty and mean what you say.

5. **T**one

   The tone of your voice and the feeling of what you say often say more than the words.

Basic communication – the four-part phrase

- 1. I feel...
- 2. When...
- 3. Because...
- 4. I would like/prefer/want/need

1. 'I feel...' State your feelings.

   - Begin with your vulnerable feelings: sad, hurt, left out, unimportant.

   - Then, if you're not being heard, say your angry feelings: irritated, annoyed, upset, angry, mad.

2. 'When...' State the situation.

   - Leave out the 'you' word.

   - Be clear and specific.

3. 'Because...' State the reason.

   - Most people respond to reasons. If they don't, then don't give one.

   - How you feel should be enough for them to take notice.

4. 'I would like...' How would you like things to be?

   - Be specific.

   - This is your strategy for fixing things so this doesn't occur again.

   - It's vitally important so that it doesn't happen again.

Remember: You don't always get what you want. This is because others have choices too. However, it's more important that you've declared who you are by saying what you want! People respect those who speak up.

Key concept

- Speaking up solves problems.

What helps me to communicate?

- [ ] Courage (to express my feelings)
- [ ] Making myself able to be heard
- [ ] Active listening
- [ ] Confidence
- [ ] Feeling understood
- [ ] Enjoyment
- [ ] Understanding the other person's needs
- [ ] Speaking clearly
- [ ] Belief in myself
- [ ] Not having to like everyone
- [ ] Money and financial well-being
- [ ] Less stress
- [ ] Relaxing surroundings
- [ ] Openness
- [ ] Being non-judgemental
- [ ] Freedom from distraction/interruption
- [ ] Belief that you aren't perfect
- [ ] Accepting everyone contributes
- [ ] Honesty
- [ ] Being clear about what I want to say
- [ ] TV/radio OFF
- [ ] Knowing what I'm talking about
- [ ] Time
- [ ] Asking permission to talk
- [ ] Making time
- [ ] Appreciating the speaker's perspective
- [ ] Knowing I can trust someone not to tell others
- [ ] Choosing the best time
- [ ] Love (of others)
- [ ] Warm feelings
- [ ] Respect for others
- [ ] Empathy
- [ ] Trust
- [ ] Staying focused
- [ ] Faith
- [ ] Common ground/purpose/goal
- [ ] Interest in the topic
- [ ] Treating others as I want to be treated
- [ ] Freedom
- [ ] No prejudice or racism
- [ ] No triggers
- [ ] No put-downs
- [ ] Sense of equality
- [ ] H.O.W. (Honestly, Openly, Willingly)
- [ ] Feeling needed
- [ ] Friendship
- [ ] Acceptance of myself
- [ ] Acknowledgement by others
- [ ] Good self-esteem
- [ ] Being heard
- [ ] Writing down issues
- [ ] Understanding others

- ❑ Letters instead of talking
- ❑ A desire to hear
- ❑ Clarity
- ❑ People liking me

Knowing or having all the above would be great. If you have half of them then you have plenty to relate well to people. Most people are still practising when they die. We just have to remember to do them until they become automatic.

Remember: STAY COOL – DON'T LOSE IT.

> ## Key concept
>
> ◆ We can develop skills that help us get on with others.

CHAPTER 19

Warrior Training

Being a 'warrior'

Being a 'warrior' when it's needed is very important; everyone needs to be a 'warrior' sometimes. Some people seem to be more naturally 'warriors' than others. Being a 'warrior' however doesn't mean just physical fighting. Effective 'warriors' have skills and training that go way beyond fighting. The best 'warriors' don't have to fight any more. They do all the work before it ever gets to the physical combat. Our movies glorify the 'warrior' who kills the baddies. Te Whiti, the great Maori chief and non-violent 'warrior', and most martial artist masters, would say that the most powerful fighting is beyond guns and happens in people's hearts. How to create the struggle in people's hearts is the secret.

We need to be sure that if we are going to go into conflict it is for the good of more than just ourselves and that it isn't coming from spite and hate. Our job is to bring things back to the good because they have gone astray. The next three pages contain some thoughts on what 'warriors' are and how they should behave. Read them and think of one conflict that you need to have in your life or community. How could you use the following to guide you?

Warriors

'Warriors' aren't scared of saying how they feel, including saying that they are scared.

Instead of fighting back or fighting against something 'warriors' fight for something.

'Warriors' know how to touch the conscience of other people.

'Warriors' aren't afraid of saying they are wrong when they are wrong and saying it without shame.

- ◆ Believe life is beautiful and worth defending
- ◆ Believe in fairness and justice
- ◆ Are smart – they think
- ◆ Are pro-active not reactive
- ◆ Fight for good
- ◆ Talk while they are in conflict
- ◆ Know what they want
- ◆ Can dance and have fun
- ◆ Are happy people
- ◆ Don't seek revenge
- ◆ Are tough and strong in their minds
- ◆ Get out of the way of out-of-control people

- ◆ Can laugh at themselves
- ◆ Don't let people push them around
- ◆ Don't steal or lie
- ◆ Have clear heads
- ◆ Struggle without giving up
- ◆ Work for the good of all
- ◆ Tell it how it is
- ◆ Bring hope to others and the world
- ◆ Don't get bought or bribed
- ◆ Protect their head, they need it for thinking
- ◆ Protect their heart, they need it for courage

- Aren't afraid to speak boldly of things that people don't want to hear, but need to

- Fight for principles not rules

- Are never out of control

- Are dignified and respect the dignity of others

- Are more careful with damaged people

- Are teachers

- Are highly trained in their use of their 'weapons', tools and techniques

- Never lash out

- Go into conflict from love not anger

- Train their minds and hearts before their bodies

- Know that bad action will come back on them

- Gets wounded sometimes, emotionally or physically; they let it heal quickly; don't fight from the wound

- Know fear is the enemy; selfishness is the other enemy; a bold conscience defeats them both

- Can finish with something when it needs to be let go of

- Are true to their word

- Think ahead so they are never taken by surprise

- Know there is always an alternative approach to conflict that you haven't thought of

- Are strong on talking – SWORD is spelt WORDS

- Know enemies are potential friends

- Practise for conflict or their cause may die

- Have a plan

- Can think four moves ahead

- Know when you engage in conflict with a person you find out who they are

- Don't stop battling until someone respects their viewpoint

- Always give their opponent a chance to change

- Know the only place you can lose is in your heart

- Believe mean is obscene

- Know love is the reason for and must be the result of the fight

- Get out of the way of big opponents – go round the side and push big opponents off balance

- Understand opponents can reconsider better when they are sitting down; if they haven't sat down to think, then help them

- Know: a 'warrior' who runs away instead of failing, can come back tomorrow to succeed

- Never meet the opponent head on – they may break their head and yours

- Always celebrate their victories – invite their former opponent to the celebration

- Know if the opponent doesn't want to come then they haven't succeeded yet

- Let an opponent who wants to go home do so freely

The following pages are lessons on being a 'warrior'. Try them out.

Think of people you can respect that use them in their 'warriorship'. Usually they respect others and themselves so much that they need to act rather than just accept a bad situation!

'Warrior' training lesson 1
Shields

Shields, protective clothing and other ways of protecting ourselves are ways of keeping us safe when we are under attack. We all need a shield to protect us when someone is being unpleasant or trying to control us without touching us.

WISE NOT WILD

BE COOL NOT CRUEL

Verbal

Put-downs

Name-calling/lies

Threats

Blaming

Bringing up old stuff

Labelling

Swearing at you

Shaming you

Subtle threats

Sarcasm

Accusing

Disrespect

Insults to self, family, gender, sexuality, race, age

Vibing

Angry looks

Heavy expression

Depressed

Black cloud vibes

Not joining in

Bad body signs

Angry body language

Turned back

No eye contact

Noises

Ignoring you

Treating you as unimportant

When someone attacks you or sends unfriendly signals or vibes it's easy for us to attack back as self-defence. Most of the time the other person wants you to attack back to get power over you. Don't. You can use a shield to protect you so that these things don't hurt or affect you.

Imagine them hitting the shield and falling on the floor leaving you untouched. Stay calm and watch the other person, knowing that you are calm and safe.

♦ Don't attack back.

♦ People who attack back are on 'automatic loser' response.

♦ You don't have to do anything if you're attacked verbally.

♦ If you're attacked physically – get out.

♦ Their problem is their problem not yours.

♦ You can watch things better from behind a shield.

♦ Shields give strength.

My personal shield

Design in your head, or draw on this page, a shield to protect yourself. It is your personal shield. It could be ancient, medieval, high-tech, force-field, magical, super-human.

Some clues for people who have a habit of attacking back:

- Do not put weapons on it

- Do not put abusive or attacking words on it

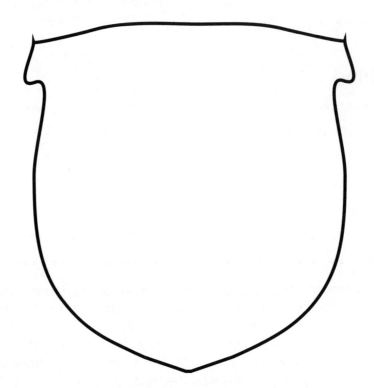

Remember:

- It is always with you

- It is your personal defence system

- You can use it whenever you want

- Do not forget to use it

Key concepts

- Knowing our triggers allows us more choice.

- We can protect ourselves from people who want to have power over us.

'Warrior' training lesson 2
Swords

The sword stands for your will to stand for good in conflict
What is written on your sword?

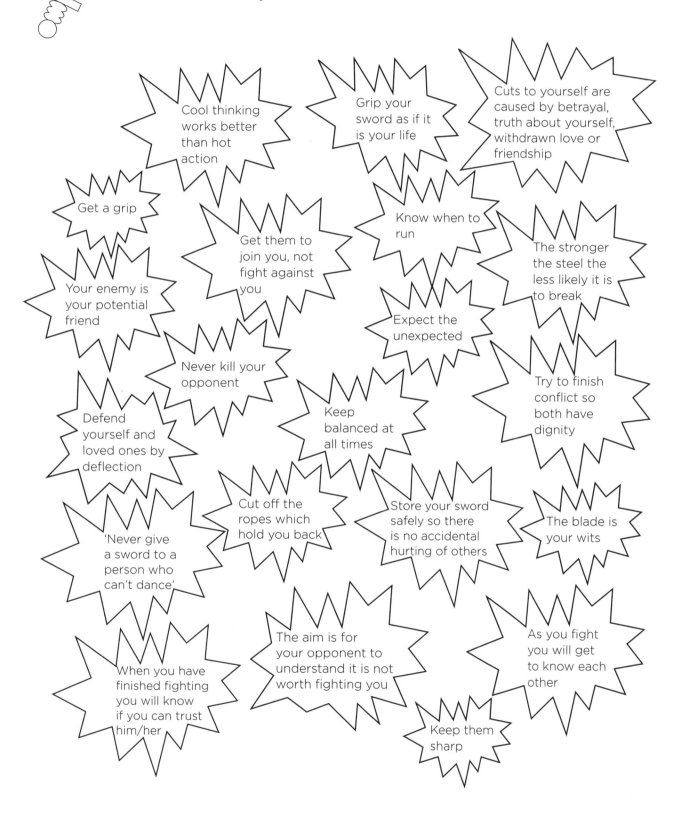

Cool thinking works better than hot action

Grip your sword as if it is your life

Cuts to yourself are caused by betrayal, truth about yourself, withdrawn love or friendship

Get a grip

Get them to join you, not fight against you

Know when to run

The stronger the steel the less likely it is to break

Your enemy is your potential friend

Expect the unexpected

Never kill your opponent

Try to finish conflict so both have dignity

Defend yourself and loved ones by deflection

Keep balanced at all times

'Never give a sword to a person who can't dance'

Cut off the ropes which hold you back

Store your sword safely so there is no accidental hurting of others

The blade is your wits

When you have finished fighting you will know if you can trust him/her

The aim is for your opponent to understand it is not worth fighting you

As you fight you will get to know each other

Keep them sharp

'Warrior' training lesson 3
Bows

The arrow stands for making your point.
The bow stands for your strength.

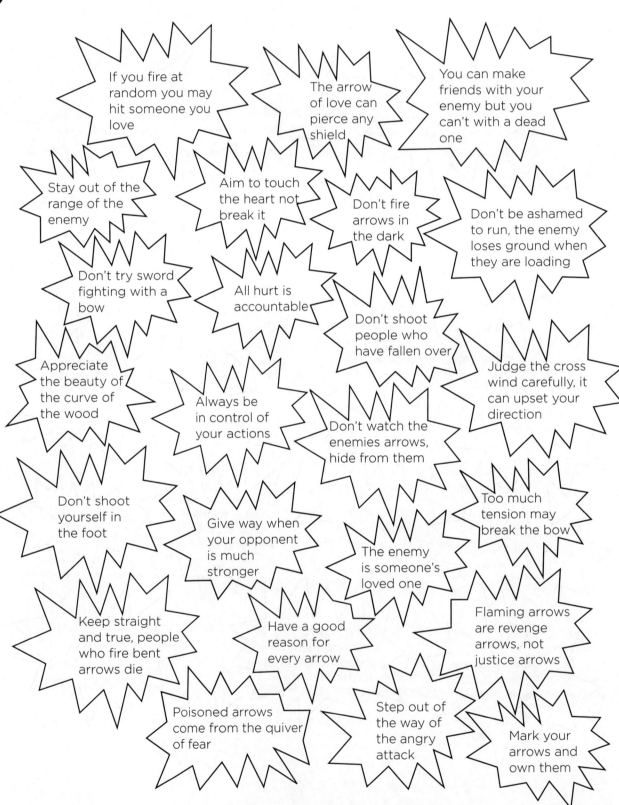

If you fire at random you may hit someone you love

The arrow of love can pierce any shield

You can make friends with your enemy but you can't with a dead one

Stay out of the range of the enemy

Aim to touch the heart not break it

Don't fire arrows in the dark

Don't be ashamed to run, the enemy loses ground when they are loading

Don't try sword fighting with a bow

All hurt is accountable

Don't shoot people who have fallen over

Appreciate the beauty of the curve of the wood

Always be in control of your actions

Don't watch the enemies arrows, hide from them

Judge the cross wind carefully, it can upset your direction

Don't shoot yourself in the foot

Give way when your opponent is much stronger

The enemy is someone's loved one

Too much tension may break the bow

Keep straight and true, people who fire bent arrows die

Have a good reason for every arrow

Flaming arrows are revenge arrows, not justice arrows

Poisoned arrows come from the quiver of fear

Step out of the way of the angry attack

Mark your arrows and own them

'Warrior' training lesson 4
The korowai training

Korowai: The cloak of protection

Korowai is the traditional cloak of the Maori people of New Zealand worn both for protection and to declare the *mana* or status of the person wearing it. The power of the korowai lies within the people who have worn it before, the ancestors' use, the patterns in the wearing and the thoughts of the person wearing it.

The power of the korowai wrapped around the person allows them to be protected from evil and bad intentions of others.

We suggest that you have a personal korowai to put on in your mind immediately someone attacks you. Some ways people may attack you are:

Verbal

Put-downs	Curses
Disrespect	Swearing at you
Name-calling	Blaming
Sarcasm	Suggestive comments
Lies	Bringing up the past
Threats	Insults to family, self, sexuality, age, gender, race
Shaming you	

Spiritual/emotional

Angry looks	Not joining in
Turned back	Not sharing
Heavy expression	Disappearing
No eye contact	Bad body signs
Depression	Angry body language
Noises	Heavy silence
Black cloud vibes	Treating you as unimportant
Ignoring	

When someone attacks you or sends unfriendly signals or vibes it's easy to attack back as self-defence. Most of the time the other person *wants* you to attack back to get power over you.

Resist attacking back.

You can wrap your korowai around you to protect you so that these things don't hurt or affect you. Imagine them missing you or dropping to the floor leaving you untouched. Stay calm and watch the other person knowing that you are calm and safe.

It says the person inside is powerful without hitting back.
People who attack back forget their dignity and strength.
You can watch things better from within your korowai.
You don't have to do anything if you're attacked verbally.
You may do something later.

Remember:

- It's always with you

- It strengthens you

- It never hits back

- You can use it wherever you want

- Hurting others damages the *mana* of the korowai

- Don't attack back – rest in your *mana*

- Don't forget to use it

- Korowai gives strength

- Korowai gives peace

- Be wise not wild

- If you're attacked physically – get out

- Their anger is their problem

✓

Design in your head or draw your korowai of protection

It is your personal protection.

It could have special patterns, feathers, colours, weaving that you want to strengthen and protect you.

It will have the *mana* of your family or people.

Name the people you respect who know how to wear a korowai like this.

Name where you get your strength from:

Where I get my strength from		People who know how to wear this korowai
. . . .		. . . .
. . . .		. . . .
. . . .		. . . .
. . . .		. . . .
What does it protect me from?		Who wore it before me?
. . . .		. . . .
. . . .		. . . .
. . . .		. . . .
. . . .		. . . .

Key concept

♦ We can protect ourselves from the anger of others.

CHAPTER 20

Self-Abuse and Other Abuse

What is abuse? What can you do about it?

Abuse can be physical, verbal, sexual, mental or to property, or people can use their power over others to manipulate them. All violence is abuse and is wrong.

For all abuse you should be able to go to your teacher or counsellor at school. If you are physically or sexually assaulted you can report this to the police. Other forms of abuse like verbal and psychological abuse are more subtle and less obvious but in the long term just as damaging. You can't report these to the police but if they persist then child and adolescent welfare agencies can be involved.

Verbal abuse can include put-downs, sarcasm, prejudiced remarks, criticism and swearing. Verbal abuse is usually an attempt to control you by making you feel inferior. It is not OK. In school or the work place there should be a complaints procedure in place. If you can deal with it yourself this is likely to be more effective because you will have reclaimed your power and the abuser will know it.

You could try practising how you will respond next time in front of a mirror or pretending with a good friend.

Read the section on bullying in Chapter 17 and remember:

- Check your body language (stand tall, head up, shoulders back)

- Use eye contact

- Use a low firm voice

- Make an 'I' statement

- Give consequences – tell them what you will do if they speak to you like that again

- Make sure that you carry out the consequences if nothing changes

If someone is abusing you speak to the abuser so that others can hear you if that is possible. You are not to blame. The shame and blame belongs to the abuser not to you.

Example: the right to be assertive

Sarah recalls being groped by a man on a bus. 'It took a lot of guts,' she said but she stood up, looked at him and said loudly, 'Get your filthy hands off me.' Everybody on the bus turned to look at him and he got off at the next stop looking really embarrassed.

Sexual abuse can be very complicated. It can affect the abused person in so many ways. Self-esteem can be affected, often severely. People can develop confused ideas about their sexuality and may find that they dislike their own body. The abuser will want the victim to take the blame for the abuse, consequently the victim will begin to blame him/herself:

'I should have stopped him/her.'

'Perhaps if I had not worn that skirt/been walking alone, it wouldn't have happened.'

The truth is that if someone uses their power over you to perform a sexual act on you (genital touching, oral sex, digital or penile penetration) without your consent then they are the perpetrator and they are at fault. They have committed a crime. If you are a child or young adolescent under 16 they have committed a crime whether the act was with or without your consent.

People can have power over us in many ways. They may be older or have a position of authority or care (boss, school teacher, parent, friend of parents, an older sibling or relative or a professional person you have consulted).

If you have become a victim of sexual abuse the perpetrator is to blame, not you.

Sexual abuse affects many aspects of the abused person's life as well as causing self-blame and low self-esteem. The abused person may have nightmares, feel anxious, depressed or exceptionally angry, have difficulty concentrating, have problems with eating and may generally feel out of control with their life. Sexually abused people often feel angry at the world and sensitive around sexual matters. Don't take your anger out on other people. If you don't feel angry then you are entitled to feel very angry during the counselling process.

If you are reading this and you have been sexually abused you can get help.

In some countries the government helps to fund counselling with an approved counsellor or therapist. Thousands of sexual abuse survivors have worked their way through their distress to lead happier, productive lives.

So where do you start? You might find it easier to get the support of a trusted friend or relative. If you don't get the help you need, go to someone else. Some people may feel uncomfortable hearing about another's sexual abuse particularly if they have been abused themselves. Parents are sometimes not the best people to talk to as they have their own shock, fears and issues to deal with. They may even ignore or tell you to forget the incident because of huge consequences for themselves.

You could try talking to a doctor, a school counsellor or a social worker. It does not have to be your own GP. You will them be referred to the correct help. Professionals are bound to confidentiality and could lose their jobs if they break confidence but they are also bound to help abuse to be stopped.

It might take some time to feel comfortable talking openly to your counsellor but if your counsellor does not feel right for you then it is OK to go to someone else.

When you choose a counsellor you have a right to ask:

- How much will my sessions cost?

- Who will pay for my sessions (if you are still at school)?

- What is your training in sexual abuse counselling?

- Do you have regular supervision?

- What professional organisation do you belong to?

What can you do to protect yourself as much as possible?

Drugs and alcohol are often taken to take away pain or release inhibitions created by abuse. Try to stay aware of why you might be taking them. Ask yourself:

- Will there be any harm to me?

- Am I doing this to fit in?

- How will I feel tomorrow?

Also ask yourself if you might need to talk to someone, even a good friend, instead of taking yourself into states that are damaging in the short or long term.

Taking alcohol and drugs leaves anyone vulnerable to abuse. We are all less aware of what is happening around us. We miss danger signals and we lack the physical strength to escape. Your judgement may be impaired and you may make decisions that you would not make if you were sober. Don't let people 'spike' your drink.

Example: self-protection

Tegan says that she always drinks from cans when she is out so that she can keep her thumb over the hole in the can. 'I never drink again from a drink I have left unattended.'

Key concepts

- It's never OK to abuse others or yourself.

- Abuse may leave the victim feeling vulnerable and angry.

- People who abuse others and people who are abused can be male or female, rich or poor, educated or uneducated, old or young.

- Most people have good intentions and care about others.

Preventing abuse of myself and others

There are many types of abuse – physical, verbal, property, sexual, spiritual and also abuse you do to yourself. None of them are OK because they all hurt someone and take away their personal rights. It's not OK to ever hurt yourself because we're all connected and affect each other.

Anger

One of the problems is that anger gets confused with abuse. Anger is not the problem. Anger is an emotion that is normal and healthy. If you don't feel it from time to time then you are likely to get abused. Anger is OK. Anger protects, motivates and energises us. Express it safely.

Abuse

Abuse is behaviour. It is something that we do. It is never OK. We were not born abusive so it is something that we have learnt. We can unlearn it. The most important thing to remember is:
We have a choice about our behaviour. That means that we are responsible for everything that we do.

Past abuse

If we have been abused ourselves, especially when we were little, then it is as if we have a recording or programme that makes us more likely to choose to abuse others. We need to be extra conscious of making a decision to not give that same abuse out to others. We can help ourselves by healing abuse from the past. Sometimes it's as simple as telling the person who hurt us that that's what they did and that you are angry and hurt about it. Other times it's much deeper and may need skilled help and years of talking to feel repaired. Things that influence the damage of past abuse are how much love and hugging we got when we were small children, whether we had a safe place to take our hurts to, how much we had to stuff the pain down and how long we had to stuff it down for.

However even considering these things there is never an excuse for abusing others or even ourselves.

We always have a choice.

Self-abuse

Sometimes an abused child or person turns the abuse inside rather than dumping it outside or getting help and healing. This may show in ways such as or unhealthy risk-taking or being careless about safety in such things as sport, nature, sex, driving.

Harming ourselves can also be in the forms of overeating, under-eating, unhealthy foods, self-cutting, self-hitting, poor tattooing, burning, dirty dressing, brawls, accidents, smoking, sabotaging relationships, education, jobs or chances. The ultimate self-abuse is suicide.

The use of alcohol or drugs is a way that many people cover up pain and feeling bad. But after it wears off you still have the problem or the feeling, plus you may also have a hangover or depression. The best way is to front up to the problem, do some hard things and make some choices that will create a change in your life. It's hard, however, if adults hold a lot of power and control. This is why support from peers or supportive adults can often get us through. Sharing, caring and trust are skills and qualities that are ultimately what life's made of. Don't self-abuse. You are worth more and there is someone out there you may not have even met yet who thinks so too. You are worthwhile.

People who feel bad about themselves may try to make others feel bad about themselves in order to feel better. People who feel good about themselves often help others feel good about themselves.

People who hurt others often hurt themselves as well.

Key concepts

- ♦ Abuse can be physical, verbal, sexual, spiritual to self and to property.

- ♦ Abuse is a behaviour and is never OK.

- ♦ Anger is a feeling and is OK.

- ♦ Having good self-esteem helps us handle anger.

The monster within

Old hurt, pain, fear and anger can become like a monster within, slowly eating us from the inside. Our monster also sneaks out to hurt others around us. Kick the monster out. Don't let it eat you and run your life.
Cross out the things you want to get rid of because they damage your life.

Key concepts

• People who hurt others often feel bad about themselves.

• You get back what you give out.

The internal success coach

Fill hurt, angry and empty spaces with useful things to help you.
Tick the things you want because they make you lucky and likeable.

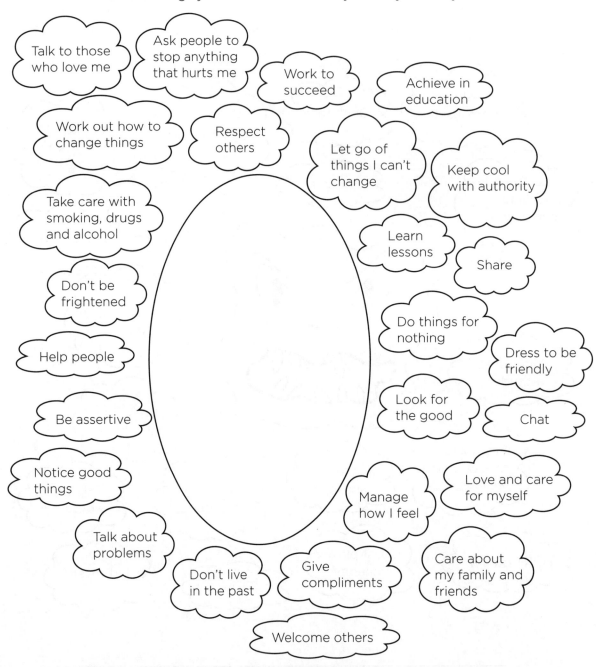

Lying and stealing

People often steal or lie about things because they feel powerlessness. It's never an excuse, but it can help us to understand why.

Fill in the two boxes below then draw lines to the reasons in the Black Hole.

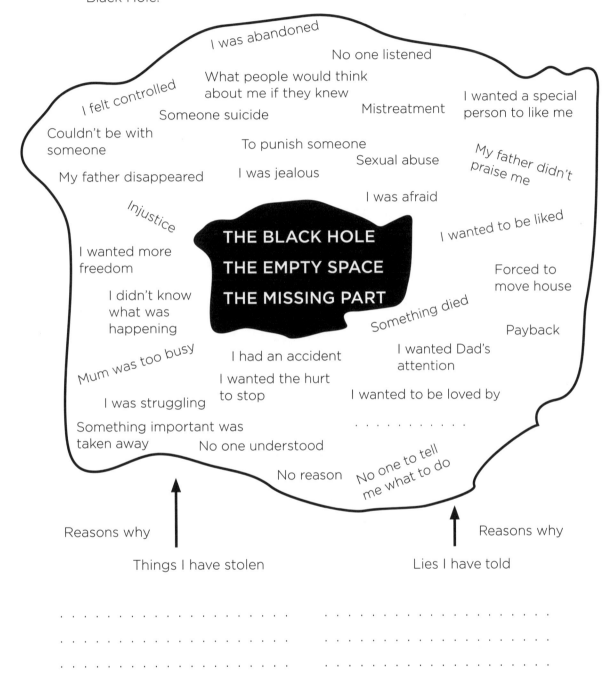

I was abandoned

No one listened

What people would think about me if they knew

I felt controlled

I wanted a special person to like me

Someone suicide

Mistreatment

Couldn't be with someone

To punish someone

My father didn't praise me

Sexual abuse

My father disappeared

I was jealous

I was afraid

Injustice

**THE BLACK HOLE
THE EMPTY SPACE
THE MISSING PART**

I wanted to be liked

I wanted more freedom

Forced to move house

I didn't know what was happening

Something died

Payback

Mum was too busy

I had an accident

I wanted Dad's attention

I was struggling

I wanted the hurt to stop

I wanted to be loved by

Something important was taken away

. . . .

No one understood

No reason

No one to tell me what to do

Reasons why

Reasons why

Things I have stolen

Lies I have told

. . . .

. . . .

. . . .

Key concepts

♦ There's always a reason for wanting to hurt others. Find it!

♦ Abuse is never OK.

Letting go of the guilt

Here are some possible examples of lying and stealing, with possible reasons:

Stealing small things from class mates:

- I didn't have what they had and had no way of getting it

- My parents were fighting a lot at the time and didn't take time for me

Stealing from my parents:

- They didn't listen and I wanted their concern for me

- I was being controlled like a kid

Stealing from my mate:

- Payback for hurting me

Lying to my parents:

- Afraid they wouldn't love me if I told the truth

Lying to my friends:

- Wanted them to like me

Lying to the teacher:

- Afraid of punishment

- Payback for controlling me

All of the above are never excuses for lying or stealing.

Get rid of the black hole.
It can suck you from the inside.
It causes depression and hopelessness.

Talk about your black hole.
Talk. Talk.
Talk about the guilt and the shame.
Fill the black hole with hope and honesty.

Think about your lies or stealing and fill in:

1. What I did: . . . .

. . . .

. . . .

. . . .

Reasons why I did it:. . . . .

. . . .

. . . .

Other things I could do instead:

   a.

   b.

   c.

2. What I did: . . . .

. . . .

. . . .

. . . .

Reasons why I did it:. . . . .

. . . .

. . . .

Other things I could do instead:

   a.

   b.

   c.

Key concepts

♦ There are reasons why we choose to hurt others. Find the reason.

♦ Reasons aren't excuses for abuse.

♦ Understanding reasons helps us plan new choices.

Tagging

Tagging is spraying a name, slogan or a comic picture on a wall where it can be noticed. Tagging is:

- A voice saying 'Notice me please'
- A way of saying I am important I exist
- Territory
- Art
- Abuse of others' property
- A silent inner voice daring to speak

If you had an inner voice waiting to be heard, what would you write? Tag this piece of paper with felt pens with your truth.

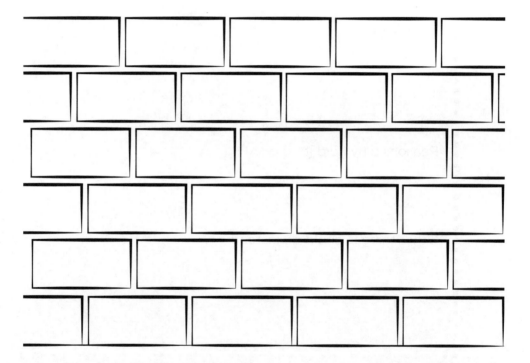

Write a letter to your local council asking for a place to tag legally. We need to say what we are hurt and angry about.

Key concept

- Damage to property is abuse.

Smoke screen – smoking

Have you ever smoked cigarettes or other drugs, or do you smoke now?
Where there is smoke there is fire.
Talk to someone about your fire.

Smoking is often a smoke screen or cover for anger, rage, hurt, loss or feeling worthless. If you are a smoker or if you did smoke, what would you be covering? Write or draw the anger, rage, hurt, loss or uselessness. They can be seen through your smoke.

Self put-down

Fear

Hurt and mistrust

Stress and pressure

Resentment and payback

Abuse

Things I hide from people

. . . .

. . . .

. . . .

Worthless and useless

Anger at...

. . . .

. . . .

. . . .

. . . .

. . . .

. . . .

Key concepts

- We often cover or hide our anger.
- Repressed anger always sneaks out.

Why children, adolescents and young adults drink alcohol

- ❑ To relax
- ❑ Socially acceptable
- ❑ Experiment
- ❑ To look good
- ❑ Avoid problems
- ❑ Belong to group
- ❑ Advertising
- ❑ Reduce stress
- ❑ Have fun
- ❑ Forget
- ❑ People might not like you
- ❑ Take away bad feelings
- ❑ Meet people
- ❑ Peer pressure
- ❑ Get to sleep
- ❑ Numb out
- ❑ Get confidence
- ❑ Hate themselves
- ❑ Get drunk
- ❑ Not responsible
- ❑ Male bonding
- ❑ Female togetherness
- ❑ Companionship
- ❑ Get happy

- ❑ Proof of manhood/adulthood
- ❑ Not got courage to say 'No'
- ❑ Inexperience
- ❑ Get courage to do something
- ❑ Escape
- ❑ Tension
- ❑ Stupidity
- ❑ Boredom
- ❑ Habit
- ❑ Lose inhibitions
- ❑ Companionship
- ❑ Loneliness
- ❑ Cover low self-esteem
- ❑ Reality too difficult
- ❑ Take away sadness
- ❑ Take away pain
- ❑ Keep up with mates/friends
- ❑ Excuse for stupid behaviour
- ❑ Quench thirst
- ❑ Who cares?
- ❑ To fight
- ❑ Because you're told not to
- ❑ Meet boys/girls

Why do you drink or want to drink?

. . . .

. . . .

Why don't you drink or want to drink?

. . . .

. . . .

If you had a wise friend (not parents or friends you're hanging out with), what would they say?

. . . .

. . . .

If you drink, how often is OK?

. . . .

. . . .

When is it OK?

. . . .

. . . .

How much is OK?

. . . .

. . . .

> **Key concept**
>
> ♦ Alcohol and abuse often go together.

The effects of alcohol

Some effects on the person who is drinking:

- Removes inhibitions
- Takes the pain away
- Happy
- Overcome fear
- Loose behaviour
- Thirst quencher
- Relaxation
- Get laid
- Horny
- Stories to tell with friends
- Mellows
- Flirt
- Say brave things
- Friends think you're cool
- Bravado
- Giggle and laugh
- Releases hostility
- Trouble with parents
- Late home
- Kills brain cells
- Disorientating
- Numbness
- Cirrhosis of the liver
- Fines
- Visit the panel beater's
- Lawyers
- Addiction
- Talk rubbish
- Isolation
- Dry horrors
- Confused
- Loss of appetite
- DTs
- Blackouts
- Vomit
- Anger
- Smell bad
- Self pity
- Euphoric
- Sad
- Headache
- Large liver
- Gastric bleeding
- Small balls
- Hostile
- Guilt
- Memory loss
- Paranoid
- Trouble with police
- Childish behaviour
- Talkative
- Bloodshot eyes
- Intensifies emotions
- Denial
- Loss of judgement
- Split personality
- Abuse
- Debilitating

- Irrational thoughts
- The runs
- Divorce
- False expectations
- Impotent
- Offending
- Urinate more
- Stomach ulcers
- Death
- Depravity
- Violence
- Changeable moods
- Bad farts
- Selfish
- Lose job
- Aggressive
- Crying
- Feel foolish
- Loss of driver's licence
- Moody
- Forgetful
- Have car crash
- Deformities
- Muscle decay
- Feel guilty
- Forget to watch yourself
- Blood pressure
- Unpredictable
- Smash things
- Decreases coordination
- Say dumb things
- Tired
- Forget condom
- Forget you even had sex
- Hurt from accident
- Cuts from fighting
- Depresses
- Homeless
- Hallucinations

**Some of these are good and some of these are not
so good. Weigh them up. Is it worth it?**

Alcohol depresses the central nervous system. The immediate effects could be:

- Relaxation, feeling of happiness and well-being
- Depression
- Decreased co-ordination
- Users often experience emotional responses out of keeping with actual situations
- Large doses cause blackouts and a hangover

The long-term effects are:

- Continued heavy use results in brain and other nervous system damage, heart, pancreas, stomach and liver damage and in extreme cases, death. Serious family, social and work problems are common

Coping with loss and hurt

Gina's parents split up when Gina was 13. She feels angry that her world was turned upside down. She lost her familiar family home, friends who lived close by and the security of coming home to the people she knew and felt comfortable with. She had to split her weekends with parents and there was less money for everyone.

Sam's best friend, Leo, killed himself last year. Sam finds he cannot stop thinking about his friend's death. He is angry that Leo did not get help and he is grieving at the loss of a friend who had been part of his life for eight years. Sometimes Sam finds himself going over and over the time before Leo's suicide asking himself, 'Could I have stopped him?' or saying, 'If I had gone to see him earlier that day, I could have saved him.'

Terri went to a small country school before her family moved to the city when she started high school. Terri misses her friends at her old school. This new school seems so big to her. She longs to be back in a place where everyone knew her and she felt safe. She often feels sad when she thinks of her old life and sometimes she is angry with Mum and Dad for moving to the city.

David is 14. He has just started high school. In the past few months he has been growing so fast that now he is taller than anyone in his class. His family makes jokes about the space he takes up in the house and his Mum complains that he is always hungry. David feels embarrassed at being different. Sometimes he longs to go back to the body he had a few months ago. He gets angry when people make comments about his height.

Soni is new to the country. She misses her own village, island and culture. She encounters racism at high school and gets called names.

All these people have experienced major changes in their lives. When a change like this occurs we experience loss and we grieve for what is now missing from our lives.

Grief and loss can send us on a roller-coaster ride of feelings that are often stronger than we have felt before.

At first we might numb ourselves against a serious loss and wander around in a daze. We might find ourselves saying, 'I don't believe it'. Then we might find ourselves feeling angry, perhaps angrier than we have ever felt before. We might feel sad and be tearful, or fighting back the tears might give us headaches. Guilt is part of grief as it was for Sam who kept telling himself, 'If only I had...' Our whole selves are affected by grief. Don't be surprised if you have trouble sleeping or have digestive problems.

You might find that you are thinking that the lost person or place is the only one in the world and can't be replaced ever. This is a part of grieving too. It is called idealising. One day you will find that, although you still feel sad when you think of the lost one, this does not happen nearly as often.

The nightmares are less frequent and the sadness and anger are less. Your grief is healing.

However, a major loss can affect us for months or even years.

So what can you do to help yourself to cope?

- Find someone you can trust to talk to about your feelings and problems.

- Find positive ways of expressing your feelings of sadness and anger. Let yourself cry. Walk out your anger. Write poems or letters (unsent) to the people you believe have caused the loss. Use a punching bag or play squash.

- Do something to give out to others who have experienced a similar loss.

> Sandy's sister died in a car accident caused by a drunken driver. Sandy decided to join Students Against Drunk Driving. She felt she was doing something in memory of her sister and she also met others who had experienced loss in similar circumstances who understood her feelings.

Remember that grieving is not a sign of weakness. Grief often gets blocked by anger especially in boys. An angry young man is often a sad and hurt young man.

It takes courage to show others your feelings and your vulnerability. Get clean not mean.

- Ask a school counsellor at your school to start a grief group that meets perhaps once a month so that people can share their experiences and not feel so alone.

- Ask your school counsellor to ask someone to come and speak at a school assembly about grief. Understanding grief helps us to cope.

It might help if you have a special place to go and grieve for someone who has died: a special tree, garden, or seat. You may ask a friend to come with you. Afterwards make sure you do something to take care of yourself such as phoning a friend, listening to a piece of music. Having a shower or bath and a change of clothes might also help.

People who care about you might think they are helping by telling you to get over it, pull yourself together or put it behind you.

We don't get over a loss. We get through it. And we do that best with the help and support of people who will listen and care.

Change and grief

Change involves letting go of one thing and taking on another. The process of change involves grief. So how do you deal with grief? Ignore it? Let it out through being angry, grumpy or always irritated? Get depressed, isolate yourself or drink? Or have a cry?

Make a list of the changes that have happened in your life in the past year. These could be changes to your family, your body, your school life, your friends or the things you own. They may involve a death.

What have you lost?

Have you gained anything through these losses?

How have you been feeling?

Change (situation)	Loss	Feelings	Gain

What you need to know about marijuana

What is marijuana?

Its botanical name is Cannabis Sativa. It's also called weed, grass, dope, green, a bud, a joint, a toke, etc.

The plant contains 419 chemicals and intoxicates its users, primarily because of the mind-altering ingredient called Delta-9-Tertrahydrocannabinol (THC).

Why do people use marijuana?

Many use it out of curiosity. They simply want to try the 'high' or the 'stone'.

Others use it because of peer pressure, a desire for excitement, a search for identity, to reduce stress, anxiety and boredom, to feel good in a social situation. Often it is used to avoid both physical and emotional pain.

How much is heavy use?

Heavy users smoke once a day or several times a week.

Can marijuana cause mental or psychological problems?

Like many drugs it brings to the surface emotional problems. People often use marijuana to treat depression, however this often worsens the problem. It's sometimes used medicinally to relieve pain.

Effects of marijuana on the body

It depresses the central nervous system.
The immediate effects are:

- Relaxation, laughter, increased appetite, slowing down of linear time, heightened sensory experience

- Dry mouth, dizziness, bloodshot eyes and decreased co-ordination

- A panic reaction in some users, with confusion and depression

- An increased heart rate by as much as 50 per cent and chest pain to those suffering from poor circulation

The long-term effects (unlikely if you smoke less than once a month) are:

- High tar intake of heavy users may cause respiratory complications. The active ingredient (THC) is stored in the body

- Confusion and depression can occur for some months after discontinuing use

- Heavy and continued use can cause personality problems, together with family, social and work difficulties and memory loss. In relationships it may seem as if the user is 'not there'

Marijuana has various effects on the nervous system. Although some of these effects are minor and will pass, they occur in users whether they are long-term users or not, for example, decreased psycho-motor performance (for instance driving). In most studies cannabis use has been reported to affect short-term memory, thinking and some types of learning. It is suspected that long-term heavy use can result in long-lasting changes to the brain, which makes itself known by memory loss.

CHAPTER 21

Expressing Anger

Transferring anger and authority

When we are small, adults seem to have all the power. They often don't handle their power well and make mistakes. Sometimes we carry anger and later transfer it to authority in other areas of our lives or we transfer it to the present time and our parents don't realise that it is anger from the past.

Anger towards adults from our childhood is often transferred to teachers, police, employers, leaders and any handy older person, even the ones trying to help us. This is transferring anger to authority figures. This stuffs up our lives. Angry young males get thrown out of school because they are angry at something from their childhood and are transferring it to the teachers. There may be trouble with the police, which is really anger at a father. A woman boss may get sworn at because of anger at a mother.

Example: transferring anger

Steve:

> 'I felt angry with everyone and was thrown out of one high school for fighting. Later I found out that it was the farmer who sexually abused me that I was really angry with and who I wanted to kill. I got help from an anger management group.'

The key is:

- Know who you are angry at

- Tell the person or someone about that old anger and get rid of it

- Treat each new person as good and friendly unless they show you that they don't want to be. If a person is being unpleasant there is a good chance that they are transferring their anger from someone else to you!

Some questions for thought

- Do you have anger at authority figures?

- Do you call authority figures names – parents, teachers, police?

- Do you have an attitude that prevents you from being happy at school?

- Who are you really angry with from your past?

- How can you get rid of that anger that you are carrying around?

Do you hold your anger in?

Do you turn your anger inwards? This will hurt you. Bottling or squashing anger inside will only mean it comes out in bits anyway. Don't hurt yourself. Express it.

Write your bottled anger in the spaces.

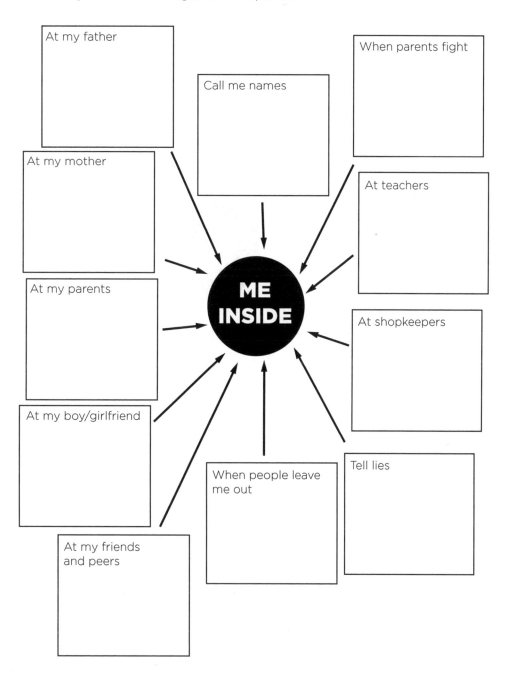

How do you express your anger outwardly?

Write the ways you express your anger outwardly in the spaces.

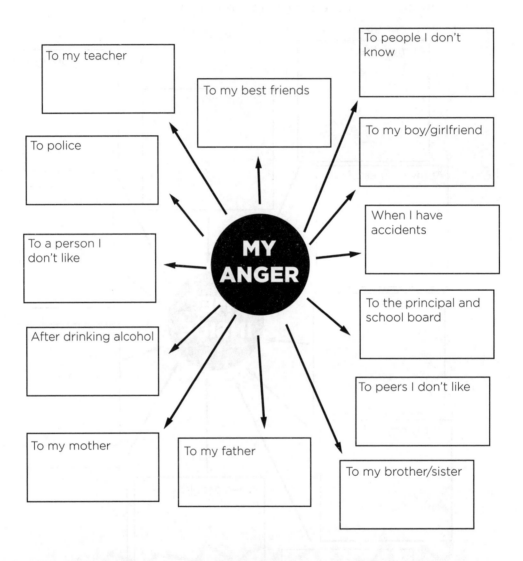

To my teacher

To my best friends

To people I don't know

To police

To my boy/girlfriend

To a person I don't like

When I have accidents

MY ANGER

To the principal and school board

After drinking alcohol

To peers I don't like

To my mother

To my father

To my brother/sister

Heavy metal rage

Draw a heavy metal poster or CD cover with one or more characters in it.

Sometimes persons, creatures, monsters or animals are just imaginary parts of our own real world. If the figures, symbols or words above were people we know or problems in our lives, what or who would they be? Write their names or situations on the blocks.

Express it in song

What sort of music do you like?
   Think of songs you remember.
   Write the titles and key lines that flash to your mind in the spaces.

What are the messages above saying about life, how you feel about males, females, sex, money, love? What do they say about anger? Is it safe?
   Is it good for everyone?

Key concept

- We need to express anger safely.

Movies

Write in the names of some movies you have seen in each circle.

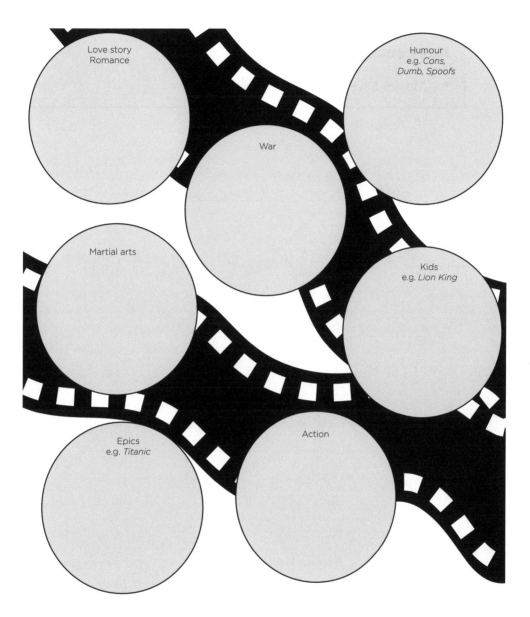

QUESTIONS

What do these movies tell us about hurt?

Who got hurt?

How did they handle it?

Who got angry?

What did they do?

How did they handle it?

Is it different for male and female?

Who is your best model?

Key concept

♦ Movies have powerful models for us.

CHAPTER 22

Making Life Better

Anger comes into play when we feel disempowered. The purpose of anger is to re-empower us, change what is bothering us, put things right or remove something that is unfair. It helps to know what we need to make life better. It creates the solution or the whole point of the anger kicking in, in the first place.

Talking to others, getting exercise, mapping our lives are all part of the 'making it better' process. Next comes the desired state, the dream, the goal or mission to be accomplished. A dream is needed. An intent for the future needs to be visible. Positive intention, self-talk and strengthened esteem lift us and carry us forward. Some things need to be let go of and new mantras and plans generated.

Visions that are strong inspire others and generate a wave of 'more than one person' in the world. Anger really is about improving life for self and others.

Expression of feelings

How do you feel today?

Do you feel the same way now as you did last night?
   Do you feel the same as you did yesterday?

Our moods and emotions change. Sometimes the change is rapid: sadness, anger, joy and excitement can roll over us within a very short space of time. We might be laughing uproariously and then find ourselves in tears. Feelings often come in waves. If something traumatic has happened to us a feeling of anger, hurt or sadness may seem to be stuck inside. At times like this we may believe that the feeling will last forever. It is important to know that you can seek help if you feel this way.
   What can we do to help ourselves if our feelings seem to be too powerful to cope with?
   Here are some ideas that may help:

* Keep a journal.

* Be kind to yourself as you would to a friend. Take some Time Out to do things you enjoy.

* Talk to yourself. No, this is not crazy talk! We all do it (in our heads of course, not out loud). Notice how you talk to yourself. Do you put yourself down? Do you call yourself stupid, or worse? Would you speak to a friend the way you speak to yourself in your head? Be encouraging and caring. Here are some encouraging statements to make to yourself. Can you think of some more?

  * You did that really well

  * You're improving

  * Wow, look at you

  * Hang in there

  * You can do it

  * You've coped with worse than this – you can do it

  * It's OK to be scared/ask for help/feel angry

* Find a positive way of soothing yourself: a favourite pendant to stroke, a charm, locket, bracelet, a smooth stone in your pocket, a photo of someone you love in your pocket, a soft toy to hold or a favourite cushion or pillow. This is not childish. Some of the greatest heroes of the past century carried a teddy bear with them. Even the toughest looking people need something to hold on to at times: a glass of alcohol or a cigarette for instance. See if you can find a more positive object.

* Write a poem about how you feel.

◆ Be mindful. Notice things around you and in your mind and body more carefully. Take a very close look at something very ordinary: a flower, a pen, your watch, even a hair from your head. See it as an object from outer space you have never seen before. Live like you are watching yourself. Notice how you feel when you are sad or angry. Where in your body is the feeling? Does the feeling remind you of a colour? Become really aware of the taste and texture of your food. Be mindful of your senses. Take a moment to pay attention to any tastes, smells, textures, sounds or sights around you. Sit quietly sometimes and watch the world go by. All this can help you feel calm and safe inside. Don't judge yourself or others. Just notice things and feelings.

Learn to use your breathing to deal with uncomfortable or powerful feelings. Here is a simple exercise to try:

Breathe slowly and deeply. Fill your lungs. Now let the breath out very slowly, as if you are sending your breath to the far horizon. Notice how you feel when you have done this.

When you feel distressed or angry and need to feel calmer, bring your thoughts and awareness back to your breath as it goes in and out of your body.

Remember to avoid doing this exercise if you are doing anything that needs your full attention, like driving a car.

◆ Get some exercise. A brisk walk, dancing to your favourite music or a game of basketball with friends are helpful when you feel angry or very sad. Exercise activates the brain chemicals that give us a feeling of well-being.

◆ Talk to someone you know you can trust.

Dream-catcher

Ever wondered why you dream?
Ever wondered what that dream that seemed so weird was all about?

Our dreams are a way of sorting out what is in our minds. Sometimes they remind us of things we have forgotten and need to attend to. Sometimes in our dreams we get to feel the feelings we stopped ourselves experiencing when we were awake. Sometimes we dream about things that have actually happened but more often we dream in symbols.

Katya dreamed that she had arrived at a building that seemed to her like a haunted house. The door was opened by a woman in a red jacket who invited her in and then locked the door. Katya was afraid of this woman who had control of her, of what she would do to her. Katya ran around the house trying to find a way out, but the only way was through the front door and the woman in the red jacket held the key.

When she thought about her dream later, Katya realised that she had been called into the dean's office the day before her dream because of a number of incidents at school. The dean, a woman with red hair, had given Katya the option of informing her parents before the school did, in order to arrange an interview the next day. 'I was trapped,' said Katya, 'and the woman in red held the keys. I had only one way out and that was to face up and tell my parents. Go through the front door, so to speak.'

Here are some ideas for making sense of your dreams and getting to know yourself better:

+ What do the symbols in the dream mean to you?

    This was Katya's symbol list:

    Door = trapped, way out

    Red = danger, the dean's hair

    Keys = the answer, an escape

    The haunted house = a scary place where I feel powerless (school)

+ Give your dream a title, as you would a film or a book. What does the title tell you about your life at the moment?

+ Write down the date of your dream and then look back at what you were doing in the days leading up to it. Does this help you understand the dream?

+ Write the story of your dream and record how you felt at the end of each step in the dream. Do the feelings in your dream relate to how you have been feeling in your waking life?

- Do you like the way your dream ended? Think of a more satisfying ending and write it out in your journal as if it is happening now. Take some time to notice how you feel as you change the ending and take control of the dream

- Ask yourself what you have learnt from the dream. How has it helped you to understand yourself and your feelings?

- Share the dream with a friend

- Leave your journal by your bed at night ready to catch another dream

Keeping a journal

You can make your diary work for you and help you cope.

Strong feelings of sadness, hurt and anger can be hard to cope with. You may even begin to believe that these feelings will go on forever. Feelings need to be expressed in some way. Keeping a journal or diary is a very effective way of doing this. You will also find out more about yourself and how you get on with other people.

When you keep a diary you are doing it for yourself. A diary needs to be confidential, so find a safe place to keep it. Other people need to respect your privacy. A diary is a very personal thing.

Here are some ideas of things you may want to use in your diary or journal:

* Write in your diary or journal as if you are writing a letter to someone e.g. 'Dear Diary...' or you might want to give the diary a made up name e.g. 'Dear Katy...' We all need someone we can talk to. A diary or journal can be a substitute friend when there is no one else around to share your feelings. If you have no real friends, it may help to speak to your school counsellor or another trusted older person. Making friends is not something we know about automatically.

* Write a list of things that have meaning just for you:

  * The things I like

  * Places that make me feel peaceful

  * Music which makes me feel peaceful, happy, excited

  * People I like

  * I like people who...

  * Important things that have happened in my life

  * Sad things that have happened in my life

  * The things I am angry about

* Write a letter to someone you feel angry with, but don't send the letter. You may regret it later. Just keep it in your diary. It may help to share your letter with a trusted friend, or you could burn it or bury it in a significant place

* Draw a mandala, a round picture that tells about you. You might start your mandala at the edge and work in or at the centre and work out

* Write your life story. You might want some chapter headings to help you start: 'My Birth', 'When I was a Toddler', 'My First Memory', 'A Birthday Party I Remember', 'Starting School', 'My Most Embarrassing Moment'

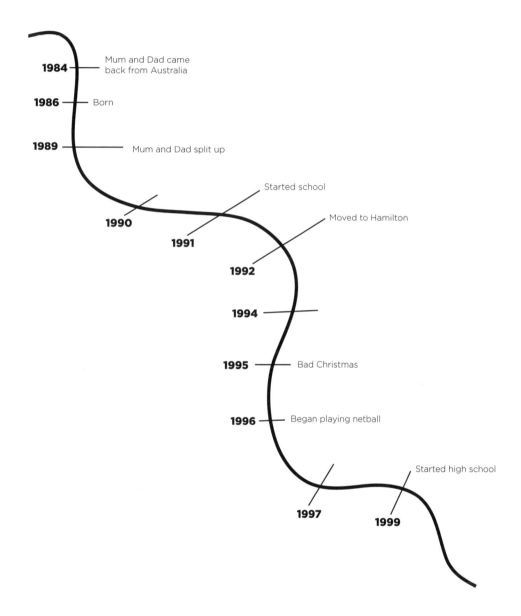

Draw a time-line of your life. Mark on it memories, special happenings and occasions, things others have told you that you might have forgotten. Draw pictures or write significant words

1984 Mum and Dad came back from Australia

1986 Born

1989 Mum and Dad split up

Started school

1990

1991

Moved to Hamilton

1992

1994

1995 Bad Christmas

1996 Began playing netball

Started high school

1997

1999

Adolescent poems

You can write your stuff too!

Angry ball

I don't understand how I feel, it's not that big of a deal

I have a great amount of anger, that's hard for me to control

Sometimes I feel like a bursting ball

I don't like to talk about it, that's why I always put up a fight

It hurts me so much, that I don't like to be touched

I just want to die so please go away, until then I'll be waiting for that day.

Do you forget

When roses stop their blooming and petals start to fall

When raindrops cling together and mud begins to form

When snowflakes blanket the earth and bury grass beneath

When grey clouds cover blue skies and the sun's gold rays cease…

Do you forget what once was there?

No – because you realise, that things are all still here –

Hidden temporarily, but you know they'll reappear.

Their beauty is still existent… Just wait and you will see,

That now it has returned and is better than you thought it would be.

Why am I so different? Something has masked me too

Why don't I get the same patience and understanding from you?

I know I'm a mess right now, dear friend, but underneath, I'm still me

I'm still the same person you've always known – I just need some TLC

Please don't desert me now, I beg you, 'cause I promise eventually

Things will start to get better, the way they're supposed to be.

My life begins to grow again, the dirt all washes away;

The coldness thaws, then disappears and the sun comes out to stay.

I may not be exactly the same, but 'cause we've made it through together,

Our friendship's stronger than it's ever been and I know it will last forever.

Left

If I was a bird I would fall

Depression creeps into the minds of all

Some look above for relation and love

Yet while they soar I am left to crawl.

Feelings

One minute I'm happy

Next minute I'm not

Others are chatty

But I'm really lost.

I don't know what to think

I don't know what to feel

Maybe some day I'll just shrink

Put me in an envelope

Sign,

Stamp,

Seal.

I'm not happy where I am

But I won't be happy there either

Maybe I should put my life in a can

And take an eternal breather.

But I'm not chicken

No, I'm not yellow

My pain will thicken

But I will bellow.

Jennie

Betrayal

Anger, pain and tears

Still build up strong inside

The guy who caused my fears

Should no longer be alive

The pains still strong I just can't release it

I've had the feeling for so long

His face is where I long to spit

Anger continuously swirls inside me

I think it has become eternal

I wish so much that I was free

But that desire isn't meant to be.

Jennie

Imagine a life on the edge, playin' puppet masta, without realisn'
you' replayin' yourself and the strings are breaking, half sunken in
an ocean of self despair, like black ink, silky yet staining, lasting
yet not as black for a lifetime imprinted on your soul.
And hollow tears, no fear, no remorse, but is this all my life was,
all criminal and drunken behaviour, soundin' like respectful love
never entered my mind, the truth be, with memories fading,
I recall, playin' kind with innocent mind, but white boy style jus'
wasn't that, there had to be more. But I should have stayed on the
clean and clear, but would I have grown up as I did, with
experience, more than anyone, emotions of several life-times, the
girls I've met, though some do me wrong, all mean life rather than
death, no boys keep me sane 'cept Krazy K, respect yourself for
you never know, you could have been a big rolla or a lil' nerd,
never born or deformed. Life be it hard or be it sad, will always be,
less Armageddon, the apocalypse comes, cherish and embrace,
for it ends in tragedy.

Josh

Positive self-talk
Saying good things to yourself in your head

Use this instead of negative self-talk which may get us deeper into trouble. Using positive self-talk helps take control of ourselves and our actions and get positive results.

When you recognise the old negative self-talk starting, stop, switch it off. Take a deep breath and choose one or two of the positive phrases from the list above.

Continue to take deep breaths and feel the energy die down before you speak out loud.

Self-esteem

Good things about me

GOOD THINGS I DO Ideas: Sport, tasks, work, money, dance, singing, cooking, etc.	GOOD THINGS I AM Ideas: Friendly, loyal, generous, talkative, happy, helpful, artistic, unselfish, etc.

Payback

The consequences of living with revenge and resentment

Give bad

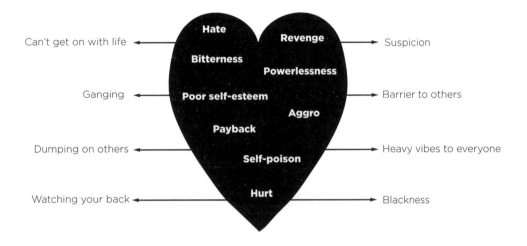

Can't get on with life ← **Hate** **Revenge** → Suspicion

Bitterness

Powerlessness

Ganging ← **Poor self-esteem**

Aggro → Barrier to others

Payback

Dumping on others ← **Self-poison** → Heavy vibes to everyone

Watching your back ← **Hurt** → Blackness

Give good

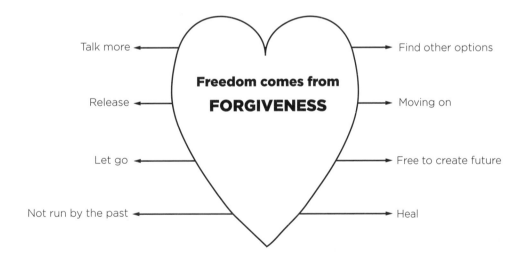

Talk more ← **Freedom comes from** → Find other options

FORGIVENESS

Release ← → Moving on

Let go ← → Free to create future

Not run by the past ← → Heal

Get good

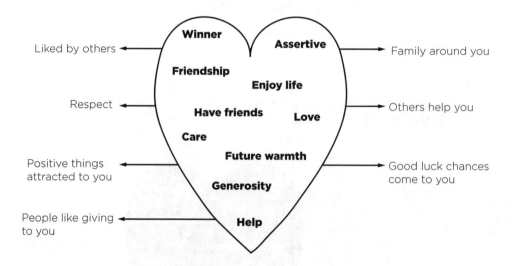

Liked by others ← Winner
Assertive → Family around you

Friendship
Enjoy life

Respect ← Have friends
Love → Others help you

Care

Positive things
attracted to you ← Future warmth
→ Good luck chances
come to you

Generosity

People like giving
to you ← Help

Key concepts

- Payback is storing old anger.

- Forgiveness is healthy for us.

Hot penning

Choose one of the quotations below. Apply it to yourself. Take pen and paper and write as fast as you can, not stopping to think, for five minutes. Don't worry about spelling or grammar. Write every little thought that comes into your head. The idea is to create personal honesty and also to see what comes to mind when you're not censoring or thinking about what you should say.

Read it to yourself.
What do you learn?
You might want to talk to a friend about it.
Which one catches your eye?

HURT PEOPLE HURT PEOPLE	LIKE FATHER LIKE SON
BEHIND EVERY ANGER THERE IS A HURT	IT IS NOT COOL TO BE A FOOL
SOME MOTHERS SMOTHER	RESISTING REACTION
BE COOL NOT CRUEL	RAP DON'T SLAP

Getting money plan

There is huge pressure on young people to have money to spend on technology, fun, education, travel and appearances. If you are not bothered by these then that is great. It leaves you very powerful and fulfilled. However if you feel the pressure to have money then the best thing is to get some. Tick the things you are able to do.

- ❏ Dress up as a clown, storyteller or magician for kids' parties
- ❏ Set up garage sales
- ❏ Buy things you know and resell them
- ❏ Teach people something you are good at – music, skateboarding
- ❏ Grow plants and fruit to sell
- ❏ Babysitting
- ❏ Work at the supermarket
- ❏ Sell food door to door to businesses
- ❏ Product promotions
- ❏ Sell products on the internet
- ❏ Walk dogs
- ❏ Deliver to letterboxes
- ❏ Wash windows door to door

- ❏ Win a competition
- ❏ Buy bulk goods and sell to people/friends singly
- ❏ Establish an automatic savings account
- ❏ Collect things from people's junk and resell
- ❏ Charge for making people beautiful – hair, nails
- ❏ Make crafts and sell at markets
- ❏ Sell fruit off people's trees with permission
- ❏ Take old people shopping
- ❏ Write software
- ❏ Wash cars
- ❏ Feed pet animals
- ❏ Save money
- ❏ Door knock for odd jobs and gardening

**Money helps us do and have.
Not needing £ is powerful.**

Key concept

- ♦ Money isn't everything.

Vision for a world without aggro

Violence and hurt are common in the world. They touch most people.
Imagine a world without violence or deliberate hurt.
How would you like it to be?

OUR HOMES	THIS COUNTRY
MY FRIENDS	TRANSPORT
THIS SCHOOL	OUR WORLD
OUR STREETS	SPORTS

Key concept

♦ We can choose to make the world happier and less violent.

✓

What do I want for my future?
Making plans for the life I deserve

Write on the lines what you personally want for your future.

My health: . . . .

. . . .

. . . .

My education:. . . . .

. . . .

. . . .

Recreation/fun:. . . . .

. . . .

. . . .

Spirituality: . . . .

. . . .

. . . .

Personal growth: . . . .

. . . .

. . . .

Community/others:. . . . .

. . . .

. . . .

Work/job: . . . .

. . . .

. . . .

My mother: . . . .

. . . .

. . . .

My father: . . . .

. . . .

. . . .

My feelings/heart: . . . .

. . . .

. . . .

Money: . . . .

. . . .

. . . .

Friends: . . . .

. . . .

. . . .

My anger: . . . .

. . . .

. . . .

Choose one a week to focus on and make it happen!

Key concept

♦ Anger is about past and present. Choose a future where you need it less.

Summary of Key Concepts

- People respond to powerlessness by feeling angry.

- Anger is OK. People feel angry for a reason.

- Trust and respect are vital to power sharing or assistance.

- It's never OK to abuse others with 'power over' attempts and domination.

- We need to talk about our powerlessness, not try to 'power over' back.

- We need to listen to people's powerlessness.

- Hurt, fear, loss and shame are forms of powerlessness.

- More information changes what we think about others. Making judgements can be risky.

- All people need and are entitled to respect (parents and adolescents).

- Abuse is never OK.

- You are entitled to respect and attention.

- You need to ensure you give the same back.

- Our children are growing up in a society that is different and untested. We need to pay attention to their real needs and meet them.

- Our community needs to take positive responsibility for our adolescents.

- Understanding and knowing ourselves helps us know and live with our children.

- Fixing it with our own parents greatly helps our parenting of our own children.

- Healthy relationships require you to communicate well.

- Good communication involves talking and listening well.

- You need to listen to feelings.

- 'I' statements promote responsibility and stop blaming.

- Feelings may sometimes be uncomfortable but they are important.

- Anger is an integral part of adolescence due to the changes, hurts, sensitivity, fragility and losses taking place.

- A positive experience with the same-sex parent and plenty of affirmation from them is essential to good identity and self-esteem.

- Be patient, keep cool. Don't meet anger with anger.

- Keep consistency in boundaries.

- Growing up is a process of negotiating power from parents to adolescents.

- People who can negotiate can retain their own power and also give away power.

- Don't release stored anger in destructive ways.

- Negotiating involves thinking, talking and trading.

- Negotiating is a learned skill and needs practice.

- We need to remove labels from our children in order to negotiate with them as they become adults.

- Clear boundaries give shape and security to young lives.

- Too much control, or too little control, generates anger.

- Stick to the anger rules.

- People who are angry need to be heard.

- Help adolescents with their anger now.

- We have a choice of positive or negative expression.

- Negative expression is abusive.

- The purpose of anger is to put the situation right again.

- Behind anger is hurt, powerlessness or loss.

- There is always a good reason for a person to feel angry.

- If you feel angry make sure you have a strategy for changing things.

- Damage can be repaired by listening and empathy.

- Knowing your triggers gives you more control over them.

- Time Out helps you to keep safe. You need to come back and complete the discussion.

- People learn by experiencing the consequences of their behaviour.

- Positive attention is much more effective than negative attention or punishment.

- Children are more co-operative if they share in decision making about their behaviour.

- Fairness and a willingness to listen will encourage co-operation.

- Short, clear, firm communication is best.

- Children have a right to their own feelings, space and possessions.

- Parents' anger at each other should not involve the children.

- Children have a right to feel hurt and angry at parents who can't get along.

- Children hate it when separated parents fight.

- Listen to others' feelings. Talk about your own feelings.

- We should never put up with abuse.

- Violence and abuse are a community responsibility.

- There is an association between anger and parental attempts to control romantic and sexual behaviour.

- Young people need support from a strong adult when in crisis.

- If parents cannot offer this support, they need to find someone, or an organisation, who can.

- Adolescents who live in more than one culture have more challenges to meet and good reasons to feel angry.

- Living in two cultures with supportive adults can be positive in terms of mutual understanding, depth of character and intellectual growth.

- Adults who live and work with adolescents from different cultures need to be aware of the additional challenges these young people face and offer support and understanding.

- With freedom and power comes responsibility.

- Handling power and freedom requires integrity, empathy and self-worth.

- Everyone is entitled to have problems.

- All people need and are entitled to respect.

- We are often strangely like the people we have difficulty with.

- People treat me according to the message I give out.

- All clothing carries a message.

- If we know early signs of anger we have more choice about our actions.

- You need anger to protect and help you.

- What you DO with anger is what matters.

- If we know the early signs of anger we have more choice time.

- You can change the faulty things you were taught about anger and abuse.

- We need to break negative cycles.

- We can change loser choices into winner choices.

- Triggers are hurts we react to without thinking.

- Being triggered gives my power to others.

- Choosing not to be triggered gives us power.

- Time Out is time in charge of yourself.

- After Time Out, come back and fix the problem.

- Fighting back makes losers.

- You always have a choice.

- If you like yourself, you can handle someone else's problem more easily.

- Some parents have abuse problems.

- Small minds live in small pictures.

- Speaking up solves problems.

- We can develop skills that help us get on with others.

- Knowing our triggers allows us more choice.

- We can protect ourselves from people who want to have power over us.

- We can protect ourselves from the anger of others.

- It's never OK to abuse others or yourself.

- Abuse may leave the victim feeling vulnerable and angry.

- People who abuse others and people who are abused can be male or female, rich or poor, educated or uneducated, old or young.

- Most people have good intentions and care about others.

- Abuse can be physical, verbal, sexual, spiritual to self and to property.

- Having good self-esteem helps us handle anger.

- People who hurt others often feel bad about themselves.

- You get back what you give out.

- Talk positively to yourself.

- There's always a reason for wanting to hurt others. Find it!

- Reasons aren't excuses for abuse.

- Understanding reasons helps us plan new choices.

- Damage to property is abuse.

- We often cover or hide our anger.

- Repressed anger always sneaks out.

- Alcohol and abuse often go together.

- Bottled anger hurts us and is dangerous.

- We express anger differently in different situations.

- Movies have powerful models for us.

- Payback is storing old anger.

- Forgiveness is healthy for us.

- Money isn't everything.

- We can choose to make the world happier and less violent.

- Anger is about past and present. Choose a future where you need it less.

About the Authors

Warwick Pudney

Warwick Pudney is a father of three children who, like him, often feel angry and, like him, don't always get it right. He lives and works in New Zealand and the UK establishing programmes, taking workshops, counselling, training and listening to people and he lectures at Auckland University of Technology in the Psychotherapy Department. His favourite things to feel angry about are violence on TV and movies, children getting hurt, wars, books not being returned and someone else finishing the biscuits.

He has worked as the CEO of Man Alive, a men's and boy's counselling and well-being centre that he established in order to better cater for male welfare. He works with men and boys in the field of anger, gender relations and fatherhood. His passion is helping men live more creative lives and facilitating social change and he also enjoys backpacking, listening to music, canoeing, life…and chocolate biscuits.

Some of his other books include *A Volcano in My Tummy* and *Beginning Fatherhood*.

In 2000 he was awarded a UNESCO Millenium Peacebuilders Award and in 2004 the Queen's Service Medal.

Éliane Whitehouse

Éliane Whitehouse lived and worked in New Zealand as both a teacher of children and adolescents and as a counsellor-therapist. She had fond memories of adults who stepped out and helped her as an adolescent and made a difference. She also acknowledged what she learned as a parent raising adolescents herself, and what they in turn taught her.

She had two children's books published: *Wood Smoke* and *Young Exile*, and she co-authored, with Warwick Pudney, *A Volcano in My Tummy* and *Little Volcanoes*.

She enjoyed connecting with her own peace through gardening, walking and yoga.

Sadly, Èliane passed away in 2010. This book is part of the contribution of her life.

Bibliography

Anda, R.F, Felitti, V.J., Bremner, J., Walker, J.D. *et al.* (2006) 'The enduring effects of abuse and related adverse experiences in childhood: A convergence of evidence from neurobiology and epidemiology.' *European Archives of Psychiatry and Clinical Neuroscience, 256,* 3, 174–186.

Bassoff, E. (1995) *Mothering Ourselves.* New York: Plume.

Bassoff, E. (1995) *Between Mothers and Sons.* New York: Plume.

Berger, K.S. (2012) *The Developing Person Through the Life Span.* New York: Worth Publishers.

Biddulph, S. (1994) *Manhood.* Sydney: Finch Publishing.

Biddulph, S. (1997) *Raising Boys.* Sydney: Finch Publishing.

Biddulph, S. (2008) *Raising Boys: Why Boys are Different – and How to Help Them Become Happy and Well-Balanced Men.* Berkeley, CA: Ten Speed Press.

Blackenhorn, D. (1995) *Fatherless America: Confronting Our Most Urgent Social Problem.* New York: Harper Perennial.

Bradley, J. and Dubinsky, H. (1997) *Understanding Your 15–17-Year-Olds.* Ontario: Warwick Publishing.

Cornelius, H. and Faire, S. (1989) *Everyone Can Win.* Brookvale, NSW: Simon and Schuster.

Courneau, G. (1991) *Absent Fathers, Lost Sons.* Boston: Shambala.

Ellis, B., Bates, J.E., Dodge, K.A., Fergusson, D.M. *et al.* (2003) 'Does father absence place daughter at special risk for early sexual activity and teenage pregnancy?' *Child Development, 73,* 3, 801–821.

Erickson, E. (1980) *Identity and the Life Cycle.* London: Norton.

Faber, A. and Mazlish, E. (2006) *How to Talk So Teens Will Listen and Listen so Teens Will Talk.* New York: William Morrow Paperbacks.

Field, E.M. (1999) *Bully Blocking: Six Secrets to Help Children Deal with Teasing and Bullying.* London: Jessica Kingsley Publishers.

Frodl, T., Reinhold, E., Koutsouleris, N., Donohoe, G. *et al.* (2010) 'Childhood stress, serotonin transporter gene and brain structures in major depression.' *Neuropsychopharmacology, 35,* 6, 1383–1390.

James, M. (1985) *It's Never Too Late To Be Happy.* Reading, MA: Addison Wesley Publishing.

Lamb, M.E. (2003) *The Role of the Father in Child Development.* New York: Wiley.

McCann, R. (1999) *Fatherless Sons.* Auckland: Harper Collins.

Mourant, M. (1991) *Understanding Teenagers.* Auckland: Collins.

Peifer, M. (1994) *Reviving Ophelia.* New York: Doubleday.

Perry, B.D. (1997) 'Incubated in terror: Neurodevelopmental factors in the cycle of violence.' In J. Osofsky (ed.) *Children in a Violent Society.* New York: Guilford Press.

Perry, B.D. (2008) 'Child maltreatment: A neurodevelopmental perspective on the role of trauma and neglect in psychopathology.' In T.P. Beauchaine and S.P. Hinshaw (eds) *Child and Adolescent Psychopathology.* Hoboken, NJ: John Wiley and Sons.

Perry, B.D. (2009) 'Examining child maltreatment through a neurodevelopmental lens: Clinical applications of the neurosequential model of therapeutics.' *Journal of Trauma and Loss, 14,* 240–255.

Pudney, W. and Cotterell, J. (1998) *Beginning Fatherhood.* Auckland: Tandem Press.

Sheehy, G. (1996) *New Passages.* London: Harper Collins.

Stewart, I. and Joines, V. (1987) *TA Today.* Nottingham: Lifespace Publishing.

Taffel, R. (1999) 'Discovering Our Children: The connection between anonymity and rage in today's kids.' *Psychotherapy Networker*, September/October.

Waddell, M. (2005) *Understanding 12–14-Year-Olds.* London: Jessica Kingsley Publishers.

Whitehouse, E. and Pudney, W. (1994) *A Volcano in My Tummy.* Auckland: Peace Foundation.